Kismet

From the Joy of Romance to the Agony of Alzheimer's

~

Elizabeth Gibbons Van Ingen

Elizabeth Van Ingen

For Patty Lee—
"Remember the good times!"

Liz

2013 · FITHIAN PRESS, MCKINLEYVILLE, CALIFORNIA

Published by Fithian Press
A division of Daniel and Daniel, Publishers, Inc.
Post Office Box 2790
McKinleyville, CA 95519
www.danielpublishing.com

Distributed by SCB Distributors (800) 729-6423

LIBRARY OF CONGRESS CATALOGING-IN-PUBLICATION DATA
Van Ingen, Elizabeth Gibbons, (date)
  Kismet : From the Joy of Romance to the Agony of Alzheimer's / by Elizabeth
Gibbons Van Ingen.
    pages cm
  ISBN 978-1-56474-545-3 (pbk. : alk. paper)
  1. Van Ingen, Elizabeth Gibbons, (date) 2. Van Ingen, Tony, 1931–2005.
  3. Alzheimer's disease—Patients—United States—Biography.
  4. Women caregivers—United States—Biography.
  5. Married people—United States—Biography. I. Title.
  RC523.V36 2013
  616.8'310092—dc23
  [B]
                2013003573

Kismet

For Caroline, Linda, and Marianne

Contents

Kismet

Take My Hand...

1958

"TAKE OFF YOUR SHOES, MARGY!" Off came our three-inch stiletto heels with the pointy toes. Big-lady purse in one hand, shoes in the other, we ran giggling down Stockton Street, dodging in and out of startled San Francisco ladies in hats and white gloves. We were on our way to *Kismet* and we didn't want to be late.

"*Kismet!*" I said. 'Let's see if we can get tickets for today's matinee,"

"You mean today for today?"

"Yes. Let's try."

We got them! Tickets for the two-o'clock show.

"Kismet" means "fate" in Turkish, and *Kismet* is a musical story of romance and exotic beauty, like the *Arabian Nights*, with jewel-colored costumes and backdrops of bright tiled mosques with onion-shaped domes and choruses of noisy marketplaces. We could almost smell the spiciness of the bazaars from our balcony seats.

We sang as we floated out of the theater after the final act. We hummed "Baubles, Bangles and Beads" and "Stranger in Paradise" all the way home on the train. The next day I went into Thos Tenny's music store on College Avenue in Berkeley and bought the 33-1/3-rpm long-play record album, took it to my room, and played it over and over again, memorizing all the words. I sank down in the soft easy chair in the corner of my bedroom and absorbed the romantic, sensuous songs and dances based on a classic symphony by Alexander Borodin.

In 1959, when I went to visit my father in Iran and decided to stay there and get married, my mother kept the album and played it over and over, thinking of me, and how I had rushed to meet my own kismet.

Now, more than forty years later, my husband and I stand hand in hand looking at our wedding photograph. The ceremony is over. We two in the droshky have said our vows. I pledged myself for life to a man I had known for four months. "I love you enough for both of us," he had said when I expressed hesitation and uncertainty about my own feelings.

Tony often calls me into his office room to look at the photo with him. He has no idea who those two people are, but he likes the forty-year-old photo. He is fascinated by that man and that girl. "Look at him," he says. "He is laughing and happy! Who is the girl? Do you see all the people chasing and pointing at them?"

I am no longer dismayed that he doesn't recognize me, or himself, in the picture, or that he doesn't know who I am standing next to him. Little by little, he has drifted away from me, and I am learning to let him go. On that long-ago wedding day, I couldn't have foreseen how firm our bond would become or that one day, it would stretch and grow thin and eventually snap.

PART ONE

Out of the Commonplace, into the Rare...

CHAPTER I

The Arrival and a Fur Coat

Tehran, 1959

IN THE NINETEEN-FIFTIES and 'sixties thousands of Americans lived and worked in Tehran, eager for high profits in the process of helping the Shah bring Iran into the twentieth century. However, it was an unlikely place to find an unmarried American girl on vacation. Nevertheless, there I was. My father, who was a civilian working for the U.S. Army Corps of Engineers, and his wife, Maddie, had been in Tehran almost two years when I went there to visit them in September of 1959.

I grew up in Berkeley with my mother and sister, Katie, two years older than I, in an extended family of women that included my widowed aunt and her three daughters and our three widowed grandmothers. Katie and I looked so much alike that teachers and friends regularly called me Katie. I heard "Hi, Katie" again and again as I tromped across the college campus between classes. I smiled back and didn't make an issue of it. I came along behind her by two years, doing everything she had done until she, following the unwritten but well understood convention of the fifties, married soon after graduation from college. Not for me! In the winter before my own graduation, I had no such plans, so when my father sent me a letter asking if I would visit him in Iran for a few months, I jumped at the prospect of adventure and I answered "Yes" by return mail. Looking back, I am sure I was relieved to have a viable substitute for what I was *supposed* to do by convention, that is, get married.

When the envelope from Pan American Airways arrived by registered mail in January of my senior year, I took the stairs two at a time up to my room and flopped into the big chair to open it, stare at the ticket, and savor the thought of the adventure that lay ahead of me. Iran! Persia! A mystical, desert land, a country with a different religion and people speaking a language whose alphabet I wouldn't even recognize, a new and exotic culture. That ticket in my hand told me the trip was not fantasy. I envisioned myself getting off the plane in Tehran, going through customs, and walking confidently out to greet my father and Maddie. However, as I sat in that chair with the ticket in my hand, it dawned on me that not only was I plunging into a foreign country halfway around the world; I was going to live with my long-absent father for three months.

My father had left our family when I was ten years old, and I knew him only from early childhood and rare visits every few years when he took Katie and me out to dinner with Maddie. My memories of him were of an overbearing, unpredictable person, one to be wary of. Now with tickets in hand to see him, I considered the situation I was putting myself in. I can't say that as a little girl I knew him. He allowed no physical affection, no cuddling on his lap, or being carried when I was tired. My mother often stood with her back leaning against the kitchen counter, arms crossed, watching my sister and me eat dinner while she waited for him to come home from the neighborhood bar. She said he was immature, a euphemism, I know now, for being self-centered, an alcoholic, and a womanizer. I can still feel the shock of his final words to us when he boarded the train from Oakland to Chicago for his new job and left all of us behind. "Goodbye," he said. "I am starting a new life. You no longer exist for me."

My sister told me the divorce was our mother's fault. She couldn't keep her man. But I saw how Mother laughed more often once she was without him.

I wrote to him a lot. Thinking he was lonely without us, I sent him cards and pictures and stories I'd written, anything I thought would cheer him up and make him notice me and remember me. He sent me a jewelry box for my twelfth birthday, red leatherette with gold letters printed on the top. Unfortunately, the letters spelled out my sister's name instead of mine. I wrote to him, "Was there a mix-up? Was there another box coming for Katie with my name on it?" "No, there's only one box. It is for you. It has *your* name on it, not Katie's," was his reply. I stared at the top of the box trying hard to make "Katherine" read "Elizabeth." I really wanted that box, my favorite color and all, and I didn't want him to be embarrassed by the mistake. Now, holding the Pan Am, round-the-world ticket in my hand, I looked over at the box, still on my bureau. The old English lettering had become indistinct in my mind as I wanted to believe he had given it to me, knew me, and had remembered my birthday and my name. I looked down at the ticket with *my name* clearly printed in capital letters. I was going around the world! I'd be stopping in Iran for two or three months, and would at least get to know my father better than I knew him now.

Within days of receiving the ticket I found an Iranian student to give me a few lessons in Farsi, and soon my bedside table held books with the titles *Iran, Past and Present* (1956) and *A Guide to Iran* (1958). My favorite was a coffee-table–sized book with 105 pictures in photogravure and five color plates. The dome and minarets of the Madraseh-yi-Madar-i-Sah at Isfahan glistened against a brilliant blue sky on the dust cover. I arranged with the University to put off my practice teaching, originally scheduled for the fall semester, to the one starting the following January.

In September, I said goodbye to my boyfriend of the moment, who teased, "Oh, you'll never come back, Lizzie," and, with the encouragement of my mother, boarded a new Pan American Airways Boeing Jet 707, bound for the mysterious Middle East.

I knew nothing of the land where I was headed, except the little I had read and memories of *Kismet*, which I had seen a few months before. "Baubles, Bangles and Beads" drifted through my mind as I settled into the seat on this Pan American flight, a jet service as far as Europe, but not yet all the way around the world. In Rome, we changed to an old turbojet that flew relatively slowly and shakily to Tehran, with a stop in Beirut, Lebanon.

We landed in Beirut in the dark of night. Lebanese men in tan coveralls got on the plane and indicated that there was some trouble with the aircraft and we would have to remain in Beirut for a while. I remembered there had been an attempted coup there the summer before. At that time, I had been in Naples with some college girlfriends, expecting to meet a couple of Marines we knew from school who were stationed there. When we arrived at the dock where their ship was supposed to be, it was gone, off to quell an uprising in Beirut. So, remembering this when we had to hand over our passports and disembark from the plane, I was a little nervous—needlessly, as it turned out.

The next day, continuing on from Beirut to Tehran, I sat next to a young Iranian woman, about my age, with bleached blond hair and plenty of makeup.

"*Hally shauma shatori?*" I said, trying out a Farsi phrase. "How are you?"

She laughed. "*Parlez-vous Français?*" she asked. My French was not good, but better certainly than my Farsi. Her name was Rosette and she was a hairdresser in Tehran returning from a vacation in Paris. We muddled along with primitive French and gestures. Rosette said, "I bought this small fur coat in Paris for my sister and this other one for myself."

"*Oui, très jolie*, pretty," I said keeping the conversation going.

"We are only allowed to take one coat in through customs without paying a high duty. I just don't know what I am going to do."

"*C'est dommage.* Too bad."

"Do you have a fur coat?"

"No, just this nylon Borgana thing that looks like fur. Fake." I had bought the coat in San Francisco anticipating a snowy Iranian winter.

"Oh, *merveilleux*! You could carry one of mine over your arm with no problem!"

"*Balli, balli.* Yes, yes, I suppose I could," was my people-pleasing response, in those days before terrorists, hijackings, or security monitors.

As the plane approached Tehran, I thought again about my father. I was nervous and had distracted myself with a book until now. Maddie had visited in San Francisco six months previously. She and my mother and I went out for dinner, where Maddie assured Mother that I would be welcome and safe in Iran. Then the three of us went to the movie *Gigi.* I was comfortable with Maddie, but uneasy around my father. He was tall, six-foot-two at least, with almost black hair, a bushy mustache, and mischievous, topaz-blue eyes. He would probably have some gray hair by now, no doubt very distinguished looking. Would he notice changes in me? I was a little taller maybe, still youthfully slender, skinny really, with very dark brown eyes and hair. I knew I looked like Mother. Would that upset him?

It was six o'clock in the morning. Would he be there to meet me? Apprehension flushed my face and I shuffled through my purse and carry-on tote to find his address. I wished I had confirmed the arrival time more recently than six months ago, and now we were late because of the long stop in Beirut. Yes, there it was, APO 506, San Francisco, California. Oh, no, that wouldn't do me any good in Tehran! I looked up at the American stewardess putting on her coat and little navy blue cap, ready to help the passengers disembark. She spoke English, of course. I could ask her. Or, there was always the American Embassy. I could go there, wherever it was, if no one was waiting for me. I nervously recalled a time when Katie and I had waited for him to take us out and he just didn't show up.

The plane circled over the city of Tehran before landing on that Friday morning in September. With my forehead pressed against the window I could see a golden sand color, the city only distinguishable from the sand because of the sharp shadows delineating the buildings. As the plane banked the other way, the window filled with brilliant, cerulean blue, the same vibrant color that was on the cover of the book back home.

As the plane taxied to the terminal, I prayed that I would see my father waiting outside. We filed out of the plane, clambered sleepily down the metal stairs, and walked across the hot tarmac and into the cavernous, marble-floored airport building. The inspectors opened suitcases of passengers ahead of me. Then it was my turn.

Two dark men in tan uniforms decorated with badges and insignias saw me waiting, then turned their backs to me and chattered together, glancing over their shoulders at me wearing the Borgana imitation fur coat with Rosette's genuine fur slung over my arm. I felt my face go red as I closed my eyes and turned my head away, not wanting to account for the apparent fact of me with two fur coats. They waved me to one side to wait.

Across the expanse, I spotted my father and Maddie! They gestured questions on the other side of the glass partitions, and I started toward them, grinning expectantly, but the two men weren't finished with me yet and motioned me back.

All the other passengers had left the area, gone by now in buses and taxis, including my hairdresser friend. I stood twisting a Kleenex in my hands while the inspectors handled the fur coats, snickering at my distress.

"No," I protested. Surely, they must understand. "This one is fake fur. Not real. No good. One real fur, only one real fur." I looked around me, feeling very small in the nearly empty space. Even the stewardesses and pilots were gone. Looking back at the inspectors, I put my hands up in a gesture of surrender and experienced for the first time the arbitrariness of Iranian rules and laws. They tired of toying with me and laughed and waved me off with nonchalance, as if the rules weren't very important or it was tea time and they couldn't be bothered with me any longer. My high heels clattered on the marble floor as I dragged my things out to meet my father. He gave me a peck on the cheek, asking, "What was going on in there?" I laughed with embarrassment and told him I had carried a stranger's coat through customs. He scowled and welcomed me with, "Oh. Lizzie! What a goddamn stupid thing to do." He was right, of course.

Maddie hesitated, then threw her arms around me with a grin and a chuckle. "You're here! We've been waiting for you! How was the trip? Welcome." I let out a giggle of relief. I had arrived.

Outside we found Rosette pacing around the taxi stand. I gave her the conventional hug on both cheeks and surreptitiously transferred the coat from my arm to hers. My father tossed my suitcases in the trunk of his car and we were on our way.

He drove us along the wide, tree-lined, divided boulevard toward the city, then slowed the car as he merged with the crazy Tehran traffic, starting, stopping, and honking through the chaos. I stared out the backseat windows, first on one side of the car, then the other, at the dusty streets and dusty trees and dusty people and shops and air, a fine light haze putting the city in soft focus. I caught a glimpse of the Elborz Mountains rising above the city into the smooth, blue sky. Sunlight filtered through the trees, dappling the people on the sidewalks. Horns blared, people shouted in unfamiliar tones, and vendors hawked strange things to eat from carts with kerosene stoves. The thick exhaust from lopsided diesel buses seeped into the car, mixed with the pungent aroma of wandering donkeys and sheep. Closing my eyes, I breathed in a fragrant unfamiliar world. Then I watched again, as pedestrians stepped in front of us and beside us, patting fenders as though they were sheep. Shadowy women enveloped head to toe in flowing black chadors, lumpy shopping bags filling out the folds of the robes, threaded through banged-up cars and overloaded taxis, in an apparently understood and accepted chaos.

My father parked the car in front of his apartment building on Khiabani Shah, not a residential street but a city street known for its exclusive shops and offices. I got out and jumped over the deep, wide gutter between me and the sidewalk. This gutter, called a *jube*, was an open waterway about two feet wide that served most water needs for people of the city as a way of controlling water distribution in this arid land, the water being directed to different parts of the city on different days. In the Koran it is said that water purifies itself every so many feet, so on that principle the jube water was used for everything.

I stopped and watched as at that moment, leaning over the flowing gutter water, a woman with one end of her chador clenched in her teeth to keep it from falling off, crouched washing a cooking pot and a little beyond her two more women sloshed clothes up and down. Upstream, a squatting man rinsed delicate gold-rimmed tea glasses and put them neatly on the round tray next to him on the street. I saw that people ignored the foot-wide, arched cement bridges and leapt across the jube anywhere.

We also jumped the jube and entered the marble foyer of the building. A strong odor came from a slowly opening door of the downstairs apartment. It was the smell of an unwashed body in unwashed clothes that had been slathered day after day in perfume. Mrs. Bitinvia, the building's owner, grabbed me with a shriek of joy and a smothering embrace and kissed me on both cheeks, squeezing the life out of me. She was my height, heavy and bosomy and tightly corseted under a black odoriferous dress. Was there perfume in the dyed black hair piled up on her head? I gasped for breath. She let go of me, and her husband, a bald doctor, round, and shorter than his wife, took both of my hands into his and with his head bobbing up and down, smiled a welcome. The Bitinvias occupied the ground floor for the doctor's office and their residence. Nodding and grinning, they watched us as we ascended the stone stairs to the second floor apartment, which they rented to my father and Maddie.

Maddie welcomed me into the room she had prepared for me with a single bed in the corner covered with a neat, white spread. She opened the wardrobe. "Will these be enough hangers, Lizzie?" she asked, and, "This straight chair, not too soft; is that all right?" Then, grinning, obviously anxious but pleased with her preparations, she opened the glass doors, where sunshine poured into the room from a narrow porch overlooking a central rear courtyard and the backs of the houses that also had access to the yard. I smiled appreciatively and though the bed tempted me, I was too stimulated by the newness to sleep.

My father and Maddie ushered me through the other rooms. In the kitchen barely big enough for two adults to stand in, a black transformer the size of a breadbox took up one counter, ready to power Maddie's American appliances. My father had built a tin tub under the shower to keep the water from running out into the hall and explained that I should turn a handle to let the water into the tank above the toilet before I pulled the chain and then turn the handle again after flushing; otherwise the tank overflowed and dripped on his magazines.

Maddie clattered in her little kitchen and soon appeared with a tray, carrying coffee cups and cookies into the living room where my father and I sat talking on the white-and-gold brocade sofa. A pair of matching brass lamps, three-and-a-half feet tall, made by hand in the Tehran Bazaar, stood on brass tray-tables on either side of the sofa. My father ignored the coffee, went over to a sideboard, poured himself bourbon on the rocks, and began telling me in his formal manner about his work. "As a civilian working for the U.S. Army Corps of Engineers, I have an office here at the Gulf District in the northern part of the city. But often I am out in the country for a week or two at a time on job sites. Then you and Maddie will be here on your own. Maddie is quite used to being alone, and she has a good friend, Lorna, whom you will meet."

We sat with our backs warm from the sunlight streaming into the living room through glass doors. We faced the dining room, which was now in shadow, with windows overlooking the street. I learned that thousands of Americans worked in Iran, some in the many U.S. agencies, others with the U.S. military, still others with private American companies. We Americans were welcome in the country, my father told me, and as long as I respected the culture, I would have no problems.

Maddie interrupted with, "Lizzie. Shall I call you Lizzie or Liz? Would you like anything else? Can I get you something? Just tell me what you need. I don't know what young girls like nowadays, ha-ha. Are you tired? You must be tired. How was the flight? I showed you your room. Let me know if I have forgotten something. Towels are…" Loneliness colored her words along with a need to please.

"Maddie, just a minute, will ya?" My father interjected.

"But Walter, I'll need to know what time you want dinner. Is chicken à la king all right? Do you like chicken à la king, Liz, Lizzie?"

"Yes, of course. Thank you."

My father went on to tell me about his plans for the next few days. He *had* expected me, having arranged a party that was to be held in my honor three days hence, followed a few days later by a five-day trip south to Isfahan and Shiraz, two ancient and historically significant cities I had seen in that large picture book.

"And then," he continued, "perhaps you'll find some way to be useful while you're here." I felt uneasy sitting there in the living room with him; it was possibly the first time I had a conversation with him without my older sister there to answer his questions and take his attention.

Looking back now, I can see that he really wanted to show me things, and was maybe even proud to introduce me to his friends. At the time, I was thinking about myself and the adventure ahead and not yet consciously appreciative of what he was doing for me.

I stood, excused myself, and took my coffee cup and plate to the kitchen, my body relaxing after the tension of the flight and the anxiety of arriving. Later I went to my new room and stretched out on the bed, but thoughts darting through my mind kept me from immediate sleep. The noise and bustle from the street rose up through an open window, urging me to come and explore. For the first time, I was not following in my sister's footsteps. No one would call me Katie. What would I find? I closed my eyes.

CHAPTER 2

Caviar and a Calling Card

Tehran, 1959

WE HAVE JOKED FOR YEARS that Tony crashed the party to meet me. The story has become family lore. He was eating a hamburger in the lounge of the American Club in Tehran when he heard the laughter and the schmaltzy music from the three-piece Italian band. He left the bar, went outside and stepped, uninvited, under the colored lights that glittered in the trees surrounding an outdoor pavilion where a party was going on.

The evening of September 21, my father drove me through the guarded gates of the American Club on Kh. Pahlavi, a wide, tree-lined boulevard named after the Shah, which led north from the city of Tehran to the suburb of Shemran. As hosts, my father, his wife, Maddie, and I, positioned ourselves to greet the guests. I was just twenty-one and though I felt confident in a slim red brocade dress, I still longed for my father's approval. He had not liked the dress I had traveled in. "Dowdy" had been his assessment when he picked me up at the airport a few days before.

Now, standing next to me on my left, my father formally introduced me to each person arriving. He occasionally touched my elbow and looked down at me, his hair, now silver, falling in a boyish wave over his tan forehead. One hand brushed habitually across his thick silver-gray moustache as his eyebrows lifted up and down over mischievous blue eyes. Maddie had dressed him in a navy suit with a tie of red brocade from Damascus.

Maddie was taller than I, and her straight, upright posture made her look taller than she was. She was on my right, tipping her blond head to one side as she shook hands, hugged, and giggled with each person. Then she turned to me to share some tidbit of information.

My father wanted me to meet the people he worked with at the Gulf District of the U.S. Corps of Engineers as well as the community he socialized with. This man was a German national from the Gulf District. The next was with USIA, the United States Information Agency, and another from ARMISH, the U.S. Army Mission Headquarters. I met Iranian Army officers, American engineers, geologists, and a young man from the U.S. Post Office service. Americans, Swedes, Germans, French, and Iranians stepped to greet us under the colored lights.

"Oh, yes. I'm happy to be here," I responded, as names and faces and acronyms jumbled in my head. Dark, tuxedoed waiters balancing trays of caviar and lamb kebabs moved among the guests. Small round tables covered with white linen cloths held down by glowing hurricane lamps surrounded a dance floor where couples swayed to music played by the Italian combo, or they stood twos and threes in evening dress, a drink in one hand, a cigarette or canapé in the other.

From a silver hors d'oeuvres tray, I accepted a small triangle of white toast heaped with tiny iridescent gray pearls. I held it up to my nose. It was fishy, yet not like a fish market, more like the ocean. I turned my back slightly in case I would gag, and took a small lick. *Mmmm*, soft, salty. Then a nibble off the top without the bread. Pretty good, not too strong, and velvety, squishy in my mouth. The little pearls mooshed together and melted into a pleasant sensation of salt and ocean. I didn't feel the separateness of beads rolling around in my mouth as I had expected. I popped the whole thing into my mouth. Caviar! Slowly, triumphantly I looked around to see who was watching. No one.

The festive lights against the black night, together with the music, the hum of foreign languages and the sophisticated men and women entranced me, made me feel like I was on a movie set. I danced and smiled and made small talk like I was a movie star. I recognize now that having just graduated from college and the rowdy, adolescent fraternity parties, I was awed by being at a "grown-up" gathering, stepping into what I thought was the real world. I glowed and wanted it to last.

I looked around. I had met everyone there. What next? Oh. Who was that tall, blond man at the edge of the pavilion looking around as if to get his bearings? He recognized my father as the host, and my father laughed and pointed my way.

"Hi, I'm Tony," he said. "Ricky, that nurse over there, saw me inside the club house eating a hamburger, and she told me there was a party going on and that I had to come over here and meet a special American girl, someone new here in Tehran. That must be you."

"Well," I answered, "I *am* new here. My name is Liz."

"I know," he said.

"Where are you from?" I asked. "You're not American, are you?"

"Oh, yes. I am. A naturalized American. I was born in Amsterdam, and immigrated to the United States when I was twenty-one, a few years ago, after the war. So what you hear is a Dutch accent mixed with Ohio and Kentucky twists that I picked up from buddies in the army. What brought you to Tehran?"

I briefly told him that I was from California, visiting my father for a couple of months before returning to Berkeley.

"Are you with the army?" I asked, "The marines? Are you an engineer like my father?"

I listened to his story, fascinated by his blond good looks, his smile, and the intriguing bit of foreignness in his voice and manner. He was not with the military, as I had supposed, but was a businessman, the Middle East representative for Firestone International Company. His sales territory included Iraq, Lebanon, Syria, Saudi Arabia, and all the countries and sheikdoms in the Persian Gulf.

The music was still playing. Tony held out his hand and we got up to dance. It was a large hand, with thick fingers, almost a mitt. A Dutch hand, I thought. He stood remarkably straight, with shoulders square and confident, leaning slightly back as he moved to the music so I had to stand on tiptoes to reach him. He tapped an extra beat with one foot and I had to scramble to follow.

When we sat down again at one of the little tables, the light from the lamp flickered as it grew dim.

"I am leaving tomorrow for Aden," he said. "Can I call you when I get back?"

"Sure," I answered, "I'd like that. My father has arranged for me to go with him and his wife to Shiraz, Persepolis, and Isfahan for a few days. We'll be back on the thirtieth."

"The thirtieth. I will call you on the thirtieth. Here, let me give you this." He leaned down and took off my shoe and slipped his business card into the toe. "I don't want you to forget me," he said. "This way you won't lose it."

As soon as he left, I took it out and studied it—the unusual name, H.A. (Tony) Van Ingen; the incomprehensible address, Sherkat Sahami Jahan Motors, Kh. Amir Kabir, Tehran, Iran; and a phone number. On the back of the card the writing was in Farsi letters and numbers. I could figure out the numbers in Farsi by comparing them with the numbers on the front, but certainly not the letters. I'd wait until the thirtieth to find out their meaning.

Back at the apartment, I used the card as a bookmark as I read about Isfahan and the centuries-old history of Iran.

CHAPTER 3

Kingdoms and Classrooms

Southern Iran, 1959

IF MY MOTHER WANTED me to have a broader view of the world, then my father surely gave it to me. Mother would have wanted to know what the people of Iran were like, how they lived, and what they wanted out of life. My father, as a civil engineer, was interested in the facts: the history of the ancient ruins, who built them, and how they were being preserved. Maddie wanted to find the best bargains on embroidered table cloths and printed material for skirts. I wanted it all. I had left the sheltered college environment of the fifties and was eager to experience the world, to learn, and to be grown up.

The trip to Southern Iran was my first experience in a "developing" country. My father organized the details like the hotels, the drivers, the guides, and the meals.

The children in Isfahan captured my attention particularly because I was planning to teach children this age in elementary school in America. On the dirt-packed floor of a home, young girls sat together in pairs, cross-legged, picking threads or whipping them together to make a design in the cloth. Chadors covered their young faces and they did not look up or acknowledge our presence. I saw only their hands, flying at their work, like hummingbirds' wings.

Small boys in another room wove bright red material used for the bath towels we had seen waving in the air outside the *humums*, public baths. We eased ourselves down a couple of big steps into the dark, dingy work area. The boys there appeared to be sitting on the ground, but actually they were standing with their legs down in a pit, their feet pushing pedals that changed the loom's threads to make a design. They too, worked lickety-split, throwing the shuttle back and forth. As we climbed up those few mud-packed stairs to leave, I looked back and saw that dim, dust-filled light softened the scene somewhat, perhaps honoring their work.

These scenes are well known today through our instant communications, but they were all new to me then. The carpets of Isfahan, the most beautiful of all the world-renowned Persian carpets, were products, mostly, of the country's children, very young children. Small girls sat cross-legged on a scaffold made of unfinished tree limbs, five feet or so above the floor, with a partially completed carpet hanging in front of them. The finished part with its jewel-like colors was rolled up below them, empty strings faced them, and a paper pattern was pinned above them. I climbed up on the scaffold to have a close look as the girls' fingers flew across the strings, tying the knots with their eyes on the pattern. The owner of the factory asked the girls to go slowly so I could see what they were doing. The number of knots per square centimeter determined the quality of the carpet, so when the girls were too old and their hands grew too big, they no longer worked on the finest carpets. I looked at these children through the eyes of the elementary school teacher I was training to be and wondered uneasily, "Do they go to school? Will they learn to read? Or is this what their life is to be?"

The thick air in the covered bazaar was heavy with dust and redolent with the pungent odor of cinnamon and saffron, cloves and turmeric; but as we walked, the air blended with kerosene, then horse and donkey dung. Squatting artisans pounded ancient motifs into copper, brass, and tin trays or pots. These designs soon became familiar as they showed up everywhere, beaten into shiny metal, stamped on fabric for clothes, and carved into stone and wood artifacts. The din of their tinkering added to the noisy exchanges between customers and shopkeepers who flung exquisite carpets onto a dirt floor for inspection. The vendor of kerosene called out *"Naaaft! Naaaft!"* as he and his laden donkey lumbered by us. Rhythmic sounds, and exotic smells and the intrigue of buyers and sellers, horses and donkeys, carts and boxes, turbaned men and chadored women all whirled around me then like the dust that danced in the smoky shafts of light from the openings in the roof.

South of Isfahan, near the town of Shiraz, in the ancient ruins of Persepolis, a once impregnable fortress and palace built by Darius I and Xerxes I between 500 and 400 B.C., I learned where the ubiquitous patterns originated. The imperial guard, with spears and various headdresses, marched in bas-relief on towering but crumbling columns, around the massive base of the great hall, and on collapsing walls. Artisans have copied those figures from the glory days of the Persian Empire with pride for two thousand years. I saw the roots of their culture, and as I watched them repeat the motifs of their ancestors, I felt their sense of belonging to the ancient, the great, and the deep.

We returned to Tehran after a mind-expanding five days. During the next few days I explored on my own, walking a little farther from the apartment each time I went out. I strolled around the vendors roasting melon-sized red beets on an open charcoal fire, the aroma following me as I stepped into shop after shop. I wordlessly nodded a greeting and listened to the shopkeepers who responded with melodic syllables and who with friendly arm-waving invited me to look at their wares. I laughed and went on my way, absorbing the street life with my eyes, ears, and nose. I stood my ground at a stop light while other pedestrians rushed by me, ignoring the red signal.

Though Maddie had lived in Iran for two years, she didn't venture far from the places where other Americans gathered. She played canasta with a few women friends and shopped often at the U.S. Commissary. There she visited with other American women and bought groceries and supplies as she would have in America. I wandered through the aisles with her one day, looking at the slightly wilted lettuce and carrots and green beans flown in from the States. There were bags of oranges and grapefruit from

Florida, a luxury because the only citrus fruit grown in Iran was limes. One lady with a round rosy face and a loud voice stopped to visit with Maddie and complained that her arm was aching from cutting up big chunks of frozen meat. I thought of the carcasses hanging from hooks in the heat on the sidewalk in town and the butcher with a bloody towel tucked into his belt, standing there by his shop stabbing at the meat with a knife. Maddie bought Minute Rice and boxes of potato flakes, cans of corn, and prepared chicken à la king. Outside, the local grocers with open air stalls along the street displayed green beans that snapped and firm potatoes, shiny red apples, purple eggplant, and sacks full of limes—all good, fresh produce. But I could understand that Maddie was more comfortable buying vegetables in cans and cuts of meat she knew than to learn the Farsi words and to negotiate with a wily street vendor. But that is exactly what I *wanted* to do. Maddie must have had some lonely times in Tehran, far from the family she had lived with most of her life. Shopping at the commissary was a familiar, social event.

I discovered the Iran-American Society just a few blocks down the street from my father's apartment, so one day I pushed open the big doors and went in to see if I could take classes in Farsi.

"Oh, you're a teacher in America?" the receptionist asked. "Are you available to teach an advanced English class here two evenings a week?"

My hand went to my throat in surprise. Daddy wanted me to be usefully occupied. "Yes, I can do it!" So with no real teaching experience, I agreed and took home the class lesson plans to study.

Two days later I stood nervously in a red dirndl skirt and blouse, bare headed in front of fifteen dark-eyed, black-mustachioed men and several serious women, only some of whom wore headscarves or chadors. Every expectant eye was on me, eager adults ready to advance their proficiency in the language of the future.

Within days, I also discovered that I could get credit at the University of California for practice teaching at the K–12 American Dependent School in Tehran. I began right away in a fifth-grade class, with Mrs. Worthington as my supervisor. The children came from all over the States with different accents and expectations, but the common denominator was that they all were trying to stay American. For some this was a first-time overseas experience, for others, just another in several moves over the years. Each morning outside the school, blue uniformed guards held open steel gates, one story tall, to allow big yellow buses and chauffeured black limousines into the yard to leave the children for the day, then locked the gates behind them. I moved in an American world during the day, eating hot dogs and macaroni and cheese in the immaculate cafeteria; then at three o'clock, I stepped into the noisy, chaotic Iranian city clouded with diesel fumes, kerosene stoves, and donkey dung.

My friends were no longer girls just like me, wearing gathered skirts and shirt-maker blouses, bobby sox and saddle shoes, who went to the Berkeley hills for beer parties on Friday afternoons. Suddenly, my associates were grown women who found themselves living in Tehran and who, like me, were willing to step in and teach at the American Dependent School. An unusual camaraderie developed among these disparate women.

Mrs. Dadgar, the third-grade teacher, was an American married to an officer in the Iranian Army, with two Iranian sons. Betty, a pretty blonde from Kansas, also the wife of an Iranian, was unhappy living in the women's quarters with other wives in her husband's household, rarely spending time alone with her husband. Mrs. Pinkerton, a Texan, and the second-grade teacher, was married to a sergeant in the U.S. Army and had commissary privileges and luxuries that others did not have. Audrey, a pretty, dark-haired girl not much older than I, became a close friend. She was an art teacher from Illinois, who had met her artist husband, Hannibal, an Assyrian-Iranian, at the Chicago Art Institute and had come back to live in Iran with their little boy. One evening while drinking wine and telling stories in their basement apartment, I was shocked to realize I had to go up two flights of stairs to the bathroom they shared with another family.

I listened to the stories of these women, and to be congenial and appear to be grown up, I learned to smoke.

CHAPTER 4

Glamour, Growing Up, and an Announcement

Tehran and Beirut, 1959–1960

I MIGHT HAVE CALLED HIM "Mister" had I met him a few months earlier when I was still in school. Tony was six years my senior.

At the Bellugette, the French restaurant he took me to on our first date, mirror-paneled walls reflected the chandeliers, white cloths, sparkling glasses, along with the two of us, at an intimate table for two. The bluest of eyes focused on me as he talked. His eyebrows slanted upwards as though questioning, waiting for my comment. He leaned back, pulled out a pack of unfiltered Lucky Strikes from his shirt pocket, and, tapping one corner, offered me a cigarette before taking one himself. I took it, possibly the second cigarette of my life, and leaned close while he flicked open his lighter. He lit mine and his own, then leaned back in his chair, brushed a blond wave of hair from his brow, and watched me pick pieces of tobacco off my tongue with the long red nails of my thumb and ring finger, pinky in the air. "Fire and Ice," the new-est color from Revlon, was the matching shade on my lips, so fashionable. We were total opposites: I dark and he fair. I sipped a gin and tonic, he a Scotch and soda. I ordered Kievski, a chicken breast wrapped around a burst of melted butter and herbs. He had Iranian lamb kebabs and rice pilaf. I felt like I was in a staged world, the exotic setting, the glamour, the handsome leading man. I had been to sophisticated places in San Francisco, but not with a worldly man like Tony.

Between courses, we danced to the three-piece combo. I quickly adjusted to that little twist of his right foot as he kept the beat and looked around at other tables and the people on the dance floor. "Where do all these foreigners come from?" I asked. "And the Iranians, I'm surprised to see them at a night club like this."

"Well," he began, "many of the Americans are with the U.S. Embassy, and many are military people, army, marines, but a lot of us are here to develop business for American companies." He explained about the Shah wanting to modernize the country, and about President Truman sending economic aid under the Point Four Program after the war. Americans had poured into the country to help. Restaurants and nightclubs with cabaret shows catered to pleasure-seeking foreigners and wealthy Iranians. Expats had expense accounts and hardship bonuses and household help. They also had to adjust to the lack of American conveniences like supermarkets, peanut butter, mayonnaise, ready-made clothing, reliable electricity, washing machines, and telephones. Cocktail parties, diplomatic dinners and nightclubs helped to assuage homesickness.

That night I listened to Tony explain things to me, as I would for the next forty-five years, breathless and impressed. Waiting for dessert, Tony suddenly said to the waiter, "Please bring me a lemon." He tied knots in the corners of the cloth *serviette*, put the lemon under the napkin and gave it a little push. The napkin wobbled across the table, kind of like a mouse. A party trick! Sophistication? Ha! He was normal and could be silly, maybe just a kid like me! We laughed at everything. The waiter brought American coffee (Nescafé), along with sugar cubes in a bowl. When he tipped the bowl slightly and a cube fell on the floor, he picked it up with a flourish, blew off the dust, and put it back in the bowl.

When Tony took me back to the apartment, he asked me to

dinner the following night; and soon, when he was in town, we saw each other every night. But he was often away on business trips for a week at a time, allowing me some time with my father and Maddie. Those evenings, Daddy taught me to play backgammon. I noticed the running score sheet for him and Maddie and wondered if she was a better player than I was. "Hot Diggety!" he called out, shaking the ice in his bourbon highball when the game went his way. I wanted to win so he would respect me but was uncomfortable taking Maddie's place. I tried to tune out the noise from the kitchen while Maddie did the dishes alone. While we played, I thought he might mention my mother, maybe ask me how she was, or notice that I looked like her. He didn't. He had been married to my mother for fourteen years but never spoke of her to me. I wanted to ask him about his life after he left our family, but I couldn't. It was too personal.

Some mornings he woke me up early to play tennis before I went to school to teach. I was aware of his trying to be a good sport and wanted to help him be a good father, but I didn't trust that he wasn't teasing me and wishing I had more spunk. "Don't be a sissy," he had said when I was a child and he wanted me to go off the high diving board or jump my horse over a log at camp on visitors' day, and I had let him down. I still had an uneasy self-consciousness around my father, trying not to disappoint him. I relaxed with Tony who had, as far as I knew, no expectations of me. I was who I was.

During the next three months, Tony and I must have hit all the nightclubs and cabarets in the city. We ate out with his many friends and business associates, sipped our drinks, and watched Spanish dancers, jugglers, gymnasts, and other circus-type performers on a gaudy stage. The performers weren't local. They were members of a troupe of musicians and dancers from Austria on tour through Europe and the Middle East.

Tony was, as I have described him, a tall man with wavy blond hair and blue eyes that almost closed when he laughed, which was often and heartily. He stood so straight, up to his full height of six-foot-three, that there were no wrinkles in the shoulders of his crisp, white shirt. He often tipped his head down slightly to hear conversation. He spoke assuredly on most subjects, and foreign languages came easily. He was a charmer, having learned impeccable manners from his aunt and uncle when he immigrated to Ohio in 1952.

His chief quality, the thing that I think people, myself included, noticed first and were attracted to, was his confidence—not a big ego or bragging, but an easy assurance that he would be noticed and accepted by any group he walked into.

On our long afternoon drives out of town over the dirt roads surrounding the city and across what I recall as desert, I looked over at him in the driver's seat, no chauffeur, and marveled at his clean-cut good looks. And I listened.

"Toward the end of the war," he said, "my school in Zaandam was closed because there was no heat, and then the Germans took it over, so I went to live with my grandparents in Amsterdam and to go to school there. I was twelve, so I never spent a lot of time with my five younger brothers and sisters. I loved them, of course, but that is the way it was. When the war was over, and I was fifteen or so, I hitchhiked with three buddies to Denmark and Sweden. We were welcomed everywhere and often given free food and lodging in a barn, because during the war years nobody had traveled and people were glad to see us. When I got back home, everyone gathered in the living room, neighbors too, and listened to me tell about my trip." *Yes*, I thought. *He enjoys an audience.*

I talked, too. And I spoke without worrying what he thought about me, because, unlike other boyfriends I'd had, I knew I'd never see him again, so it really didn't matter that I say the "right" thing. I was honest and comfortable with a man for the first time in my life.

I learned that Tony's goal was not to make a lot of money, but to do a good job. He respected excellence and had no use for shoddy or careless work, even if the worker was his superior. He judged people by their work, not by their ethnicity or social position. His acceptance of people made me, too, eager to meet people as individuals, giving me a freedom from conventions that

I didn't know were binding me and a new ease in moving about in the world.

One afternoon he drove me to the house where he lived in Shemran. A mud brick wall surrounded the property, as it did every private home in this area, to keep intruders out and privacy in, each residence identified, not by a house number but by its uniquely designed iron gate. Tony stopped the car at the sign of the Big Red T and honked the horn. Reza, the houseboy, appeared, running backwards, grinning as he pulled the gates open, and the car passed through.

"A Persian garden!" I gasped at the rush of color. Rose bushes, pink and red, lined the drive, and pansies, purple, red, and yellow formed circles on the bright green lawn, and row upon row of orange and red zinnias edged a small swimming pool sparkling blue in the autumn sun. We stepped from the car onto a broad terrace and through the sliding glass doors into the living room.

"*Salaam Aleichem, Khanoom,*" Reza said, nodding his head in greeting. Reza was a young man from the countryside who had been a watchman at the house before Tony rented it, and Tony had kept him on, introducing him to electricity, women without veils, and Nescafé.

We sat on the couch while Reza boiled water in an enamel pan on the one-burner gas plate, put a teaspoonful of the Nescafé coffee powder in two cups, and carefully added the water. He stirred each one and inched his way toward us, one saucer and one gently rattling cup in each hand. Then he left us alone.

I spent the afternoon there, and though I was attracted to Tony, we did not sleep together. Sex before marriage was simply not imaginable for me. This was 1959, before the Pill, before the sexual revolution. Of course, some girls "did it," but I naively knew nothing about contraception and was sure that if I dared I would get pregnant immediately and everyone back home would know I had broken the taboo.

One evening, at a table in the Park Hotel lounge sitting with business associates, we listened to a trio of Italian musicians playing romantic songs. (All songs were romantic in those days.)

When the business talk was over and the band took a break, Tony suddenly got up and went over to the piano and started playing "The Third Man Theme." Lovely! There was a slight applause from the few people in the lounge, but Tony modestly declined to play more.

Not long afterward, at a friend's house, Tony impressed us all by a second performance of "The Third Man Theme," this time followed by "La Mer." He played with ease and feeling in front of people, but I soon discovered those were the only two songs he knew!

Over his lifetime, his piano playing would improve, his repertoire would grow, and his music would become a source of real pleasure for him and for me. He would play the piano while I fixed dinner. Strangely and fortunately, it was an ability that never left him, even as other attributes that made him who he was disappeared. Tony and his lifestyle captivated me, but when he asked me to join him in Beirut over the Christmas break, I hesitated. I still thought of him as a casual boyfriend.

"I don't want him to think I like him *too* much," I told my supervising teacher.

"Don't be silly," she said. "Go and have a good time. You'll get to see the Holy Land and Beirut and Lebanon and he'll pay for everything. What an opportunity!"

Yes, I thought, this is what people do. I can handle it, and I'll get to see another part of the world. I was ready for a break, and Lebanon and the Holy Land sounded like a great adventure.

I thought about consulting my father about the trip, but by then I was beginning to gain my confidence and wanted to show my independence. Our backgammon evenings had become less frequent, though I still got up early sometimes to play tennis so as to be a sport with my father.

When I had accepted the invitation to visit him in Iran, I had been thrilled by the prospect of adventure, and even though I appreciated this trip as a huge gift, I also felt it was my due. My father had not sent child support payments for years—in fact, not until he married Maddie and she saw to it that he sent them. It was too late for him to come see me in school plays, or be my guest at Dads' night, or counsel me through the high school years. I thought by going to Iran I could somehow make up for lost years and become truly my father's daughter, but I still carried some resentment, which may have prevented us from talking in a more personal way. Instead, what I discovered in Iran was that I had grown up fine without him, and sadly, I didn't need him anymore.

"I have a place to stay in Beirut," I reassured them, "with the Morrisons, business friends of Tony's. Everything will be all right."

"You are no longer a schoolgirl, Liz," Maddie said. "You should fix your hair. Get a permanent before your trip."

So I took a taxi to the salon of my friend Rosette. Arriving at her address, I entered the building, climbed a dark stairway, and found my way to her shop. It was dark there, too, with green walls, scarred and marked, maybe with splattered hair dye, maybe just peeling from age. Rosette's face lit up when she recognized me and she ran over and planted a kiss on each cheek.

From the hoods of two dryer chairs a whirr of hot air blew out onto the concealed heads of the two women sitting there. Other customers looked up at me, obviously *farangi*, a foreigner, without the traditional all-covering chador. The Shah's father had actually banned the chador in 1921 as part of his push toward modernization, and many women, but not all, enjoyed the freedom of going without the black robe.

In 1959, hair was teased up high into "The Beehive." That meant big rollers to give big hair, with lots of backcombing to create the bouffant. No more bobby pins. Rosette sent me to the shampoo girl before she pinned two-inch pink plastic rollers in my wet hair and settled me under the hood of an old-fashioned dryer, hot air hitting my head. Immediately, the electricity went off. "Never mind," Rosette said. "This happens all the time, and this is what we do." She shook open several newspapers from a waiting pile and clipped them tent-like all over my head. Then she positioned me over a kerosene gas heater. Whoosh! I was out of the chair, dancing around the room with flames leaping from my head. The other ladies in the shop waved their arms around and called out advice while a laughing Rosette threw towels on me and grabbed at the burning tent. The fire was out quickly and she fussed and whisked away the ashes with a towel. What could I say? Nothing that could be understood, so I laughed too, and then sat mutely with my hands folded and let her do it *again*! I sat very still. No fire this time. My hair dried quickly and I left the place looking like other fashionable Iranian women on the street.

I got off the plane in the airport in Beirut, somewhat self-conscious with my new hair-do, but the day glistened with sunshine. Had the world changed so much since I had landed there three months ago in the dark of night? I scanned the milling crowd for Tony, when our friend, Glenn Morrison, rushed up to me. "Tony's not here," she told me. "The small plane that he was in had engine trouble and made an emergency landing. He's okay, but has to wait for another plane to pick up the three or four passengers and bring them here. He should be in tomorrow." My heart sank. Emergency landing in the desert didn't sound very good. Was he all right? I was alone. My hostess, Glenn, was a woman I had only just met, but, for that matter, I didn't know Tony much better.

Glenn and I sat in the back seat and her driver took us to the apartment where she and her husband, Walt, lived. She opened the door to a sunlit room, and I walked toward the breeze from the open French doors and onto a balcony overlooking the blue bay of the Mediterranean. Any qualms I had left me.

When Tony arrived the next day, I greeted him with joy and relief. Up to this point I had considered Tony a "date," another one of many boyfriends I had been out with for varying periods of time. When he rushed over to me waiting at the gate and took me in his arms, I knew this was different. But I was going back to Berkeley in January. This feeling must be just infatuation. Later, sitting at the bar of his hotel, I was rapt as he told me the tale of his night in the desert, pacing the cold sands with the pilot. They had left the plane to the few other passengers, local people, who squatted in the aisles burning charcoal in samovars to heat water for tea. I loved being so close to him and to adventure!

Today the mention of Beirut or Lebanon brings to mind Middle East chaos and a world in turmoil. Back then, after my initial apprehension, it meant to me romance and sophistication. During the one week I was there, in 1959, I focused on Tony and me, having no awareness of rumblings of political discontent.

Together Tony and I discovered the souks, small open shops with colorful wares lining both sides of narrow streets, not unlike the covered bazaar of Tehran. In the evenings, we dined and danced. The city was full of European restaurants, nightclubs, and cabarets.

An extravagant casino had opened in the nearby town of Jounieh, just north of Beirut; it was a holiday destination for sheiks from the Persian Gulf, fun-seeking people from eastern Mediterranean countries, and, of course, for us. Arm in arm, *almost like a couple*, I thought, we stepped into what seemed to be a true life movie set with dazzling people, earnest conversations, and elaborate cabaret acts. On the stage was a constant rotation of belly dancers, men juggling knives while balancing pyramids of glasses and plates, trapeze artists, and tumblers. I had left the college world behind and was acting the sophisticated lady, drinking gin and tonics, smoking cigarettes, and dancing in nightclubs with a man of the world who switched easily from English to French and occasionally to Arabic or Farsi.

Tony's counterpart in Lebanon, Jim, and his wife Alice, invited us to their home for a Christmas party. She, blond and beautiful, and he, dark and good-looking, had been college sweethearts in Ohio and now lived here with their two little boys. They welcomed us into a reception room and then into a large living room in an upstairs apartment with a view of the city lights and the Mediterranean beyond. The room bubbled with conversations in Arabic, French, and English. I reveled in the atmosphere, chit-chatting with the men and women in this eclectic crowd.

Alice was a few years older than I, maybe twenty-six or -seven, and I asked her what her life was like there.

"Oh, Liz, you wouldn't believe it. Look at this fabulous apartment. It is a dream. I have a live-in nanny for the boys so I can go out and shop, play bridge, and have lunch with my friends any time. Another servant cleans the house and does the cooking. I belong to several international women's groups, so we do some charity work, like putting on fundraising galas and things like that. Wonderful parties."

"What about your family back in Ohio? Don't you miss them?"

"Oh, sure but we get three months' vacation, home-leave, every three years, and I have gone a couple of times for a shorter visit with the boys."

"Do you feel safe going out?" I asked.

"Oh, yes. This is like the French Riviera. That shooting business that Tony got caught up in 1958 is all over with and we can go out safely and buy everything we need here. I am really very happy."

Shooting business? Oh, yes. The coup! Tony had been caught in the same event that took the marines from Naples the year before. His original assignment from Firestone had been to Beirut to use as his base while he traveled through his Middle East territory. They wanted a man without a family because of the unrest at the time. The week he arrived in the summer of 1958, he and several others were caught in the crossfire in an apartment building, slithering across the floor to avoid gunshots and to get martinis from the refrigerator. A few days later, he packed up his things and left for Tehran as a safer place to live.

Fifteen years later in 1975, Lebanon, which had been the intellectual capital and financial center of the Arab world as well as a prime tourist destination, erupted in civil war. Muslims and the Christian government backed by the U.S. were caught up in a continuation of the unrest that Tony had seen in 1958. In 1983 the bombing of the U.S. Marine barracks publicly resparked the clashes that had been simmering in the whole region, leading up to the chaotic, militant, never-ending strife that continues today in the Middle East.

But in the fifties and sixties, after the Second World War, American companies had raced into the Middle East to expand their businesses worldwide. They sent trained representatives into these hardship posts, enticing them to stay for three years or more with perks like subsidized housing, an entertainment allowance, and provisions for household help. Communication with the head office took place by air mail letters and telegrams. There was no fax or satellite TV. No computers. No credit cards. Tony traveled with a letter of credit from his company, which he took to the local bank or business to exchange for local currency. However, I knew nothing of that at the time, and knew nothing of the *real* challenges of living in a foreign culture. I was oblivious to the undercurrent of discontent that surely was there.

The world that I knew was safe, organized, and predictable. Though the U.S. military draft was still active, my own world was peaceful. Soon after college, I expected someone would show up that I would marry. We would live in a suburb of San Francisco and raise our children. He would put on a business suit and hat and go to the City to do some mysterious work and come home in the evenings. I might teach school to help out with the finances, but I'd certainly not have a career.

Now I had spent a week in Beirut and been to a Christmas party as Tony's partner and witnessed another way to live. I had glimpsed the glamour and vibrancy of Alice's life, and I liked it.

Tony and I were to fly back to Tehran on Christmas Eve. I had shed the role of visitor since we had met three months before, on September 21, though I still had a temporary feeling and the knowledge that my experience in Iran would end. I was teaching, moving in an adult world, and had absorbed an awareness of other worlds and possibilities. The night before we were to leave Beirut, we sat smooching on the couch, very late. The Morrisons were asleep. The house was quiet. Tony snuggled up to me, then sat back and said, "You know, when you leave Tehran next month to go back to California, well, that's pretty soon. I might call you in a year or two when I am back there and you'll say, 'Tony who?' You won't remember me. Won't even know who I am.

"Well, that could happen," he went on, "or, we have two other choices." He held up his thumb and forefinger in a gesture I would see repeatedly over the years. "One, we could live together, or two..." Tony inhaled deeply for a moment as he lowered his forefinger "...we could get married."

Oh, I thought, *he's not kidding. Is he asking me to marry him?* Softly, I said, "People who get married usually love each other."

"Well, of course, that goes without saying," he teased.

"It does?"

"I love you enough for both of us," he said. "But don't answer me now. Just think about it."

"But—"

"No, just think about it. I'll ask you again later. In fact, I'll call you the day after we get back to see if you want to go ring shopping."

"Oh...."

Think about it? Think about it?

I tried. I tried to think. I made lists of pros and cons. He was mature. He loved adventure and said he loved me. I'd never been in love before—lots of boyfriends but never *in love*. Was this what love was? Having a magnificent man in love with you, spoiling you and offering you an exciting life with him? Was it the thrill of finding a handsome, intelligent, educated (he could speak five languages!), interesting, exciting man whom I could love in return and trust and care for? True, we had met just three months before, and I didn't know his family or his history, but I knew *him*. We were in a place where even his friends had known him less than a year, but we had talked honestly with each other about our concept of marriage, agreeing that it was a lifetime commitment to our partner, without games, jealousy, or rivalry.

Tony had planned his life carefully, and now, when he was settled in a career and a citizen of the United States, as he had always wanted to be, he was ready for a family, and I came along. It seemed right. There was truth in what he said that evening, for who hasn't had a vacation flirtation, fallen madly in love for two weeks, then gone home and forgotten all about it? Perhaps Tony had had such a love and let her get away? I never asked him.

Somewhere in my subconscious mind, I knew the alternative to marrying now. I would lose him forever. I would go home and live with my mother while I did my practice teaching. My college community had dispersed, no more sorority, and the five girlfriends in my close group were already married, meaning they were no longer available to me. I had no model for that kind of life. I imagined boredom and a dead-end—and no Tony, ever.

My conscious thinking was that all summer and early fall I had been to weddings. Maybe it was my turn now, time to be married and get on with what I really wanted in life, a home and children. Nobody could fault my choice; I had fallen in love with a "catch."

He was my fate, my *Kismet.*

The morning after we returned from Beirut, I was up and dressed, walking from room to room in my father's apartment, trying to be helpful to Maddie, trying to keep busy and nonchalant while waiting for Tony to call. I jumped when the phone rang and I lifted the receiver.

"Shall we go ring shopping?" I recognized the slight Dutch accent, the warmth and confidence, the short, directness of his few words, words with life-changing meaning. If I answered as directly and said yes, we would be engaged to be married. I took a big breath, and cleared my throat, suddenly gone dry.

"Yes, okay," I heard myself answer. "See you in an hour."

I put the phone down.

"Maddie!" I said, taking a step into the kitchen, "Maddie! I'm getting married! Tony and I are engaged!"

"Oh! Oh!" she said. "I knew it! When? Here? Now? Will you wear a white dress?"

"A white dress?" *Oh, yes, a white dress. I'm getting married!*

Tony and I went that morning to Lalazar Street, and among the gorgeous princess rings and other dazzling elaborate settings, we found only one ring that looked like those on my sorority sisters' fingers and in *Vogue* and *Madamoiselle* magazines. It was not the most perfect diamond, but that was the one I wanted.

Not more than an hour after I got back to the apartment,

my father called from his office with the news that he had finally finagled a ticket for me so I could accompany him and Maddie on their cruise through the Suez Canal, when they returned to the States in February, their overseas assignment completed.

"Daddy?" I said into the phone and hesitated. "Daddy? I'm not going with you. I'm staying here and marrying Tony."

"Oh." He paused. "We'll talk about that when I get home."

That evening we sat opposite each other in the living room, just as we had on the morning I had arrived in Tehran. We were as formal and uneasy as we had been then.

"Don't you think you should go home and ask your mother?" he said, taking a large sip of his drink.

I sat up straight and clasped my hands tightly in my lap. "No, I'm staying here and getting married. Mother will be thrilled for me, I know."

"Tony has an accent, you know. He'll always have one."

"Yes, I guess he does. I find it intriguing." I thought how Maddie's Midwestern manner of speech startled me a little and probably bothered my father, too, or he wouldn't have mentioned it.

"He seems to be well employed."

"Yes."

"And you feel all wiggly inside when you're with him?"

"Yes."

And that was it.

My father had given me so much with this trip—three months of unimagined experience, but most of all the knowledge that he was interested in me. I knew now he loved me and cared about my well-being. I also knew he would never be the affectionate, demonstrative father I had created in my imagination, but he was the person who provided opportunities for me and finally, the environment for me to meet Tony and start my new, adult life with confidence.

And so, the next day, without any indication that I had disappointed him, my father began the process of reversing the extra Suez Canal ticket he had pulled strings to arrange.

Now, to tell my mother. I had started a long letter a few days before so across the top of the first page I wrote, "SKIP THE FIRST 8 PAGES! GO TO PAGE 9! BIG NEWS!!!!"

She responded with a telegram asking me to phone her immediately.

To make an international phone call Tony made an appointment at the post office. We were shown to a small concrete room where we sat on a concrete bench and placed the call through an operator. We waited for about half an hour. Mother and I talked over a cable line, making for a stilted conversation.

"Are you sure?" she asked, and waited. "Yes, Mother, I'm sure," I answered, thinking, *Mother told me she was sure when she married my father and fourteen years later they were divorced.* Suddenly, I wasn't sure! My hands were sweating. Tony had already started the complicated process of changing my visa from tourist to resident. I couldn't back out! I loved him! I was starting my life! Making a choice…and hoping it was the right one. I wanted to say it out loud, to make my decision real.

"Oh, yes, Mother, I am in love and I'm very sure." Tony stood across from me, grinning so widely that I thought he would burst.

"I just wanted to hear it from your own voice," she said. "I often play the records from *Kismet* and think of you in that beautiful setting. I wish you and Tony a lovely life."

Tony put his arms around me, cradling my head against his chest. The call was over. I stopped, and with tears filling my eyes I envisioned the scene unfolding at home. I could see Mother sitting at the little yellow telephone table in the kitchen. She would have placed the black receiver in its cradle and sat for a moment, slumped against the wall. I could see the kitchen wallpaper, forest green scattered with white and red chickens, and the round walnut table where she and I had shared our meals and talked about the world. She would sit there alone now. I wasn't coming home. She didn't know the man in my life. She wouldn't be at my wedding.

"Oh, my romantic mother," I said. "She's been listening to the *Kismet* music, 'Stranger in Paradise.' I want her to know you, Honey."

That afternoon he wrote her a letter.

Dear Mrs. Gibbons,.... I was born in Amsterdam on October 24th, 1931, and besides being my parents' first child I also was the first grandchild on both sides. I believe the resulting amount of attention and "guidance" of relatives may have been one of the reasons to help me decide to leave Holland and make my home in the United States. I received my high school and college education in Holland (Zaandam, Amsterdam and Groningen) which was interrupted for nearly one year at the end of the war during which period I received private lessons at home. My major subjects: Languages (Latin, Greek, Dutch, German, French, English and Spanish) in high school and Exact Sciences in college. I entered the military service in Holland in the summer of 1952 but was discharged in October 1952 as I had received my visa for the U.S.A. I left Holland in December 1952 and arrived in New York January 1, 1953. Shortly after my arrival I was hired by Firestone International Company. I attended the University of Akron, Ohio during 1953 and '54 and again during 1958 and part of '59 (Accounting, Business Administration and Foreign Trade). I was drafted into the U.S. Army in January 1955 and received my American Citizenship in October 1955 while stationed in Fort Carson, Colorado. In December 1955 I sailed for Korea and served in Tank Company, 17th Infantry Regiment till January 1957. Upon my return to the States I was discharged from the Army and placed on stand-by reserve....

He listed relatives he had in the United States, including his Uncle Sam, his grandmother's youngest brother, in Akron, Ohio, who had sponsored Tony for U.S. citizenship.

I am very happy that Liz and I understand each other on the subject of religion. Regardless of what we believe, it is essential that our children will know that their parents agree and understand each other....

I'm glad Liz and I often talk about things. It is all right to be in love and all that but it is so infinitely more important to be in love AND be able to talk things over with sense and understanding....

But the main thing is that Lizzie and I want to make our life together a good life. The short time Liz has been here has been a long time in many respects because we got to know each other. Liz has made a marvelous adjustment here and is flexible enough to be at ease with the rather large variety of different sorts of people we associate with. This is a wonderful quality and I am sure it will be one of the important parts of the foundation on which we build our marriage.

"Flexible enough to be at ease..." When Tony read the letter to me before mailing it, I noted that phrase. That was what I would need to live life as Tony's partner, flexibility and adaptability. I knew I had that. I would have no commissary privileges as Tony's wife. Besides no peanut butter or mayonnaise, I would have only fruit and vegetables in season and only those that could be peeled or scrubbed because of the use of human fertilizer, so the picture-perfect strawberries in the markets were off limits. We would buy only powdered milk because the cows were not tubercular-free, nor was the milk pasteurized. I would buy whole chickens, and purchase meat cut from those carcasses that hung outside in the sun. I would give up driving myself. An Iranian chauffeur would take me to do my shopping, which I would do in a language I had never heard six months before. I couldn't even decipher signs as I could in a European language because the letters and numbers were in Arabic writing. Every item had to be haggled over, every tomato, every slab of bread.

I would have no friends or relatives in Tehran when my father and Maddie left two weeks after our wedding. No telephone, no TV, unreliable electricity, a wringer washing machine and no dryer—and this was in the days when every shirt was white and had to be ironed. But I was in love, and eager to accept the challenge of living a new life. Many American women had difficulty adapting and made themselves and their spouses miserable or went back to the States. I, never having been a wife in America, had nothing to compare with or miss, really, except vanilla flavoring for cookies.

Though Mother and I never again lived geographically near each other, all my life I would depend on her encouragement and belief in me. When I was growing up, she had said to me, "Liz, I can not promise you your life will be easy, but what ever happens, I know you will be able to cope with it."

CHAPTER 5

Champagne and a Swish of a Tartan

Tehran, 1960

I DOUBT IF I WILL EVER see that place again. It was a non-denominational Christian Community Church on Khiaban Qavam-os-Saltoneh in the heart of one of the most fundamentalist Muslim cities in the world, Tehran, Iran. Walking down the aisle, my arm linked through my father's on my wedding day, Friday, February 7, 1960, I was aware of the gentle shaking of the apricot-colored carnations grasped in my sweaty fists. *What am I doing here?* I thought. *That tall, blond man standing down there by the altar is about to be my husband, forever.* "Watch out the Shah doesn't get you!" my friends had warned me as I left home in California. The Shah didn't get me, but Tony did.

I stared up into Tony's eyes. We repeated the ritual "I do's." I tried with difficulty to focus on their meaning, on what I was doing. We slipped rings onto each other's fingers and we were done. Tony took an audible deep breath and I knew he was as nervous as I was. We turned with wide grins to face the congregation, really the audience, when our best man, Doug, with a swish of his tartan kilt, lofted a three-foot sword to bless the union. Startled, I laughed and hung onto Tony with a full and happy heart as we galloped down the aisle to a back table, where we signed papers with the representative from the American Embassy, making the ceremony legal in the U.S. Our wedding guests clapped and cheered when we stepped outside and ducked under an arch of swords held aloft by Tony's buddies, geographical bachelors in their army dress uniforms.

In front of us stood that rickety droshky dripping with nonsense, a JUST MARRIED sign flapping in the breeze, pots and pans and streamers drooping under the old horse's hooves. We climbed up on the worn-out seat, to be carried away by a driver who peeked around to see what apparition was behind him, as the horse ambled through the streets of Tehran. Tony's friends, foreseeing a party, had petitioned the Iranian Minister of Transportation, who had in turn organized the police with megaphones to escort the carriage through the streets, keeping the crowds at bay in case someone might think we were royalty and take a pot shot at us. Ignorant of political tensions, we bounced along, laughing and waving as if we *were* royalty.

In anticipation of the reception, my father had used his engineering skills to test the second-floor apartment he shared with his wife Maddie, to determine how many people it would hold without collapsing, then watched in disbelief as several times that number climbed the stairs and jammed into his living room to celebrate. Everyone we knew was looking for a party. My father had opted out of my life years ago, but he turned up in time to be a great father of the bride, hosting the reception, even buying a second case of Champagne because he and his friend Dave had tested out most of the first one.

After greeting each of our guests, Tony and I stood hand in hand and looked eye-level at Doug's bare knees as he stood on a chair, his legs naked from his kilt to his socks, his sword swinging at his side, reading congratulatory telegrams from all over the world. Oh, the strange-sounding names of the well-wishers! Greek, Norwegian, Spanish, French, and especially Arabic and Farsi. Tongue twisters all, and Tony repeated them in my ear, never forgetting anyone. I knew I had married someone very smart.

The guests cleared a path. Doug stepped down from the chair and led the way to the cake table, gleaming with white linen and silver. He swished out his sword and bowed as he placed the carved golden handle in our two joined hands. Together my husband and I sliced down into the small top tier, lifted the blade up, and then in again for the second tier, and finally pulled it through the thick base of the cake. We fed each other the first bite, hilariously signifying the care we promised to give each other in the years ahead, in sickness and in health, not even thinking what that might mean in reality. I tossed my bouquet down the stairwell to waiting single ladies, and Tony, to the astonishment of the Iranian waiters, lifted my skirt above my knee and pulled a lacy blue garter from my thigh and tossed it out to the boisterous bachelors. With that, the party was over. We were chauffeur-driven up Pahlavi Road toward Tony's little house in Shemran.

After changing our clothes, we poured another glass of Champagne and snuggled somewhat nervously on the couch. Tony put a small box into my hand. I looked up at him, pulled gently at the ribbon and lifted the lid. Nestled in white cotton was a gold link bracelet with two gold charms from the two countries where we had been together, a round locket from Lebanon and a delicate cross from Jordan. "It's for you, Lizzie, for both of us, for our life together. We'll add a charm for each country we visit for the next fifty years or so." My hand brushed across the empty links. Who knew the future? At that silent moment, I was secure and in love, confident that I would be taken care of, but barely grasping what the day had meant. I reached for the box I had for him, but before I had a chance to show him the gold watchband I knew he had seen in Beirut and wanted, the stillness was broken by sudden clatter and banging on the steel gate.

Reza, the houseboy, came running in, waving and shouting, "Agha! Agha!" We jumped up and looked out the patio doors to see arms and legs dangling over the iron gates, fists pounding on the metal. Laughing and whooping, our friends dropped to the ground on our side of the wall. The first ones over yanked on the bolts and let the others in. Champagne glasses still in hand, our celebrants stumbled up the drive and burst through the front door, demanding more drinks and more party. I dashed into the bedroom and covered my wedding negligee with a fuzzy, wooly bathrobe and joined the party. Ah, the party, our first party. The evidence our friends left behind when they finally retreated was dirty glasses, overflowing ashtrays, and a banana between the bed sheets.

CHAPTER 6

Arabian Nights

Persian Gulf, 1960–1962

WITH MY FATHER AND Maddie's departure for the States, suddenly Tony and I were on our own. This time separating from my father didn't feel like abandonment. After all, I was leaving him as much as he was leaving me. I continued to write to him throughout his life much as I had done as a child and felt his responses were much more personal. In later years when we visited, he often marveled at the fate that had brought Tony and me together and delighted in his part of it.

Tony and I packed our bags for a business trip/honeymoon to the Persian Gulf. Watching me, Tony said, "You can't go through customs with a suitcase like that. I'll show you how to pack." He didn't understand about the slippery clothes that women have but he took everything out and repacked for me as neatly as he could.

The pilot, with his young son on his lap, waved to us from the open window of the cockpit of the small propeller-driven plane as we climbed the steps that bright early morning.

At the southern city of Khoramshar, we disembarked to go through customs before leaving Iran. Tony took my passport and our luggage to be inspected while I took his camera and jacket with me to the restroom, not wanting to leave anything on the plane. As I left the washroom, I turned back to get the camera from the faucet where I had hooked it. Impossible. There wasn't a person in sight but the camera was gone. I ran to tell Tony and the inspector. The official waved his arms and shouted, but I realized it was only for show. He had already found the bottle of Scotch tucked under the clothes in the suitcase that Tony always brought for him. I knew I wouldn't get the camera back.

"My camera! My new Leica that I just bought in Germany! Gone?" Tony saw the distress on my face and hugged me close. "Don't worry, Sweetiepie, I can get another one."

I felt dreadful but then grateful that this man I barely knew forgave me. I didn't want to be a disappointment to him.

We flew on to Kuwait, a small, oil-producing sheikdom on the northern end of the Persian Gulf and still a British protectorate. We looked down on the blue-green water of Kuwaiti Bay, then circled mainly sandy and barren terrain before landing. We were chauffeured through the hot, humid air to the guest house of the Firestone dealer. This was traditional Bedouin hospitality, a sacred obligation to offer lodging. To sell hospitality as in a hotel was not an option, which made it hard for Hilton or Holiday Inn to get a foothold in the country. Kuwait is now the largest exporter of oil in the Gulf, but for centuries, Kuwaitis had made their living selling pearls.

"How about these roses?" Tony asked me as he moved the vase from the table and shoved twin beds together.

"Pretty," I answered.

"Is that all? Lizzie, look around you! That's desert out there. Our hosts had these roses flown in from Beirut just for us."

After Tony concluded his business in Kuwait, we flew on to Dhahran, Saudi Arabia, a city settled in 1938 when oil was discovered in the area. By 1950 there were 7,000 inhabitants, including employees of ARAMCO, the Arab-American Oil Company. By 1960, all the amenities of a small town were provided for 14,000 employees of ARAMCO, 2,100 of whom were American, as well as personnel of the U.S. Army Corps of Engineers. We stayed in a small hotel outside the compound and sweltered in the March heat.

Tony was up and out of the room before dawn to stand in the

early morning sun and adjust tires. He, in short sleeves and no hat, worked with men in *jalabas*, which protected them from the sun, and white head scarves that flapped and fanned in the hot breeze. The Saudis rolled out truck tires taller than they were which had blown out or fallen apart while working on the desert sands. Tony inspected them for reimbursable factory defects. A hot, sweaty, dirty job.

Back at the hotel, I noticed a curious cardboard poster-clock about three feet square with movable hands standing on an easel outside the breakfast room. Saudi Arabia ran on sun time, which meant when the sun came up, it was six o'clock, always, every day. A mullah stood atop the minaret at dawn every morning and blew his horn when he saw the sun so people knew it was six o'clock and they could set their watches for the day. The hands of the clock in the hotel were adjusted every morning at the sound of the horn. This made for a fuzziness around appointment times, transportation schedules, and meals, and created a casualness that didn't disturb me much, as I had no appointments. It was more difficult for a fast-moving businessman from the West, wanting to get the work done and get out of there. Tony once sent me a postcard from Saudi Arabia saying, "I really got Abdulla moving today. When I got to his shop, he was at his desk swatting flies with one hand. When I left he was swatting flies with two hands."

Alone at breakfast, I thought how arbitrary time was. People created linear time, man-made, and then gave it the power to structure our lives. Humans seemed to need a framework, or ladder, to step on solidly, something irrefutably true like gravity. But couldn't I turn the stem on my watch and make it a different time? Time wasn't solid, after all, only a convention agreed upon, or not. In that sense, as I read about women of ancient Persia, time narrowed and I became their contemporary.

So reading in the hotel room in Saudi Arabia, I was startled by a knock on the door. An employee dressed in a *jalaba* asked if we had any laundry. Being the new wife that I was, I thought I had to come up with something. Tony had been a lonely bachelor for all those years with no one to look after him and probably never had his ties cleaned. I went to the closet and pulled out the three ties he had brought with him and handed them to the man.

Tony came in that evening, hot and tired from working outside and gave me a big, sweaty hug. "Get dressed up, Lizzie. We're going to the Officers' Club for dinner."

He showered and changed and…reached for his ties.

"Oh!… I sent them all to the cleaners!"

"You what? Oh, Lizzie! They won't let me in the Officers' Club without a tie!" He turned from the closet and threw his head back and roared with laughter, rushed over to give me a hug. "Don't worry, Sweetiepie, I'll call Ahmid and borrow one of his."

Ahmid came to our room with a beautiful silk tie for Tony and a large bottle of Ma Griffe perfume for me. Tony kept the tie for a long time, as Ahmid refused to take it back.

A few days later, we flew the short hop to Bahrain and stayed at the Speedbird Hotel, which I understood to be the only hotel in the country. It was built to accommodate the British BOAC pilots and crew and allowed traveling businessmen to congregate at the bar to socialize and form business contacts.

Mohammed, the Firestone dealer, invited Tony to an open house party where he would be the guest of honor. "He said to bring you, Lizzie. He was chuckling as he said it, though, so you may be the only woman."

I had heard that in the strictest interpretation of Islam, all the wives, mothers, and young children of the extended household live together in the women's quarters, called a harem, and do not see and are not seen by men other than their husbands. The word harem means "forbidden because sacred" or "something forbidden and kept safe." Women could only go out if they were completely covered, and then only if accompanied by a male. Even a young child was accepted as an escort as long as he was male. Each Muslim country was more or less rigid in enforcing the traditional laws. Saudi Arabia was the most strict, as far as I knew, being the birth country of Mohammed, and Iran at that time was liberal under the Shah, even discouraging the wearing of the chador, or cover-up.

Mohammed sent a car to the hotel to take us to his house. Straight-backed chairs lined the four sides of the salon and elaborate Persian carpets covered the empty center space. Escorted into the salon, I realized I *was* the only woman. Tony and I were seated side by side at the center of one wall. Our host sat opposite the entrance, watching his guests arrive in a stream of twos and threes, all dark men in the white *jalabas* and head scarves anchored low over their foreheads with a black coiled braid. They entered with heads lowered but when they glanced up and saw me, a young female person with no head covering in that full, red dirndl skirt and short sleeved shirt-maker blouse (I was careful not to wear sleeveless), they quickly looked away in embarrassment. I watched our host, Mohammed, throw his head back in silent glee, enjoying the joke he'd played on his friends by having me there. Tony told me later he thought Mohammed was trying to show that he was modern and "progressive."

Tony and I were the first to be served, while the others watched us in silence. Two servants entered the room and crossed the carpets toward us. One held a stack of six demitasse-sized, handle-less cups in one hand and a brass coffee server with a long curved spout in the other. He poured the strong, thick, black coffee, lifting his arm high in the air as the coffee streamed down. The second man handed one cup to me and another to Tony. The aroma wafted through the air and into my nostrils. Beads of perspiration broke out on my forehead. I was going to vomit. Cardamom seeds and other unknown things were ground up in the coffee, giving it a foreign and, to me, nauseating aroma. I looked up. Everyone was watching me. My eyes turned to Tony, desperately pleading. *"You drink it!"* he hissed. And I did. While everyone watched. A gag gripped my stomach and rose up in my throat. I smiled and sipped, feeling the sweat drip from my hairline. Politeness required that I drink at least two cups, but I knew that I had pushed my limit with one. The customary signal to show the server that I didn't want a refill was to hand the empty cup back with an obvious wiggle in my wrist. I wiggled vigorously after one cup.

Around the room, velvet curtains covered several doorways. As the servers went around the room with the coffee, I distracted my mind from sweat-producing, recurring gags by watching the curtains move and slightly part. Dark eyes peeked through the openings. The wives, mere black shadows, were looking at me.

On this first trip together we found a gold charm to represent each of the Gulf States, a pearl in a tiny, golden shell from Kuwait, and from Bahrain, a miniature, gold coffee server.

We had known each other a little over four months by the time we were married. Though it sounds like a whirlwind romance and, in a storybook sense it was, it wasn't unconsidered. We knew the facts about each other and that our goals, standards, and ethics were the same, but we did not know how our temperaments or habits would fit with each other.

Those first years of our life together, 1960 to 1962, living in Tehran, our driver took Tony to his office in a dealership downtown and then came back to take me to school, where by then I had my own classroom and a small income.

One weekend morning Tony and I sat together at our new glass-top dining room table, Tony working on his papers, I working on mine. Tony had two stacks of paper squared up in front of him and several sharpened yellow pencils lined up to his left. He picked up one and began to write small, perfect numbers in precise, lined-up columns. In front of me were red paper hearts for Valentine's Day, and a scattering of scraps and somewhere underneath the scraps and valentines, a ragged pile of arithmetic papers to grade. I shuffled among the scraps and kicked at the red paper pieces on the floor around my chair, looking for my red and blue grading pencil.

"Have you got my pencil?" I asked.

"What?" Tony answered.

"Have you seen my red and blue pencil?"

"Your what?"

He didn't look up from what he was doing. He kept working. I had never seen such focus and concentration. In half an hour, Tony was finished with his work. He looked over at me, opened his brief case, tapped his papers straight and laid them in the bottom of the case, put a rubber band around the pencils and returned them to their specific pocket, turned the stapler on its side and fit it into its place, and shut the case. He carried the case into the bedroom and stood it next to the door, ready to go when he was. He came back to the table with a satisfied smile and picked up a pair of scissors. He cut out a few valentines with me, the scraps of red falling directly into the wastebasket. He corrected some of the fifth grade arithmetic papers with precise little checkmarks.

"How did you ever learn to focus like that? You couldn't be budged."

"Well, when I was a little boy…" (many of his stories began like that) "…during the last part of the war, we had no electricity. One lamp hung from the ceiling in the center of the dining room table lit by gas from the meter. Every evening the whole family—six kids, remember, and sometimes a few neighbors, too—sat around that table. Oh, and we were hiding my uncle, my mother's eighteen-year-old brother. If the Germans found him, they would cart him off to work in the German factories. As a little kid, you learned to keep a secret.

"My father might be discussing the war and the Dutch resistance with a friend; my mother had a baby on her lap or she was knitting and chatting with the lady from next door. The younger kids were either playing a game at the table or running around it. A couple of us older ones did our schoolwork there. That must have been where I developed that ability to focus."

"Oh, that big family and no electricity. At least you had gas for a lamp."

"Not always. Sometimes the gas ran so slowly that it didn't come in strong enough to turn the meter and the light went out. My father got up and went in the other room and kicked the meter to get it started again. I helped him rig up a rope and a log so he could stay where he was at the table and yank on the rope so the log would swing and kick the meter. No one looked up. We just heard the thump and went on with our work. You learn to concentrate when all that stuff is going on."

I was to meet my Dutch in-laws in June. Tony took time off and arranged a non-working honeymoon in Europe. We rented a car and spent a few days in Germany, appropriately purchasing a small golden beer stein for my bracelet and in Denmark, where we selected the top hat of Hans Christian Andersen, whose fairy tales I had loved as a child. Holland welcomed us with bright red and yellow fields under clear blue sky, as did Tony's parents when we pulled up in front of their house, 35 Rood, Schoutjeslaan, in Haarlem. Tony and I took time to wander into a jewelry store on Kalverstraat, the shopping street in Amsterdam, and found a tiny gold windmill with moving sails to add to our bracelet. In spite of, or maybe because of, his parents' minimal English and my non-existent Dutch, we got along well, and throughout our marriage it was so.

Back in Tehran, we ate out several times a week, often at the American Club, sometimes at a nightclub, and frequently at parties given by diplomats or other business associates. One evening I danced with the representative from Ford Motor Company, the man who had traveled to Beirut and who had brought back the gold wristwatch band for me to give to Tony for a wedding present. I was fond of him. "What do you know about Tony, really?" he asked.

"I know he is wise, and smart, and honest, and clever, and he loves me!" I answered. "And I've met his parents in Holland. Great people."

"You've known him a couple of months, right? How do you know he doesn't have a wife and kids somewhere else?" he teased.

"Oh, ridiculous," I laughed. "Quit teasing!"

In August, the hottest of hot times, we were in Baghdad and I had to cut the trip short because I was sick, and not just because of the heat. I was pregnant.

Our baby, Caroline, was born in Berkeley while we were staying with Mother for home leave. Tony entranced my mother as he had me, taking us out to nice restaurants before and after the baby was born. At breakfast, my husband and baby joined Mother and me at the table in the kitchen with the white and red chickens on green wallpaper. I was content and proud. Home for two months. When Caroline was seven weeks old, we packed up and shipped the baby paraphernalia and left Berkeley to return to Tehran, stopping in Amsterdam to show her off to Oma and Opa. I was nursing and didn't have to fuss with bottles and formula, but it was the first trip of many over the years where I washed cloth diapers in hotel bathtubs.

Back home in Tehran with my Caroline, I didn't travel with Tony anymore, nor did I resume teaching. I took care of my baby and became a housewife. Tony's house was beginning to look like *our* house, even though Tony arranged the furniture. He stood in the doorway, studied the layout of the room and immediately moved each piece just once into the most pleasing place. I would have had to shove and tug and try this and that before arriving at probably the same arrangement.

We had been given wedding gifts in the custom of the Middle East, not toasters or tableware, but jewelry for the bride, including several gold and diamond pieces. In the center of the blue and red Persian carpet that Tony already owned, he put the brilliant copper and tin tray table, a gift from Jaleh, our maid of honor. On lonely evenings with Tony away, I took the tray off its stand and put it on the floor. Then, sitting with a rag blackened with Brasso, I rubbed and polished those Persepolis Guards that marched around it until their shields and spears gleamed like pink mirrors and my arm ached from the effort.

With Tony's encouragement, I took painting lessons from Hannibal Alkhaus, studied Farsi, and joined the American Women's Club. But when I told Tony I had volunteered to chair their annual fashion show, he jumped right in to organize me and it. "As insurance," he said, "I don't want to be associated with a failure." I backed off, hurt, but afraid he might be right; maybe being in charge was more than I could handle.

One day I asked Tony if I could buy a lamp I had seen downtown. "Of course," he said, "you don't have to ask. We have plenty of money." That was the time we should have had the Money Talk. But we didn't. I didn't ask how much he made or how much I could spend. His salary was deposited half in Iran and half in the States, so no matter how much we had in Iranian Rials, there was, theoretically, more we could use in dollars. I gave my dollar paycheck from the school to Tony to deposit in the States and had no idea how much I was contributing, or how much anything was worth. Though I had worked various jobs through high school and college and knew the value of money in that context, I had been schooled not to talk about money and I didn't want to pry into Tony's domain as head of the household. So I didn't.

Tony had rented our first home in Tehran before I knew him and had furnished it with a worn, gray velour couch and two matching armchairs, a wooden bar and coffee table, and a particularly ugly lamp, wrought iron with five hanging plastic lamp shades, each a different color. I couldn't wait to get rid of it all. Yet, when he came home early one afternoon in May of 1962 with "news," I scanned the room with a loving heart if not loving eyes.

"What do you mean, 'We're moving'?" I clutched my one-year-old Caroline as if he was taking her from me.

"I got a telegram today that says the Firestone man in Casablanca has quit, and they want me to take over immediately and run the Casablanca office. Be the manager of the retread plant there and handle the imports and everything! It's a wonderful opportunity and a great promotion."

"Oh? Well? That's good. I guess," I stammered, trying to understand the import of what he was telling me. "Where's Casablanca? Isn't it in North Africa? Is it French?"

"It's Morocco! You're right! And I can use my French. It'll be perfect! You'll love it!"

"But I haven't finished up the American Women's Club fashion show, and what about my art lessons, and my Girl Scout troop? I'm just getting a handle on Farsi. And I just found out I'm pregnant again, remember? I'm not ready to leave. Mother's already bought a ticket to come and visit us here next month!"

"You'll love it, Sweetiepie. You took French in high school, didn't you?"

"Yes, but... When do you have to be there?"

"They want me there in two weeks to have some training and orientation from the guy who's there now. Before he leaves."

"Two weeks! Two weeks?"

We did it. When the idea settled in my mind for a day or two, I couldn't wait to get going, to start a new adventure. Suddenly, Tehran seemed old and stale. We sold the furniture and the food from my cupboards, packed up the Iranian treasures we had received as wedding presents, and left.

Tony went directly to Casablanca and I went to Holland with the baby to stay with his parents until he oriented himself and found out about housing. Tony arranged everything—the packing, the shipping, the visas, the tickets, everything—and I waited for his call, curious and eager to know this French-Arab country and Casablanca with its mysterious allure, ready to make a comfortable home for our growing family.

CHAPTER 7

Privilege and Lemon Meringue Pie

Casablanca, 1962–1966

TONY, WHO HAD BEEN IN Casablanca for two weeks before I got there with baby Caroline, asked me that first morning if I would buy fly spray for the hotel room. That meant I had to find a *petit taxi*, go to downtown Casablanca, and find a store that might have what I wanted. Galleries Lafayette department store on Place Mohammed V looked promising, so I asked the taxi driver to stop there. I got out with little Caroline in tow and went into the store. *"Je veux le psssssst pour le bzzzzz,"* I had said, waving my arms in the air to the lady behind the counter, and so, with my high school French and dramatic gesticulation, I got the fly spray.

The night before, Tony had greeted us at the plane, grinning and laughing, his long arms embracing us both. Taking Caroline from my arms, he nuzzled her and held her tight while he guided us through customs. In the dark of night, it seemed to be a makeshift sort of airport, and the voices sounded strange and mysterious, sometimes French, sometimes Arabic. As I remember, our passports were checked at tables set up outside a small shed with uniformed men milling around. Tony was driving the car he had inherited from the former manager, and he quickly gathered our things together and put them into the trunk. I held Caroline on my lap. The moon showed itself, blinking through a canopy of eucalyptus trees on the boulevard as our car crept through the silent night to the hotel.

"I have a surprise for you," he started. "I bought you a present. It's at the hotel."

"Oh?" I answered.

He opened the door to the hotel room and there it was, sitting on a suitcase.

"A birdcage! Is it a birdcage?" I laughed. I put Caroline down to have a better look. A two-foot-high arrangement of fine wire scrollwork formed an onion-shaped dome over an airy filigree square box and sat absurdly on top of Tony's hard, blue Samsonite suitcase. The white wire was hand-bent into curves, which were attached to each other at close intervals by small clips of sky-blue metal. A canary-sized door, with the same undulating shape, closed with a simple hook like a twisted paperclip.

"I went to Tunis and the whole town was like this, blue and white. Every window has ironwork shaped like this as burglar proofing. I don't know what we'll do with it but I just couldn't resist. I brought it back with me on the plane in a big wooden crate on my lap."

"We'll keep it forever," I said. "But it's empty! Let's get a yellow bird to keep us company in the hotel." Over the weekend, we bought a little budgie and a small sack of birdseed, but after two days, we realized the top part of the birdcage was bigger than the tray at the bottom, so there was a real mess scattered over the top of the suitcase and the floor around it. Our little songbird went back to the store the next week, but the birdcage, we decided, would stay. Years later, while in Rio de Janeiro, we found an exotic, iridescent blue-and-green stuffed bird that looks so alive people are still fooled today after thirty or more years.

Casablanca's Anfa Hotel sat on the top of a hill in a residential district of private villas, where magenta bougainvillea dripped over garden walls, fragrant eucalyptus trees lined gently curving streets, and lavender agapanthus splashed color in the medians.

From the top floor of the hotel, we looked west over the rooftops and swaying palm trees and eucalyptus to the blue of the Atlantic Ocean. In the port area, we discovered La Mer, which had a balcony that stretched out over the gentle waves and became our favorite restaurant. It was right at that spot that American and British forces invaded in 1942. Morocco was then nominally in the hands of the Vichy French, a government that collaborated with the Nazis and had resisted the Allies.

Morocco had been a French protectorate from 1912 to 1956, and had established an efficient, functioning government and bureaucracy, a system of roads, communication, and thriving industry. Just six years before we arrived, France had recognized Morocco's independence under the absolute monarchy of Mohammed V. When he died in 1961 his son, Hassan II, became the king. From the Anfa Hotel where we stayed, we could see the red flag of Morocco flying over his palace when he was in residence. We arrived in May of 1962, and the following December the king established a constitutional monarchy and held the first elections in 1963. The French government personnel had left the country and the new civil servants were struggling to keep the post office and communications systems working efficiently. But all the French people did not leave. Many stayed but remained French citizens and lived and worked independently or for international companies, as we did for American companies. They had little patriotic allegiance to Morocco. They could go back home to France any time, but under the new Moroccan government, no one could legally take their money out with them. We couldn't take money out either, which is one reason Tony was paid half in Moroccan dirhams and half in U.S. dollars.

The Anfa Hotel, where we stayed for two months, provided a recreational gathering place for families of the small American community, as well as for visiting tourists and businessmen. The sensuously curved swimming pool attracted Europeans in skimpy bikinis, while Americans played bridge at tables in the shade, drank Boulaouane, a dry Moroccan Rosé, and flirted with each other's spouses.

At a table by the pool that first Sunday, we ordered Salade Hawaiian, a composition of lobster and pineapple and caviar mixed in a dark pink dressing of mayonnaise and ketchup and zapped with a generous splash of cognac. An attractive American woman came over to our table and asked if one of us could make a fourth for bridge. Anne soon became a life-long friend. She invited us for dessert and bridge on a Saturday evening two weeks later. This would be our first social event to meet some of the other Americans living in Casablanca. In the meantime, she gave me the name of her obstetrician, as I was several months into my second pregnancy.

I made an appointment with Dr. L., a kind Frenchman whose wife did the well-checks for new babies. Of all the clinical situations I have been in, this one was the most bizarre.

"Take your clothes off," I understood him to say in French, "but leave your shoes on and walk over and get on the table." I looked around for a gown, hoping I understood him correctly and was not making a fool of myself tap-tapping across the parquet floor in three-inch heels with not a stitch on my pregnant body. I lay on the table with my eyes closed and pretended I wasn't there.

After the exam, I dressed and sat in front of his desk, where he explained in French that I must not get too fat. The French were always concerned about the appearance of the woman's body. I was okay with that. He picked up his pen and started scribbling what I thought was a prescription. But when he turned the pad toward me and tapped his finger on a drawing, I saw it was a sketch of a Swiss Guard at the Vatican with his puffed-out pantaloons. *"Ce serait vous si vous mangez trop!"* (This is you if you eat too much!) He picked up the phone and called Tony at work and told him to make sure I didn't gain too much weight. I was mortified and angry.

The day after my appointment with Dr. L., Anne and Alain welcomed us to their villa with graciousness and a drink. The other guests were lovely people and I felt lucky that we were to meet them so soon after arriving in Casablanca. After a few rubbers of bridge, Anne brought in her specialty, lemon meringue pie, and placed a generous slice in front of each of us. With the doctor's admonition fresh in my mind, I looked at the golden custard, the crisp piecrust, the lightly browned meringue on top, and thought, *I can do this, just one bite to be polite. I don't have to eat the whole thing.* I could feel the anxiety building up inside of me.

From across the room, Tony regaled his table with stories. Then I heard, "Hey, Lizzie, look at that gorgeous pie. That's your favorite, isn't it? Remember what the doctor said. Don't eat too much. What are you going to do with that pie, Lizzie? What are you going to do with that pie?"

"What do you think you do with lemon meringue pie?" I said and then I picked up the pie from my plate and threw it at him. I missed. I hit Charlotte instead, but in one step I was there scooping the dripping goo from her bare arm and nailed him the second time.

Tony howled with laughter. Everyone else was stunned into silence. Anne rushed to the kitchen. "Don't worry," she said. "I'll get a towel. It's okay. Never mind."

Tony laughed, I laughed, and soon the others were laughing, too. I blush today, thinking of my disgraceful behavior. Tony helped me out of a horribly embarrassing situation.

In spite of the pie-throwing incident, Anne and I and the women I met at her house that night became close friends. We raised our children together for the next five years and supported each other through the challenges of living in a foreign country. Whereas in Iran there had been thousands of American families, those in Casablanca formed a small community. They represented private companies like Firestone, Caterpillar Tractors, John Deere, General Tire, Pan American Airways, TWA, and oil companies like Richfield, Mobil Oil, and Esso. The American Embassy was in Rabat, the capitol of Morocco, but the Consulate, which employed many Americans, was in Casablanca, a busy port and the largest center of business.

Jim, the Consul General, and his wife, Henrietta, lived in the Anfa district a few blocks from the hotel. They invited Tony and me to elegant soirees, and soon we knew most of the Americans as well as French and Moroccan business people and their wives. At our first such affair, in the summer of 1962, we mingled with other guests on their spacious lawn with cocktails and hors d'oeuvres and stared up at a large black-and-white movie screen. The film, sent from the U.S. State Department, showed Jacqueline Kennedy walking through the White House, speaking in her delicate voice, showing off to the world the rooms she had famously redecorated with exact historical details.

In the library of the Consul's house, a small inconspicuous plaque hung on the wall commemorating the historic meeting that had taken place there in January 1943 between Roosevelt and Churchill. It was there that Roosevelt announced that the end to World War II would only be by unconditional surrender of the Axis powers.

By fall, after living for several months in the hotel, caring for a one-and-a-half-year-old, washing diapers in the bathtub and draping them over the furniture to dry, we settled into our own villa. An Englishman now living in London owned the house. He wouldn't be able to take his money out of the country if he sold it or rented it to Moroccans, so we Americans were ideal, as we could pay in dollars from the part of Tony's salary that was deposited in the States.

To my joy, Mother changed the plane ticket she had for Tehran, took three weeks off from work and arrived in Casablanca ten days before the baby was born. In the middle of the night of December fourteenth, we woke her with, "It's time, Mother! We're going. Listen for Caroline!"

Tony drove me through the dark night to the small, intimate birthing center, Clinique Conte. A single bare light bulb dangling at the end of the dark hall led me to the delivery room. "*Sur la table, Madame,*" the nurse said, and I climbed up on the delivery table. The doctor arrived, checked me, then stepped out in the hall for a cigarette with Tony. While I was in labor I could hear them laughing and having a great old time. They came back into the delivery room at the right moment for Tony to witness the birth of Linda, our second daughter. He was the first to hold her.

Mother and I spent a close week together at home with Caroline and our new baby, Linda, so when Mother flew off for California the day after New Year's, the house was palpably empty, and I put all my energy and love into the children, once again completely dependent on Tony. We were now a family of four, bound to each other in a land of strangers with unfamiliar customs and difficult languages.

Tony immersed himself in his work as the manager of the Firestone Branch office and the retread shop thirty miles from Casablanca, which had sixty to seventy Moroccan employees. *"Oh, mais oui! Bien sûr!"* I'd overhear him say with a dramatic flare, laughing and gesticulating the way the French did. Soon he was able to understand nuances and even jokes in French, and he became socially at ease and confident in his leadership ability. He traveled to Europe occasionally in search of tire casings that he could import and retread in Casablanca and thrived on the challenge of being his own boss and directing every aspect of the business. It was intense work for him, and it took him out of the world of our family and into a new sphere that I was not a part of.

During dinner in a restaurant with a French-speaking couple one night, I nodded off to sleep a couple of times because I couldn't follow the conversation. I got a few words here and there and then was done. I knew I needed to focus on learning French again. The Alliance Française taught classes to foreigners, so that's where I went for six hours a day, five days a week, for six weeks. I reinforced the lessons with daily stops at the market. *"Ah, j'ai de la chance!"* I exclaimed when finding a ripe tomato, repeating the phrase I had just learned from Mme. Thebout on the audio-visual tape at school. "I am lucky!" I had said, and I knew I really was.

I gradually learned to ask politely for *viande hachée* and *entre-côte* at the butcher, and soon I ventured downtown and approached the daunting Grand Marché Central with a wicker basket over my arm. Masses of flowers—gladiolas, irises, birds of paradise, and all manner of vibrant-colored bouquets—banked the entrance to a maze of open-air alleys and paths. I followed my nose to the fresh fish stalls where, if I was there early in the morning, counter after counter was piled high with silvery, gray fish, sole, slippery and scaly, heads and tails intact, mounds of raw *crevettes*, and unopened *huîtres*. Moving on to the meat and poultry area, I noticed unusually red ground meat and steaks. Backing a few steps away from the stall, I looked up for the store's sign and saw a life-size model of a horse's head staring down at me: *viande de cheveaux*, horsemeat. Farther along the aisle, I noticed a pig's snout and a lamb's head also hanging out above their respective meat counters and at last I found the cow's head, its big brown eyes staring languidly into space.

There were bins of artfully arranged artichokes and asparagus and piles of *haricot verts*, arrays of polished carrots and beets, *escarole*, endive and Romaine, all glisteningly clean. Courteous and flirtatious vendors beckoned as I walked by. I filled my basket and stopped last at the *boulangerie* for irresistible *pain au chocolat*, croissants, and stalks of fresh bread, crunchy on the outside, warm and soft on the inside. Often, by the time I got home, I had eaten the insides of a whole loaf of bread, leaving the hollow crust to dip in sweet butter later.

Some vendors came to our garden gate, notably the *escargot* man, unkempt and shaggy, with live snails crawling all over his basket and oozing up his arm. I had cut out a recipe from the newspaper for *escargots* which involved starving the snails for days to clean them out. I dared myself to try lots of things, but not that. Sometimes we treated American visitors to a favorite restaurant in the mountains called *La Cuisse de Grenouille*, where we ate garlic-and-butter-smothered, caught-on-the-premises, frogs' legs.

Everyone we knew, French and American, had at least two servants, an easy custom for me to adopt. Kaya lived in a room in the basement of our rented villa and helped with the children, the laundry, and the kitchen clean-up. From the age of two-and-a-half, the children went to nursery school, and when they weren't at school, Kaya was at the house to look after them if I wasn't. Mohammed, a houseboy, came every day to clean. He always had a rag or a broom in his hand and often took our copper tray-table outside with a can of Brasso and polished those Persepolis figures as I had done in Tehran, until they shone like headlights.

This arrangement left me with a lot of free time to play with the children without having to scold them for running in the house with muddy feet, to explore the Moroccan culture, to play bridge with the ladies several times a week. Tony had begun to stop for a drink after work on a regular basis, so after the children were in bed, I was often home alone in the evenings.

One evening, November 22, 1963, we were to meet at the home of friends for dinner. Tony stopped for a drink at the El Mansour Hotel near his office while I was waiting at our friends' home. The phone rang and Jack, our host, answered. "Yes? So? What's the joke?" we heard him say. Then he was silent. He hung up and turned to us, suddenly pale, and gasped, "President Kennedy has been shot. Probably dead."

We looked around at one another, silent with disbelief, until someone grabbed the radio and began fiddling with the knob to get an English station. Tony burst in with more news. The bar at the El Mansour Hotel near his office had been filled with people trying to get information and translating from the French and Arabic TV. Kennedy *was*, in fact, dead, and our new president, Lyndon Johnson, was already sworn in. We huddled, stunned, in the small living room comforting each other, making calls to friends at the Consulate, bewildered and feeling out of touch with the world.

The next morning a grieving Mohammed arrived at our house holding a transistor radio up to his ear. "So, so sorry, Madame, for your country." Kaya, too, clasped my hands and wailed in sorrow. The vendors at the outdoor market all had radios blaring next to the tomatoes and the beans. With compassion in their eyes, they expressed their regrets. I had no idea so many people I dealt with every day were aware of America and what was going on in the world. It had never occurred to me that they were interested in anything other than my groceries or my household issues.

I was the one who was out of touch, but what was I supposed to be in touch with? Some Americans adopted the French way of setting the table and had their maid serve dinner the French way. Should I try that? The first maid I had spoke only Arabic, so I had to look up words first in my English-French dictionary, and then in the French-Arabic dictionary, and try to pronounce them to her in Arabic. What could I teach her? Were the children safe with her? Mohammed cleaned the floor with a good hand-towel from my grandmother. Did it matter? It seems trivial now, but I was confused. Did I need to have my hair done and combed out nearly every day, like the French women? Husbands of most of the other Americans didn't stay out in the evenings. Was it okay for Tony to do that? I missed my mother. Who could I talk with to ground me?

We had slipped into the life style of the privileged French expatriates and Americans finding themselves transported to a multicultural society, with servants and time on their hands. The Churchill Club was a place where English-speaking people, and those who wanted to speak English, gathered to socialize. English, German, Dutch, and Japanese, as well as Moroccan and French, entered our circle there, and socialize we did. We wives made American hamburgers every Thursday night and played bridge, and Tony joined the men in a friendly game of poker. We formed a little theater group and put on plays in which I acted and sometimes Tony worked on the sets.

Our lives swirled on a stage filled with the color, sounds, and smells of Morocco. I reveled in the vibrancy of the medina of old Casablanca, a maze of open shops and stalls offering traditional crafts, foods, and wares of all kinds, separate from the modern, European-style city. I often strolled by myself without a specific errand through the mysterious paths, enjoying the assault of color. Red, gold, and emerald-green kaftans floated in the breeze from hangers above shops; bright copper and brass Fatima pots flashed like beacons. The medina was similar to the bazaars in Iran, but brighter, and full of more color and sunshine. Shafts of sunlight streamed through slits in the woven reed mats overhead. Artisans sat cross-legged on the ground, twisting golden threads for embroidering on black or magenta velvet cloth. Little boys carved wooden handles with a razor blade held between their toes while their hands pulled back and forth on a string which turned the wood like a lathe. The wood became handles for crude iron skewers for lamb kabobs, or brochettes. Sharp-to-the-nostrils paprika and cinnamon, coriander, cloves, and saffron blended to fill the air with bewitching potpourri. And mint—everywhere the fragrance of mint tea.

Kismet had brought me here, and I was again swept up in the aura of the Arabian Nights, complete with accompanying music. Tinkling bells announced the man selling a drink of water that he squeezed into a small brass drinking bowl from a leather flask slung over his arm. A flute whined out an alluring lament, and the lyrical voices of Arabic and French intermingled to make my meandering otherworldly and fantastical. I laughed and teased with the shopkeepers calling for my business, and learned how to bargain for the best price on copper pots, leather bags and hassocks, touristy camel saddles and brass candlesticks, gold brocade fabric and turquoise pottery for couscous. "You win, Madame, I lose," they'd laughingly call after me.

A few steps away from the medina and I was back in a European world, but I kept the swirls of color and the contrasts of culture in my drawings and paintings of that time. The backdrop of my life changed constantly, from bikini-populated beaches under a hot blue sky, to dark, smoky nightclubs and bars; from the snowy Atlas Mountains to parties with limitless cocktails; and from charity work with American Women's Club to entertaining American senators on fact-finding tours.

We became accustomed to the warm weather and Mediterranean-style work hours. Sometimes, during the three-hour midday break, Tony joined me for lunch and a glass of wine at a beach restaurant or the pool where I took the children. Lunchtime included the typical "siesta" hours, when shops and offices were closed until mid-afternoon. After work, Tony would stop on the way home for a drink at the El Mansour Hotel or Chez Pierre and come home late or not at all for dinner. I held dinner and fumed, but excused his behavior, thinking it was important for his work.

There were times when he didn't come home until early morning, and I would lie in bed in the dark room, my thoughts alternating between anger and worry. More than once, I was so peeved that when he inevitably slept all morning, I went downtown and bought a new dress. One woman remarked that I had a new dress for every party. Yes, I thought, I do. Occasionally, Tony would call and invite me to meet him downtown, so after the children were in bed, I'd call Kaya to watch them, and at nine or ten o'clock I drove to wherever Tony was for a late dinner.

That didn't happen often, and one night when he came home late, laughing and happy but tipsy and decidedly unattractive. I asked, "Where have you been? Why are you so late?"

"Well," he said, "if you're going to be angry, I won't tell you."

Thinking about it the next day, I decided I didn't want to be the nagging wife, and had to find something to *do* so I wouldn't count on him for so much of my sense of worth. I began art lessons with a woman who used her lush back yard, tangled with marigolds, pansies, and violet agapanthus, as inspiration for drawing and absorbing a calmness of life. I spent hours there and at home in creative work and developed some degree of self-confidence that I could develop my own life.

For Tony's birthday, I rented a piano, thinking it might bring him home earlier in the evenings. He didn't come home any earlier—in fact he sometimes came home at three or four in the morning—but he did play and was soon banging out "Frère Jacques," "Fait Do Do," and "Happy Birthday" for the children.

Though we joined each other in various projects, Tony's world was with the French, mine with the Americans and British. The other American women became my extended family as we worked together on crafts to sell at a yearly Christmas bazaar to raise money for an orphanage. One woman in our community created clothing based on the very feminine, flowing, often gold-brocaded Moroccan kaftan, so as a fund raiser we staged a fashion show one summer evening on the lawn of Jim and Henrietta's residence. Several of us floated barefoot down a makeshift runway covered with Moroccan carpets, swishing the updated kaftans.

Tony was completely bilingual by then, so the women asked him to be our commentator.

Every New Year's Day we invited everyone we knew to an open house (no TV, no football). Our friends came for American waffles, fried eggs, bacon, and London Fog, which was a mixture of one third vanilla ice-cream, one third black coffee, and one third Bourbon served out of a punch bowl. One year someone started playing the piano, so another went home to get the trumpet he hadn't played for years, and the man across the street actually dragged in his vibraphone, and the party and the music went on all day and into the night.

With all this socializing, time with just our family was a special occasion, and I began looking toward the day that our lives would calm down and Tony and I would have time for each other. One day when we had been in Casablanca for several years, I broached the subject with a friend.

"What are we doing, Fernanda? Are we contributing to anything? Our husbands are busy and involved in their work and don't really need us. My children are speaking French in their sleep and I can't even understand them! Tony and I are with different people nearly every night. We see each other at parties, he on one side of the room and I another. I am lonely. I don't know who he is anymore. I wish he really needed me for something. I don't even polish my own copper tray-table anymore. I don't know what my purpose is."

"I'm not bothered," Fernanda answered. "I know exactly my purpose in life. I am a hostess for my husband. He needs me."

"Oh." I hesitated. *A hostess?* I loved being a hostess, but my purpose? To be a hostess for parties? Was that *it?* Was that how the world and Tony saw me? Surely, there was more. I had two healthy daughters, help in the house, and an exciting, vibrant life. Was I a good wife? I hardly saw Tony. A good mother? I had Kaya to help me. A good hostess? Maybe. With all the comforts of living I had, what was wrong with me?

I *knew* what was wrong. Could I admit it even to myself? When Fernanda left later that day, I sat down at the patio table under the acacia tree and talked to myself. Through the glass doors, I could see the bouquet of red roses on the table in the living room—roses delivered yesterday. The director of the play I was currently rehearsing for and I had developed a strong attraction for each other and he had sent them. He was a gentle soul and kind and infatuated with me. I thought I might be falling in love with him and I was afraid. I was afraid of my emotions and afraid for my marriage.

"Meet me at ten o'clock for coffee on Sunday," he had said at the Friday night rehearsal. Sunday morning while Tony slept late, I left the house to have a simple cup of coffee in broad daylight with a friend. We were so drawn to each other, leaning head to head across the small table, I was sure the waiters at the café would think we were having an affair. I *felt* like I was having an affair! Guilty! When I got back home, Tony was still in bed. He didn't know I had gone. He hadn't noticed the red roses, did not notice my turmoil. I wanted the security that only he could give me, but he was too involved with his own life to notice me. I would have to make some decisions *myself*.

I read about women in America who were not "fulfilled" with babies and housework. But "consciousness-raising" didn't apply to me. What was that? I was far away from that world, wasn't I? I knew of Betty Friedan and her book, *The Feminine Mystique*, published in 1963, but I didn't read it until 2004. Only then did I see my former life described, living overseas or not, as a woman wanting to discover her talents, feeling useless, wasted as an individual, yet still holding herself to the standards and security of known expectations of the fifties.

I stood up, went inside, and fingered the velvety red petals on their thorny stems. I was flattered and deeply appreciative of the attention, but I knew what I truly wanted. I made a conscious decision that I would do whatever it took to stay faithfully married, forever, even if I was no more than a hostess for my husband. I did not want to jeopardize what I had grown up to value: my family. Much as I enjoyed the lavish attention of strangers in Casablanca, it couldn't be real or lasting. My marriage would be.

By the time we had been in Casablanca for four and a half years, the business and political situations had changed. In 1965, there was serious rioting between different political factions in Morocco, and Hassan II dissolved the parliament and imposed a curfew for several days. French citizens were selling their businesses to Moroccans and going back to France. General Tire had built a factory which cut deeply into Firestone's business of importing and retreading tires. Finally, the Firestone International Company sold the retread shop, *Pneu Firestone Rechapage*, to a Moroccan company, so there was no job for Tony in Casablanca anymore. This time I had no ambivalence about moving. I was ready to close the social calendar and live as a family.

Once more, I left the packing to Tony and took Caroline and Linda, now five and three, to Berkeley to stay with my mother, three weeks ahead of Tony. He arranged storage for our now considerable household goods while we waited for Firestone to decide what to do with us.

Leaving Morocco I was like a tag-along with no direction of my own. I realize now that I wasn't the only one. Tony also was being told what to do and where to go. We were both waiting for instructions. Waiting.

CHAPTER 8

Interlude, or a
Blip in the Fairy Tale

Akron, Ohio, 1967

TONY'S EMPLOYER PROVIDED an apartment in Akron for families in transition like ours. So after vacation in California at my mother's, we moved to Ohio and Tony started training for his new job assignment, while I put the children in nursery school and shopped for things we wouldn't be able to get overseas. I had great fun selecting books at the school book fair, including *Harry the Dirty Dog*, that would see the girls through several years. I knew wherever we were sent we wouldn't be able to get books like these in English. We were drifting but still tethered to the company and I expected the future to be nothing but wonderful, secure that Firestone had something good ahead for us.

But I was blindsided, shattered. Tony came back to the apartment one evening after meetings at the office and, ignoring the shopping bags on the couch, sat at the dinette table, his usually straight shoulders slouched, his clasped hands between his knees. He looked over at me and shook his head. His eyebrows furrowed together in pain, questioning. I stepped toward him and put my hand on his shoulder.

"What's wrong?" I asked. I sat down.

"We're in trouble," he said. "I need your help. We're out of money. In fact, we're in the hole."

"No money? What do you mean no money? In the hole? We owe money somewhere? How could that happen? What's going on?"

"I didn't want you to worry. I thought I was on top of it," he said. "We owe a lot…a lot of rent on the house in Casablanca."

"Rent? You didn't pay the rent?" I said. "I thought you made plenty of money. Why didn't you pay the rent? What happened?"

"Well, Lizzie, you see…it was business." He explained that he had agreed to pay our landlord, an Englishman, in U.S. dollars from the part of his salary that was deposited in the States as a way for the landlord to get his money out of Morocco. But Tony also had made a deal with one of his Moroccan customers who also wanted dollars in an account in the States. The Moroccan paid Tony in dirhams in Morocco for the American dollars that were deposited in his account in the States. That meant all of our money was in a checking account in dirhams in Casablanca and we had no dollars in the States for the rent. Looking back, it must have been easy to let the money flow out with no budget and my ignorance. We had spent all of it and then some in Morocco. It was not illegal, just stupid.

The landlord had informed Firestone that he hadn't received the rent for several months and he wanted his money.

"Firestone won't send us out on assignment until we settle this, Lizzie. We need a lot of money right away." He told me the amount, and my mind reeled.

I stared at Tony. That was a lot of money. *Yes, I was reckless in my shopping*, I thought, *but* you *never stopped spending…. the lavish parties, the trips, the restaurants, first class everything, the gallon bottles of Scotch.* How could I have known? Or even suspected? *I'll have to cancel my order for the books,* I thought.

But, it wasn't all Tony's fault.

I was twenty-seven years old, mother of two, university educated, widely traveled, worldly, and yet I expected to be taken care of like a child, blithely and unquestioningly ignorant of our financial situation. A flash of anger nearly choked me, the same feeling I'd had as I lay in bed in Casablanca worrying about him until three in the morning while he was out spending money on liquor and…what else? I let the anger subside and remembered how our friend and banker, the one who had organized the poker games at the Churchill Club, arranged for me to have an overdraft available so I wouldn't have to worry about over-drawing our checking account. *Had* I overdrawn our account? I didn't even know if I had, or by how much.

I reached over and squeezed Tony's hands, trying to grasp what he was telling me. My brain went fuzzy. I hung on to the edge of the table for balance.

"Lizzie? You'll have to ask your father for a loan. I can't think of any other way."

"*Ohhhh*," I moaned and held my head in my hands, thinking. We had no collateral, no car, no house, a minus in our bank account, and no credit. We had to come up with actual money. I couldn't think of any other way either. "You call, Tony."

"He's *your* father."

I picked up the phone and, noting the time difference, dialed my father's number in Hawaii. My heart beat and my voice trembled, just as it had when I'd called him years ago to say I was going to stay in Tehran and marry Tony, but this time I hesitated. There was no joy or confidence in my voice. Just halting, flat words as I explained what had happened. Daddy listened. He, himself, hadn't always been financially responsible. Maybe he would be sympathetic now. He was. Yes. He would help. The next day he had an agreement drawn up with regular payments including interest, and forwarded the money to Tony.

But we weren't finished. A few days later, Tony sat down again and told me he had been wrong about the amount. We needed more. I didn't even ask why more. We needed an additional five or six thousand dollars, miniscule compared to the first loan needed from my father. I assumed this was due to my extravagance, possibly that overdraft at the bank, and, sobbing with shame, called my mother. "Of course," she said, agreeing to loan us what we needed, "but don't let it happen again."

I didn't try to figure out what had happened, but understood this crisis as simply bad judgment and felt Tony's desperation as my own. We needed the money. I got it.

The next day, head lowered, I went to the school and cancelled the books I had lovingly picked out at the book fair, all except *Harry the Dirty Dog*, which became a family favorite. The little white dog rolls in the mud until his family doesn't recognize him, but after a bath is once more hugged and loved.

Nowadays, there seems to be no disgrace in going into deep debt with credit cards and over-blown mortgages while bankruptcy runs rampant. But then, in 1967, the shame attached to owing that much money, and having to ask my parents for help was mortifying.

Tony was able to pay the landlord and he paid the bank. Firestone was satisfied and gave Tony his next assignment. We packed up our things and left. For Tony, that was that. As far as he was concerned, the issue was handled. Done. He never mentioned it again. And somehow, when Tony assumed his confident attitude and sunny outlook, my respect for him returned as though, indeed, this affair was trivial.

However, I took over paying our bills, so I was the one who was reminded every month as I wrote the checks to my parents, month after month, year after year. When the last one to my mother went into the envelope, I addressed it with a flourish and kissed the stamp. But the payments to my father continued for years and years. With this episode we had another connection, my father and I, and I will always be grateful for the help from him without condemnation or his expression of disappointment in me.

As time went by, and I could see we were gaining ground in the financial department, my panic and shame mellowed and I began to think more rationally about what had happened. We were both responsible. Now I felt pride in living more frugally and seeing results.

CHAPTER 9

The Wrong Hat and Apartheid

South Africa, 1967–1974

WHAT COULD BE MORE appealing than a seaport town on the southern coast of the African continent with clean, smooth beaches, a moderate climate, and English-speaking people?

This was what we had waited for. Tony was now sales manager at the Firestone Tyre Factory in Port Elizabeth, South Africa, where the night sky turned around the Southern Cross instead of the Big Dipper and December 25th was right in the heat of summer. He would no longer be working independently as he had been in Casablanca, but would be reporting to the South African management of the American-owned company. I was thrilled with the news, not expecting that our years in South Africa would turn our lives in an unexpected direction.

We arrived in Port Elizabeth in March of 1967 and stayed for seven years. The physical landscape was similar to that of Casablanca, and a rush of familiar feelings came over me on our first drive out of the city center, down the broad boulevard toward the beach area. The center medians were lush with pink and white oleander bushes and spikes of purple agapanthus as the road edged the coastline with its clean white sand of King's Beach. We could look forward to blue skies, breeze enough to blow away smog from industry and harbor activities, and mild winters. Because of the sunshine, I expected the same warm openness from the people here that I had known in Morocco and California with similar climates.

Though the South Africans I met were friendly and cordial, our social interactions were not much influenced by the sunshine. First of all, people were separated from one another by skin color and ethnicity—not just by custom, but by law. Heritage further divided them, there being many rival African tribes, and two distinct and competing groups of white South Africans, each with its own language. History and gender informed interaction that the law didn't prescribe. Divisions showed up everywhere, lines I had to learn not to cross. We were not unwelcome as Americans, but the United States at that time had begun to apply political and economic pressure on South Africa to end Apartheid. South Africans did not speak freely with one another about it, and certainly not with an American who might be critical. An undercurrent of tension about racism that couldn't be admitted or talked about hovered beneath lively social chitchat.

To be honest, I carried my own gray cloud, a left-over from our financial crisis in Akron. The valuable jewelry I had been given as wedding presents in the Middle East weighed on my conscience. *I didn't deserve to have such luxuries when we were so much in debt.* Without telling Tony, I took a diamond and turquoise ring to a jeweler downtown and sold it. I walked into the shop glancing around. *Does the jeweler think I need money for drugs? Does he think I stole the ring?* I needed to suffer, rather like the self-flagellation some Muslims perform as penance with stones tied to whips that they lash on their bare backs. I understand better now how that works. The money made no difference to our debt, but it assuaged my guilt some so I didn't want to sell anything else.

The King Edward Hotel, where we stayed while we looked for permanent accommodations, stood like a manor house on top of the historic Donkin Reserve, a grassy park overlooking the har-

bor and Algoa Bay. I woke on our first morning there with great
expectations. I kissed Tony off to his new job and took our little
girls to the dining room for breakfast, on the way picking up a
newspaper at the desk. The high ceiling loomed over a vast room
with tables set formally with white cloths and silver cutlery. Smiling brown women in black uniforms with white aprons and caps
scurried here and there with menus and dishes.

After ordering, I opened the newspaper. "White by Night!"
the headline blared. My instant reaction was that pedestrians were
being told to wear white at night to keep from being hit by traffic.
What? I quickly realized it meant that Natives, or Bantu, people
who had black skin, were to be out of sight at night, inside if they
had jobs that required them to stay in town or back in their own
township, leaving the streets of Port Elizabeth "white by night."
The Group Areas Act of 1962 legalized the relocation of the entire
non-white population, so in 1965 the whole South End area of
Port Elizabeth had been forcibly depopulated, the buildings flat-
tened, and the Natives who lived there moved outside of the city
to a new township of their own called New Brighton.

This was Apartheid, the name given after 1948 to legal government policies designed to separate the races. Our plane from
Amsterdam had taken the long way south, skirting around the
western bulge of Africa because other African nations did not allow planes headed for South Africa in their air space. But here
it was. Right here in the newspaper! I had experienced subtle
prejudice in the States, but this blatant, legal separation of races
shocked me.

Our weekend explorations took us to the coast road beside
beaches labeled WHITES ONLY, and then as the shore became rock-
ier, BLACKS ONLY, INDIANS ONLY, COLORED ONLY, ASIAN ONLY, with
the Afrikaans translation printed underneath the English. Tony
and I looked at each other in dismay, but did not discuss it. We
were guests in the country and my first priority was to help our
children adjust to this new place without constant criticism from
me. I meant to teach them to respect their new friends but still
grow up knowing a very different world turned above us. Apart-

heid meant we wouldn't experience the colorful culture of the Xhosas or Zulus, wouldn't hear their music or see their dances or wonder at the rhythms of their languages. Natives became almost invisible as they worked in the city's homes and businesses and factories.

We rented a pleasant house with a narrow deck overlooking the port and Algoa Bay. The girls started school, for whites only of course, but the school was also divided in another way. Caroline and Linda were in classes for English speaking South Africans and only mixed with the white Afrikaans speakers during morning assembly, where the announcements were given in both languages—one, then the other.

As in all schools, Summerwood students were distinguished by their school's uniform. I walked Caroline into the principal's office on her first day after taking a picture of her in her navy jumper, white blouse, gray wool blazer, and matching hat. "What's this?" the principal asked, looking at six-year-old Caroline pulling at the elastic under her chin. "That's not *our* hat! That's the hat for our rival school! She cannot come to *this* school in *that* hat!" I felt my face go red and put my arm around Caroline. "Can she stay today? I'll exchange it. She'll have the right hat tomorrow." I thought I had checked everything, down to the regulation handkerchief in the pocket of her "brookies" and the prescribed brown oxford shoes.

Learning was based on rote memory and respect for authority. The teacher wrote on the board and the children copied it in their notebooks and memorized it. They learned two poems by heart each week, one in English and one in Afrikaans. I signed their homework every night. They acquired good study habits, and later, in the States, they used those skills to do research and to think.

Our permits to live in the country assumed we were immigrants and, as such, the girls were required to learn the Afrikaans language in special after-school classes. It was not a complicated language grammatically, mostly a simple derivation from the language of the Dutch Boers, farmers who had settled the country.

Tony, still fluent in Dutch, liked the idea that his children and I would be able to carry on some kind of conversation with his parents using this old-time language when we visited them again in Holland. He laughed at the quaint phrases he heard and looked forward to doing business in the Afrikaans-speaking farming areas of the Transvaal and the Orange Free State.

I conformed. I entered the whites-only door at the post office and bank, sat in the Europeans-only section of the theater, did not take the kids to the top of the double-decker bus, did not expect a Native to look me in the eye, carefully kept the children off the swings marked for non-whites only, and built castles with them on clean, sandy, whites-only beaches. I never went in the bar of a hotel where the men met, but was served a drink in the lounge, where I waited with the other ladies. A woman was not permitted to see her drink poured; it was poured behind a screen and brought to her on a tray.

I learned whom I could invite for dinner and with whom and I learned to make conversation in inconsequential generalities. I had help in the house, a "girl," or "gull" with the South African accent. Malfie was a cheerful, chubby, Xhosa woman who loved and spoiled the children. She lived in a room attached to the back of our house and went to her own home and family in New Brighton only on Thursday afternoons for her half-day off, as did all household help, returning the next morning.

Our days were good, happy, and pleasant. Choosing not to think too much about the subculture of black and brown people who worked among us largely unnoticed was part of my adjustment to living there. I read many books defending the "Case for South Africa" and I could see the twisted logic, but the enforced separation of the races was still thoroughly incomprehensible. I couldn't allow myself to think about it. On vacations, we spotted wild animals in Krueger National Park and Addo Elephant Park, and we involved ourselves in fund-raising events with the American Women's Club. The South Africans we met were not glamorous like the French, with no dressing up or high-society airs. At social gatherings, the men wore blazers with school emblems on the pockets and grouped together on one side of the room, and the women in plain dresses and flat shoes discussed servant problems and children. I didn't know any women who worked outside of the home.

Tony, always in a good mood, found buddies to have drinks with on the way home in the evenings, and I took up my art again and started knitting. We still didn't talk about our money, and I did the best I could to save. Tony traveled to the other South African provinces to dealers and brought back stories of the Boer farmers and the flashier coastal cities.

I assumed Tony was happy at work, because that's the way he was at home and around our friends, cheerful and happy. I was cheerful too, and ignored my deep knowledge that Apartheid was wrong, disgusting in fact. I acquiesced. What could I do anyway? It was the law of the land. We were guests. Everything was right with the world, except it wasn't.

The birth of our third daughter, Marianne, in Port Elizabeth's Provincial Hospital in November of 1968 was pure joy and gave me a new focus and Tony another daughter to love. I took her everywhere with me while the two big girls were in school.

Eight months later, July 16, 1969, Apollo 11 launched from Kennedy Space Center with Neil Armstrong, Buzz Aldrin and Michael Collins aboard. On the 21st, a camera in the Lunar Module provided live coverage so the world could witness Neil Armstrong climbing down the ladder of the module to the surface of the moon. "That's one small step for man, one giant leap for mankind," he said to the world.

July was not summer vacation for us but wintertime, and school was in session. Seven-year-old Linda came home one afternoon with a drawing her teacher had asked the class to do. "Draw a picture of the man stepping on the moon," she had said. Linda pulled from her little brown school suitcase a picture of a vivid yellow moon with a man standing on top of it wearing red pants, a yellow shirt and a straw hat. "Linda," I said, "this looks like a farmer on the moon! Where is his space suit? Where's his life support system on the back?" South Africa was one of the few countries in the world that did not allow television. We had not witnessed Neil Armstrong step on the moon as had the rest of the world.

In 1973, in the United States, President Nixon was in deep trouble, while in South Africa the whole political system was on a path of self-destruction. I hadn't voted anywhere, hadn't taken a stand or felt responsible for anything. I was floating, disenfranchised, and disillusioned; I desperately wanted to be a part of the real world. Not only did we miss televised coverage of the moonwalk, but we missed the shock and horror of the Vietnam War being televised to the American public. I was angry. I felt as if *I* were on the moon, isolated. I was tired of censored journalism, with pages ripped from the middle of my magazines and blacked-out paragraphs telling me what I could and could not read. At the same time, I scolded myself for complaining when I had the beaches, sunshine, good schools, and a healthy family.

We had several home-leave trips back to the States to see relatives and keep Tony in touch with the home office. On one such trip, passing through the airport in San Francisco, we saw unkempt young women in flowing dresses wandering trance-like through the passageways handing out flowers and pamphlets, while young men, long hair shading their faces, strummed guitars and sang mournful songs. Not yet understanding the peace movement, we were embarrassed for them and looked the other way. We were unaware of a new outlook that much of the world was adopting. The same sort of strange people gathered in the Dam Square in Amsterdam, where we stopped to see Tony's parents.

Our returns to South Africa were difficult for me. The atmosphere of cheerfulness, sunshine, prosperity, and blue skies was smothered between an oppressive weight of denial and guilt and an undercurrent of suspicion and defensiveness. In South Africa, we lived within this emotional vise for seven years. As the plane flew south and further south on that last return, I leaned my head against the cold plastic window and cried. We were headed again to the bottom of the map.

One Sunday afternoon, as we were entering our seventh year

there, Tony and I relaxed with a glass of wine in lazy chairs on the balcony after a late-afternoon barbeque of "Daddy's juicy meat." We stared silently out in the distance at the dazzling water of the bay under the ever-blue sky. What could be lovelier?

Suddenly, Tony sat straight up in his chair, turned to me and blurted out, "I can't stand this, Lizzie."

I sat up, startled. "What?"

"For the first time in my life, I don't want to go into the office." I looked at him quizzically. This was not like him. He continued. "I can't get anything done! There's too much bickering between the Afrikaners and the British South Africans about what I should be doing." When he had arrived six years before from America, well trained in the tire business and speaking both English and Afrikaans, he hadn't imagined they would be suspicious of his and the company's motives.

"Do they think I'm going to take over?" Tony continued. "Those people are pompous, hanging onto their seats in the elite dining room and their precious parking spaces. They dawdle over lunch and talk about soccer scores, old boy stories, and problems with the 'kaffirs.' I can hardly sit through lunch. They have no idea what's going on in the country, and they're afraid to find out, hiding behind their desks and spending hours in an executive dining room. They must know their world is going to change. Nobody dares mention anything about politics or the effects the international sanctions will have on business and their insulated lives." The United Nations had begun economic sanctions against South Africa because of Apartheid, and Americans were clamoring for faster action and more boycotts.

Gradually Tony had become uneasy, and so he focused on his own job and tried not to get involved with all the in-fighting and divisions and crossing of lines. He had never mentioned this to me before. The past seven years had trained us not to reveal what we were thinking, even to each other.

"It's no wonder they're suspicious of you, Tony. You remind them of what the rest of the world thinks about South Africa, and they put their defenses up."

I leaned over and touched his arm and realized we hadn't been even *this* honest with each other for a long time. How had it happened, that we had each slipped into our private selves and not spoken truths to each other? Now he stretched back against the chair and looked at me, his legs straight out, crossed at his ankles, his feet twitching in the calfskin slippers he always wore at home. I wish I could say we continued this conversation, sharing our hearts with each other. But as I had learned since the day Tony asked me to marry him, he discouraged discussion and worked out problems, making decisions in his head, by himself.

"Well," I said, "now what? What's going to happen?"

"I don't know. Something. I will *do* something."

PART TWO

Somewhere in Space
I Hang Suspended...

CHAPTER 10

A Job and a Cornfield

Muscatine, Iowa, 1974

"I WILL DO SOMETHING," he had said, and I waited. Within a few months, Tony had created a new job for himself in Johannesburg, still working for Firestone South Africa, but away from the nonsense at the head office. I had had enough of Women's Club activities, and once settled in Jo'burg, started a graduate course in Library Science at the nearby university in Pretoria. However, during the year we were there, we came to realize that this move was not the solution we wanted. Together we decided it was time to move the family to the United States, where the girls, about to start high school, would be Americans in America. That meant quitting Firestone all together and starting out new somewhere in the U.S. We called in the packers and put our things in storage and made flight arrangements.

Our children climbed the stairs ahead of us and stepped into a giant TWA 747. "Welcome aboard!" I heard, in a fresh, wide-open, Midwestern American accent. I laughed out loud with relief. After twenty-one years, Tony had quit Firestone and we were free in the world.

Free in the world this time meant no home, no car, no job, no company to tell us what to do. No address. Fifteen years of marriage, and we had nothing materially to show for it. We were financially even, still owing my father, but otherwise solvent. My mother offered us the use of her home, moved into a smaller bedroom and took up the white rugs in the bathroom. The five of us squeezed into her Berkeley house that summer of 1974, while Tony explored job possibilities.

Mother and I spent afternoons on her deck. At age sixty-five, she had just retired from twenty years as an administrative secretary at the University of California, not knowing how she would fill the next perhaps thirty years of her life productively. And I, at thirty-five, was just beginning my heaviest responsibilities as a mother, not knowing where we would be living, or if I would be starting a wage-earning career of my own. However, I was at home in a way I had not been for a long time, secure with my own mother and with time to be a mother myself.

Tony got up early every morning, put on a suit and tie, and got busy looking for work, treating the search itself as a job. He was forty-two and expected to work another twenty-five years or so, plenty of time to start a new career. He researched companies in the libraries of San Francisco, Berkeley, and Oakland. He filled the house with neat stacks of newspapers from all over the States, precisely clipped ads, and pasted them on blank pages in a three-ring binder. He followed up on every one, investigating every possibility. He clattered away on Mother's old manual typewriter, sending out hundreds of letters to companies, old friends, and business associates, adding reams of carbon copies of the letters, along with the responses he received, if any, to three-ring binders. Each letter was individually typed, and given the lack of technology, retyped if there was a typo. He came close to taking a job with a bathing suit and lingerie company where he could use his international experience, and was tempted by an offer from a small-town tire company in Nevada because of his tire background. I shuddered at the thought of either, but he knew what he wanted was a combination of both and was willing to keep searching.

Summer became fall and fall became winter. As our savings dwindled, Tony cashed in his life insurance. Caroline and Linda started school at the same junior high where I had gone, Marianne started first grade, and I began a secretarial course to learn typing and shorthand.

"What if you don't find a job, Tony?" I ventured.

"Don't ever say that! It's not a possibility!" he snapped, and I kept quiet and used my new typing skills to help him.

Christmas came and went. We bought a small tree and I saw my childhood ornaments once again, but no splurge on decorations or gifts. I began knitting once more, as I seemed to do during times of stress.

Finally, in February, after ten months in Berkeley, the job search paid off. Tony found the perfect fit as Director of Far Eastern Sales for Bandag, a tire retreading company beginning to expand internationally but based in Iowa, where we would live. And so, after living in Iran, Morocco, South Africa, and Berkeley, we packed up once again, returned the house to Mother not much the worse for wear, and left for Muscatine, Iowa, a town of 24,000. Just what we wanted.

Cornfields and hog farms formed a three-quarter circle around Muscatine, with the Mississippi washing up against it on the south. The river runs east to west right there, just below the bump on the map that keeps Iowa from being a square. Empty brick warehouses, a couple of button factories, and abandoned lots edged the river. A time long ago, whole families took turns stamping buttons out of clam shells from the Mississippi in shacks that they appended to their small cottages, making Muscatine the Pearl Button Capital of the World. From time to time, the Rock Island Line rattled and creaked along tracks at the river's edge, stopping conversations in the dining room of the old Muscatine Hotel, where Rotarians held their weekly meetings. They could look out the windows and watch barges loaded with coal or grain push gently north toward Lock and Dam Sixteen, or float quietly south toward St. Louis and New Orleans.

In "south end," the Grain Processing Company and a Monsanto chemical plant provided jobs and a unique blend of the putrid odor of fermenting grain and chemicals which, depending on the wind, drifted up into the center of town. Uptown,

Hon Industries made office furniture and Stanley Consulting, a world-wide engineering firm, had its more glamorous head-quarters.

When we arrived in Muscatine, Bandag, Tony's new company, had small offices scattered up and down Second Street, which were later consolidated into one modern facility on the north edge of town. Seasonally, a delicious aroma came from the Heinz tomato ketchup plant, and in the hot summer months the kids held their noses when we passed near the hog farms and cattle feedlots.

All of this industry contributed to Muscatine's having some wealthy, old families who supported the arts, the country club, the schools, and the city. Names in the phone book like Freyer-muth, Sywassink, Kautz, and Johannsen suggested people of German descent, or Scandinavian. There were a few black families in town and several Hispanic people who had lived in the area for years. In appearance only, it was a homogeneous white population, reminding us more of the South Africa we knew, rather than Berkeley where we had spent the last ten months. Bandag was among a few local companies that were beginning to reach out to international markets, but at that time not many people were moving in or out of Muscatine.

Our first glimpse of Muscatine was at night. We rented a car and drove south from the Moline airport on the Illinois side of the Mississippi River, through cornfields, slowly creeping through a couple of dark, quiet river towns. We crossed the drawbridge into Iowa and onto Second Street, the main street of Muscatine, found our way to the motel, and the next day started house-hunting. Within a few days, the girls were in school.

For several mornings, with the newspaper spread over the breakfast table at the Country Kitchen, Tony and I scoured the ads for a house to rent. Bandag personnel were asking around, too, but there didn't seem to be anything in town. "Ah! Here's something," I said. I read, "'Farmhouse for rent, Muscatine school district.' Now that would be different!"

Tony went to look at it that day and came back to the hotel in the evening. "Well," he announced, "it's way out there, but livable and it could be a lot of fun until we decide where we want to live permanently, and even *if* we want to live here permanently." Underlying our conversation, unspoken, was the fact that we had no money for a down payment on a house and too much furniture for an apartment. We had no choice.

I went out the next day to see for myself. The house was at the end of a long lane, isolated from others by acres of stubble-strewn cornfields. I waded through unplowed, ankle-deep snow to the front door and knocked loudly several times. A young woman rattled the door handle inside, clicked some locks, and, pushing aside the curtain that covered the door to keep out the draft, she pulled on the front door and pushed the storm door out to let me in. "Sorry, about the snow. We don't scrape in front," she laughed. "You're not from around here, are you? Nobody uses the front door around here."

She and her husband were moving out, she explained, because the house cost too much to heat. "Fortunately, the one bathroom is on the main floor, right off the kitchen, so we keep the doors to the upstairs closed and sleep down here in the living room," she said as she led me through the archway between the living room and dining room. "The house is available right away. We're moving in with my mother." There were four bedrooms upstairs, and the rooms downstairs were large, large enough to hold our carpets and big furniture. Looking out the dining-room windows, I saw two thick-trunked oak trees, now leafless, that would shade the south side in the summer and could possibly hold a tree house or a swing. Beyond them stood the barn and a hog house with, I guessed, pigs. On the north side of the house stretched a narrow, fenced-in pasture, where Danny, the old pony, would graze in the summer. Behind the house in a field of snow, a windmill stood with half the sails missing, like a photo that was attempting to be picturesque. It *was* picturesque, a rural American home waiting for a family.

"It'll be another adventure," I said with a brave heart to the girls and Tony that night. "Just think, a farmhouse with barn cats, and a pony, and baby pigs, all right there. Maybe we can get a few chickens."

We were now able to give an address to the storage company in Richmond, California, where our furniture had been waiting for eleven months. Tony was already at work somewhere in his new territory in Asia, when, two weeks later, I got a call at the motel from the truck driver saying that he was in the vicinity and would deliver the next day.

In the early morning chill, the steering wheel of the '69 Oldsmobile Cutlass Supreme that Tony had picked out for me was icy in my hands. I bounced over the gravel roads to meet the moving van at a local bar in Blue Grass, a small town where two roads crossed in the middle of cornfields. I led the way along back roads to our rented house. We could see it and the barn from quite a distance, because the fields were not yet planted. It was the first of April, and the black dirt, just disked, glistened richly in the early morning. *When Mother comes to visit*, I thought, *I want her to come in April, so she can smell the freshness and experience the spring-blue sky and haze of new green over a tree, and the black, black earth.*

The moving van lumbered behind me, spewing gravel, and followed as I turned down our lane, swerving around the ruts and the mud puddles from last night's rain. The house stood gray and alone, waiting, like the last one to be asked to dance. *We're coming. We'll have you dancing in no time! People don't landscape around here*, I thought, looking at the two old oaks, bare yet from winter, and a few scrawny sticks around the house. The warm welcome I'd come to expect in sunny climates was not here. I had no experience with winter but I guessed that color hid in bulbs under the ground and buds on the branches, which in May would explode into purple irises and large, floppy peonies and boughs of delicate, white bridal veil. I turned my head at the sound of a red-winged blackbird chirping noisily on top of a dried cornstalk, a warm spot of color on that chilly, gray morning.

Our hands were stiff with cold as we carried packing boxes in from the truck, letting the porch door slam shut with each coming and going. To find the warmest spot, we arranged the cartons in patches of sunlight on the hardwood floor in the living room and sat to open them with the sun pouring through the windows on our backs. I started unpacking in the kitchen and, over the clatter of dishes, heard the muffled sound of ripping cardboard, crunching paper and girlish squeals as my daughters, now fourteen, twelve, and six, lifted out treasures we had carefully packed in Johannesburg over a year ago.

All day I fiddled with the thermostat, expecting to hear the furnace kick on. I put my hand over the vents. Nothing. The electric stove worked, so I opened a couple of cans of vegetable soup, and we let the steam from our own familiar bowls warm our faces and remind us that we were home and not in a motel. We got the beds made and that night shivered under heavy blankets. Early Sunday morning I called our farmer-landlord, Roger, and asked him to come over. I knew I could call early. He would be just in from doing chores, his worn coveralls already smelling like pigs and his John Deere cap thrown in a corner exposing a white forehead above a weathered, tanned face. Seeing him without his cap gave me a feeling of embarrassing intimacy.

"It's *cold*, Roger," I said. "Do you think the pilot light's out?"

"Weeellll," he drawled, "see that big, white tank beside the house? That's for propane for the furnace. That could be empty. You'll have to call the Co-op. They'll deliver. But not on Sunday."

I called the number he gave me and pled my case. "I'm new here. I didn't know about propane. We're freezing! Pleeeze!"

The loaded gas truck swayed down the lane that afternoon and stopped. The driver dragged its heavy hose across the lawn and hoisted the nozzle up to the top of the big, white tank. "Just half-full," I called out when I found out how much a full tank would cost. I wrote a check on the spot and paid the extra charge for Sunday delivery, hoping this one delivery would last a very long time. The smell from the fuel fumes reminded me of jet travel, but this time it meant staying in one place, home, and warm.

Monday morning we woke up to sunshine and I walked with the girls down the long lane to wait for the school bus. We watched the top of the bus, a thin strip of yellow, slide over the dark dirt of the flat land miles away, as it crept finally to our little family standing, waiting, by the country mail box on the gravel road. We were far enough out of town to be the first family to be picked up in the morning and the last to be brought home in the evening. I waved as my children climbed the steps and disappeared into the big yellow bus. It bumped away from me and I stood alone, watching that symbol of America disappear in the dusty dip of the road. *America*, I thought, *I am glad to be home.*

I turned and looked back down the long lane that was our driveway. Our farmhouse stood like a child's drawing—square gray stucco with a peaked roof, two windows upstairs, two below, with the front door in between and the requisite shade tree on either side. Without much effort, I could imagine childish black "Vs" for birds in the blue sky above, and smoke curling from a chimney. With the sophistication of our life overseas stripped away, was I back in my childhood? Certainly I was entering a simpler way of life.

When Tony returned to Iowa two weeks later, he found everything in place in the house and the children established in school. He was overflowing with tales of his travels through several countries of Asia and was challenged and enthusiastic about his new job. I smiled and nodded and got out the atlas and found all the places he was talking about. During a brief break in his stories, I blurted out, "Tony, what am *I* going to do here? The house is done, the kids are gone all day, and I don't know a soul." There was no welcoming community of Americans like those I had found in foreign countries.

"I don't know. What *are* you going to do? You can do whatever you want. You know I'll support you whatever you decide. Just go and do your own things, Lizzie. You'll figure it out."

We looked at each other in silence. What *did* I want? I could teach again, go back to school myself, get a job, join a club, volunteer somewhere, play golf, paint, write, or just sit and read. I was not a guest in this country. I belonged here. It was America, after all, and Tony had just given me a nudge to strike out on my own. Going to work would certainly be helpful, but I had lost all confidence in myself and had not been a great success at that secretarial school. Who would hire me? For what?

How perfectly Tony and I had settled ourselves into the socially conditioned roles of the fifties. World War II was over. The men were home from the front and needed jobs in factories that were converting from war machines to domestic goods. And where was the consumer to buy these new domestic products? I grew up reading magazines full of ads for washing machines, toasters, and vacuums, diamond engagement rings, Betty Crocker tableware for the hope chest, and recipes to make her man hurry home at night. The pictured woman, dressed in a full-skirted cotton dress, nipped in at the waist with a ruffled half-apron, stood with one high-heeled foot on a step ladder, arms above her well-coiffed head, waving the wand of an Electrolux vacuum cleaner over the top of the curtain railing. Behind her on the counter, wiggly lines of steam rose from a plate of freshly baked chocolate chip cookies. In my required high school Home Economics class, I had learned to make a basic cream pie, into which bananas could be folded, or strawberries, or chocolate. We were graded on a floral centerpiece, a requirement for the dinner table every night in a happy home. In general, women graduating from high school and college in the nineteen-fifties soaked it all in, until our daughters came along and showed us there was more than one way to live a life.

I thought I was different from my college friends who had married right after graduation, if they had not quit school earlier, but I had done the same thing, just in a different place. I had then followed my husband literally, not unhappily, all over the world, changing the focus of my interests with each move to match where we were.

About this time, I read a memoir by an American artist who, in the sixties and seventies, had created an arena for women artists to show and judge their works, free from the boundaries that had been set by men. Judy Chicago was born in 1939 and so came of age in the fifties as I did. In her memoir *Through the Flower*, she describes her personal development. I recognized myself in her words as she referred to her life with her husband. "During his absence, I lived my life in terms of my own needs, but as soon as he returned, I 'put down' my life and began to rearrange my schedule to suit him. This reflected the fact that I felt that his needs were more important than mine and also that I still assumed that my life should be open-ended to accommodate his demands."

Tony's life also illustrated the expected role of the Organization Man of the fifties. After his initial, independent decision to immigrate to the States, he had taken a job with a large corporation, expecting it to be his lifetime career. He moved himself and his family without question at the whim of the corporation.

When Tony quit Firestone, he cut a tie he thought he would be loyal to forever. Firestone had been a haven for him when he emigrated from Holland twenty-three years before. Firestone International was almost a family business, as Tony's great-uncle was president and another uncle was employed there as an auditor. Now Tony had made the break. He had found this new job with Bandag on his own and was free to quit again if he so chose.

Now I, too, had a new freedom.

In those early Iowa days, Tony's trips abroad involved great distances. To make them worthwhile, he was gone from home for three to six weeks at a time and I was alone in the farmhouse. When in Iowa, he spent time in the office and with our girls, encouraging them in their studies and cheering them on at their swim and track meets. He told them tales in the evenings while they sprawled in the big chair in the living room, while Asian-costumed dolls accumulated on a shelf in the living room.

With Tony at home I was fully occupied, but when he was gone, time dragged.

One day, Linda got off the bus and skipped down the lane ahead of the other two. "Mom," she said, "I saw an art store near the school. You could draw and paint again!"

A few days later, I was sitting outside on a stool with pen and ink, drawing what I saw around me, corn, pigs, trees, the house, the fields of Iowa. In town, I discovered an artists' co-op, where I volunteered my time and sold my drawings and note cards. For the first time people knew who I was without first identifying me with my husband or my children.

In winter, I set up my drawing things inside at the dining room table. Out the window, the spectacular oak tree, bare of leaves, branches twisting, cast strong shadows as the midday sun rose behind it. Pen in hand, eyes on the tree, both of us growing strong roots, roots in Iowa. My adjustment to Iowa was made easier by those years on the farm. The land and the activity and the weather and the serenity became a part of me, so I loved Iowa and its cornfields before I had to figure out how I fit into a small, Midwestern town.

One day as I focused on my drawing, a fuzzy spot flashed in my peripheral vision. I shook my head and rubbed my eye. It was gone. Then the shadow, like a floating feather, was there again. I sat very still, bent my head to work, but again, the flash over the top of the piano. I lifted my eyes and stared at the piano. A mouse! A mouse? Gone as soon as it came. I slammed down my pen, got up, and left the room. I didn't want a mouse here. It couldn't have been a mouse. It wasn't a mouse. I hate mice!

I did not do any drawing the next day. But, the day after that, I dared myself to go into the dining room and sit down. I slowly picked up my pen, carefully unscrewed the lid of the ink bottle, then sat stock-still, moving only my eyes to the top of the piano. The mouse sat still, too, and stared back at me. I ran into the kitchen and slammed the door behind me.

I shuddered, remembering Mohammed, our houseboy in Casablanca, running around the kitchen with a broom in his two hands raised above his head like a flyswatter—*Whack! Whack!*—until he finally got that mouse. I couldn't do that! Kill a mouse like a fly?

How convenient it is to not see or acknowledge what is unpleasant; because once you admit that there is a problem, then you have to do something about it.

This case of the mouse was fairly simple. I went to town, bought a dozen traps and figured out how to put a little chip of cheese in the right place and pull the spring wire under the thin trigger hold-down. Slowly, carefully, I eased three traps onto the floor in corners of the kitchen. I warned the kids. The next morning, three fat mice. Ugh! I closed my eyes and scooped them up with a dustpan and dumped them, trap and all, into a brown paper bag and took it all outside into the garbage. Shivering with revulsion, I did this for several nights. But in time, I discovered that I became hardened and was able to raise the metal spring, free up the mouse, slide it into the brown paper bag and then re-use the trap. It seemed as if the mice were marching in from the fields, a late-fall parade, with no apparent end.

Finally, early on a Sunday morning, I phoned our farmer-landlord, Roger. "Weellll," he drawled, "see, the mice come in this time of year to get warm."

"Yes, I know, Roger. I don't *want* them in the house. How can I keep them out?"

That afternoon his truck bounced down the lane and he and his son got out armed with small pieces of plywood, a hammer and a brown paper grocery sack.

"See this here?" he said, pulling a wad of gray steel wool out of the sack. "When you find a small hole or opening around a pipe, stuff this into it. The mice ain't gunna chew through this." I stood in my fluffy pink house slippers and watched as the two men mouse-proofed my house. Unlike some of the difficulties I faced in later years, this problem had a quick solution.

Above: The journey begins.

Left: We are a couple.

Left: Congratulatory telegrams from around the world, read at our wedding reception by our colorful best man, Doug Guy.

Below: The wedding party: Jaleh; my father, Walter; his wife, Maddie; and Tony and me.

Above: Tony at work, 1959.

Below: Tony at work, 1997.

Right: The Tunisian birdcage in its custom-designed spot in the new house.

Below: With Tony as MC, I modeled up-to-date Moroccan style.

Left: On the farm: Linda, me, Tony, Caroline, Marianne, and Zulu.

Below: Our first home in the U.S.

I sat on the porch and
watched the world turn.

The tree and I sent down
deep roots in Iowa.

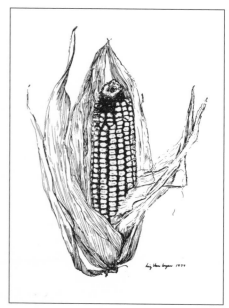

I drew what I saw—
corn and more corn, luscious.

February 7, 1960.

February 7, 2005.

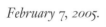

Right: Celebrating our 45th wedding anniversary in our new home in Denver, with Elizabeth, Katherine, and Nicholas.

Below: One soothing continuity in our lives was Tony at the piano.

CHAPTER II

The Rip Van Winkle Effect

Iowa, 1975–1981

WHILE LIVING ABROAD, we had often talked about what it would be like when we got back to the States. But *back* implies a return to somewhere we had been before, and Muscatine was not a place or time either of us knew. Rural Iowa was far from California's Bay Area, and 1975 was certainly not like 1959.

During the fifteen years I was out of the country, Johnny Carson's hair had gone from black to white, Eisenhower's interstate highways moved traffic from coast to coast, and it was no longer exceptional for women to work at jobs outside the home. I had left Berkeley in 1959 before the Pill, Betty Friedan and Gloria Steinem, and Roe vs. Wade. It was before the divisive Vietnam War, before the Beatles and Laugh-In, even before McDonalds and Barbie. When I left, going to a concert meant Beethoven or Bach. In 1959 a few department stores had their own charge cards. In 1975 a universal MasterCard was coming into use, but when I went to Sears to apply for their card, I was denied, which embarrassed me. We still had no collateral and a very slim bank account and of course, we had no history in that small town. South Africa was so news- and truth-deprived that I literally didn't know what was going on in the world. I even found holidays popping up that I had forgotten about or ignored, the 4th of July, Halloween, and Thanksgiving, Mother's Day, Labor Day, and Memorial Day.

In the foreign countries where we had lived I *knew* I was odd—didn't speak the language, didn't know the customs—but I hadn't expected to feel so awkward and out of place in Iowa. When I had last bought stockings in the States, it had been from a woman in a department store who stood behind a glass counter and put on white gloves so her rough hands wouldn't snag the sheer nylon when she held her hand inside of one of the legs to show me the shade. Now I found panty hose in plastic eggs in Walgreens. I felt like Rip Van Winkle.

Tony had lived in the States for five years in his twenties, about the same amount of time we had spent in Morocco and two years *less* than we had spent in South Africa. He wasn't raised in America. He didn't notice the changes I did. I don't think he ever considered we were going *back* to anywhere; he was always going forward, to the next place, the next language, the next adventure. So the farmhouse in Iowa was not back to anywhere, not a return for either of us, but another starting out. New again.

I took Caroline and Linda into town a few Sunday mornings to go to church. We were in small-town America now, and that's what people did. I was looking for community, and perhaps a return to the rituals of my childhood, hoping to find "roots." But I had changed too much, had discovered different ways to find connection with the Source and Force of my life. After a few visits, I stopped singing in the middle of the old familiar hymns, unable to continue when I didn't *believe* the words that came out of my mouth. I have regretted that I didn't have that kind of community, especially in times of trouble.

Tony thought for his family to be truly American we didn't need to go to church, but we did need to be up-to-date with the normal amenities in the house. I was curious one evening when he walked into the farmhouse carrying a big carton. It was May, but the kids and I gathered around the box like it was Christmas. Ripping open the top, he pulled out a small, black and white television set, with a pair of rabbit ears for the antenna. We had watched some television in Berkeley with my mother, but we hadn't learned to be quiet and focus, except during the quick, clever commercials for Alka-Seltzer, ("Plop, plop, fizz, fizz, Oh, what a relief it is"). It was 1975 and we had not had television since Tehran in 1962, where we had occasionally watched a six-month-old Perry Como canned program from the States. We never did get the hang of sitting around watching TV.

The first time I brought groceries into the farmhouse and found the breakfast dishes still on the table where I had left them, I laughed out loud. What had I expected? Kaya or Mohammed to appear? After the first couple of weeks, I came to my senses and stopped ironing the sheets and underwear. Caroline, at age thirteen, took on the job of cleaning orange rust out of the bathtub left there by the hard well water, because she didn't think I knew how.

Over the next year, I weeded a vegetable garden and canned tomatoes, raised, plucked, cleaned, cooked, or froze a dozen chickens, herded six turkeys with a golf club, became a 4-H Club leader, learned the difference between green beans and soy beans, put up and took down storm windows, painted the picket fence (or "thicket fence," a malapropism from our landlady), chased fat hogs out of our yard, and became friends with good people.

Look at me! I thought, appraising my canned goods and the garden, *"All by myself!"*

And I watched.

One morning in June, suddenly, all at the same time, faint rows of spring green appeared in the black earth, surprising me. The corn was up! I watched as it grew. "Knee high by the Fourth of July," they said. Our front porch faced west, and in the evenings, as I sat in an old red rocking chair we had picked up at a yard sale, I waited for the sunset and watched the corn stalks grow, green, green, all shades of green. I listened to the whish of the wind and saw silver-gray tassels emerge straight up in a delicate spray above the straight stalks, soon to be taller than I. A few days later, the tassels burst open in a spray of golden color topping the graceful, curving leaves. I got out of my chair and off the porch and wandered onto that black earth, thrilled when I found the immature cobs hiding deep down where the leaves join the stalk.

Here was the Creator performing in front of my eyes. Instead of red and gold kaftans waving over the medina, golden corn tassels seemingly floated over deep green stalks.

From the red rocking chair, I had a 180-degree view of summer passing, of the sun descending a little farther north each day, and the fields of corn maturing, eventually losing the vibrant green and turning a pale gold, then brown. I sat still and heard the rustle of the dry leaves instead of the gentle bells of the Moroccan water seller. I worried that my neighbor farmers would leave the corn too long and it would be all dried out. Of course, that was the purpose, to let the corn dry in the field so it wouldn't need expensive drying machines and could be stored without rotting moisture. When the corn was finally harvested in late fall, the kernels were stripped off and funneled into a waiting truck and the cobs tossed out onto the field for the cows. Who knew there was so much to learn? My thrill was a ride through the rows with Roger on his giant John Deere tractor.

I watched storms far in the distance as they approached our house. There could be a sunny, blue sky on the south and black rain clouds in the north coming toward me, all viewed at the same time from the calm of the red rocking chair. The days of July and August were hot, humid, and buggy and I waited in vain for hot, dry summer days I remembered from my childhood in California. The farmhouse had no air conditioning, so the windows were always open, letting in gentle breezes from time to time, but also fine dust, and when the wind was right, the pig smell. "That's the smell of money," Farmer Roger said. *Ah, money. Does Roger have time to spend his money? Can he leave his cows and corn to take a trip? Does he want to?*

Autumn came and the brilliant show of red and gold and flood-light yellow surprised me. Fall was a welcome, warm season, but with an ominous undercurrent. Winter was just ahead, and I was frightened that first year. I didn't know what to expect. The seasons here didn't morph into one another. They changed with sudden passion and made the passage of time too obvious.

On voting day in November 1976, the year of the Bicentennial, I jostled the car over gravel country roads from our house past the farms of our new friends, the Jewetts and the Nicewarners and the Daufeldts, and pulled up next to other dusty cars and pickups in front of the old Crabapple School House. The building stood alone, surrounded by cornfields, with a single oak guarding the entrance. I went up the few wooden steps and opened the door into the old-time, one-room schoolhouse. Two neighbor ladies in print house dresses greeted me from behind a table, offered me cookies, and found my name on a long printed list in front of them. Then I stepped behind a curtain and cast my first ever ballot for President of the United States.

The first snow fell the day before Thanksgiving that first year, the same day Tony left for Japan. On the way back from taking him to the airport, I suddenly decided the girls and I should have a real American Thanksgiving dinner. We detoured through the snow to the nearest little town and bought a small turkey. The next day was cooking day. Caroline pulled bread to bits for the stuffing, Linda peeled potatoes, and Marianne poured the frozen peas into the pan. I pared and sliced Jonathan apples and rolled out crust for the pie. The pieces of dough I trimmed from around the edge of the pie fell into the children's waiting hands to pat and roll and bake as they wished.

The aroma of cinnamon and apples, onions, thyme, sage, and the roasting turkey filled our farmhouse while we placed the good china on the table with cloth napkins. I lit the candles in my grandmother's silver candelabra and the four of us sat down at the dining room table as though we had a table full of guests. We were quiet. Then, in a true Norman Rockwell moment, we expressed our thanks for each other and for all we had been given.

For fifteen years, I had been the erratic creator and keeper of family traditions in an effort to give stability and consistency to our otherwise peripatetic lives. I knew that ritual gives comfort and a sense of belonging, like the repetition of ancient designs which rooted the Iranian artisans to their history. Our family had lived with change; Santa Claus meant wooden shoes and St. Nicholas's Day, the sixth of December. All these customs enriched our lives, gave us depth and understanding of others; but with *this* Thanksgiving, I was starting a new tradition for our family, an American one. "Mom, we always do it this way," was a phrase I wanted to hear. And Tony? Where was he? *Next time*, I thought.

I had never experienced cold like Muscatine in the winter. I was shocked by a reading on the bank thermometer of eighteen degrees, not realizing it was on the way down to below zero. When I was busy, I didn't notice the cold much, and certainly didn't let the snow stop me from doing the things I wanted to do, unless, of course, the country roads were drifted in and impassable. We had no garage and I learned to keep a shovel, scraper, and mittens available.

After Christmas, the gray skies blended with the somber, corn-stubbled fields and steely-branched, leafless trees. January, February, March.... Then, finally, April again, with the promising green shoots popping up in the black dirt, the sun warming us again through the farmhouse windows. April made the whole of winter bearable. The last few months of winter carried the expectation of spring just as the red and gold days of autumn threatened winter. I witnessed it all for the first time from the porch and windows of that farmhouse.

Time was passing. I'd experienced a whole year of seasons. *What's next?* I thought.

As Tony's job became increasingly secure and I found myself driving back and forth the fifteen miles from the farmhouse to the school two or three times a day, we were ready to think about moving into town.

One evening in the summer of 1977, Tony and I stood together in the damp grass on a rise and looked down the slope to a fence beyond which ran a trickle of a creek and a pasture dotted with oak trees. The pasture on the other side of the property line would most likely remain in its natural state, making the lot where we stood ideal for building a house without another structure interrupting the view. "Imagine, Tony," I said, taking his hand. "This patch of land, in all the world, could be ours. I feel like we are buying a piece of the sky."

"The oak trees here must not be touched," he answered. "Any house we build will have to go around them. I think we can do it." We committed to buying the land.

That fall, when Tony had a few weeks off from traveling, he came home one night with a pad of graph paper and sat down at the dining room table with several sharpened pencils, a ruler, Scotch tape, and scissors. He amazed me as, over the next several evenings, he used the graph paper to draw plans for our dream house.

"Hey, Lizzie, what do you think of this?" I stepped from the kitchen and stood next to him. With one arm around my waist, and the other moving over his drawing, he pointed out the living room that would be two steps down from the entrance area, like the Casablanca house. "When you come in the front door, you will look straight across the living room and out the sliding glass doors to the view beyond, to the hill with the oak trees."

"I love the openness, just like the house in South Africa."

"And here we can put in an arch between the living room and the dining room, like the Casablanca house...for the birdcage. This alcove can be a little library with shelves on both sides, with the camel saddle there for a reading stool. We will finish off the basement later, but it will be a good place for you to paint and sew, and the kids can bring their friends there, a rec room. What do you think?"

"Tony, it's a dream. Are we really doing it?" I hugged him and left him to his work.

The next night when I came from the kitchen to see, he was cutting and pasting the house together in three dimensions. The roof was on, and the garage and the driveway in place.

"Now the lot. Where are the old newspapers?" I grabbed one from the pile in the kitchen. "Watch this," he said, as he opened it flat and began measuring. He cut the shape of the lot to scale and taped it to the table. "The house will have to be just here. No, here. Let's see, the sun..." And he proceeded to place the house on the lot this way and that to get the best angles of the sun, summer and winter. He looked up. "Don't we have a little car around here somewhere?" Linda ran to get one of her Matchbook cars, red, and Tony carefully parked it in the circular drive.

We engaged a contractor, and soon the building began, with Tony's plans pinned up on the foundation. "I get a kick out of watching the men with the backhoe stop and look up at my piece of paper tacked up there with my plans," he laughed. The lot was three miles from his office, so he stopped to watch the progress every evening on his way back to the farm, until he reluctantly went off on a working trip again.

I answered the phone early one morning when he called just before he went to bed in Japan.

"Have they finished digging the basement yet?" he asked.

"Not yet," I answered.

"Tell them to add another three feet to the living room." And so the house grew. When the framing went up, Tony was there. "Here, you hold the birdcage, Lizzie, I'll measure." He took a marking pencil and drew the arch that was later cut to fit our treasure. I put up sawhorses in the new garage and stained miles of baseboards, panels for the cathedral ceiling, and spindles for the railings. By August of 1978, the house was ready for the finishing touch, the Persian light fixtures in the entranceway. Tony stood on a ladder and twisted the wires and screwed the screws, and when it was nearly dark outside, flipped on the switch. Tiny beams shone through the filigree brass lamps, making a lace pattern on the blank walls and, in a way, allowing our bright past to light up our home of the future.

At the farmhouse, we piled bureau drawers and boxes full of dishes, gently cradled in towels, into our cars. The expert packers we had had for our other moves would have been horrified! The copper tray and birdcage went on top of clothes still on the hangers flung in the back seats. Lamps, books, pillows, and paintings went carefully into the trunk of Tony's car. We rented a U-Haul, borrowed a pickup truck, and hired two hefty boys from the YMCA to lift the piano, the dining room table, and heavy chairs. Back and forth we drove, hillbilly style, slowing traffic on the fifteen-mile, two-lane road from the farm to our new home. There we spread out our life into our own suburban, American house. Tony ceremoniously hung the Tunisian birdcage in its custom-designed arch between the living room and dining room.

Tired but exhilarated that first evening, we worked till dark. Tony found two lawn chairs and carried them to the deck off the living room. "Let's stop, Lizzie. Come and relax for a minute." He poured us each a glass of wine, and we sat side by side with our backs to the boxes and piles of furniture yet to be sorted and put in place. We looked out over the expanse of dirt and rocks below us and watched fireflies darting over our back yard, our bit of America. "Next summer, I'll be mowing the lawn out there, Lizzie."

"This is it, isn't it, Tony? The American dream. Isn't this why you immigrated to America? To have a family and a home, and a lawn to mow, work you like, and opportunities for your own kids?"

"Sure. Sure, Lizzie." He leaned over and squeezed my hand. "Congratulations, Honey."

By the time the older girls were nearing the end of high school and Marianne was nearly there, I was ready for something of my own, something creative and worthwhile on which to focus my attention and energies. I had completed several pen-and-ink drawings, and even sold a few, but I knew I would never be a great artist like Judy Chicago. However, I wondered if I could be successful at *something* and was increasingly alert to discovering opportunities around me.

Caroline and Linda joined their new friends from farming families in the local 4-H Club. All year the girls worked hard on their projects and in July presented the home-made skirt, the refinished bookcase, or the glossy, home-grown tomatoes to the judges at the West Liberty, Muscatine County Fair. This gave us the chance to spend several days at the fair, strolling the muddy paths among the animals, carnival games, and cotton candy kiosks. I stopped at every advertising booth under the grandstand and picked up whatever they were giving away, a yard stick from an insurance company, a calendar, a nail file. I giggled to myself as my hand hesitated over a form for a free magazine subscription.

The first line stumped me: NAME. Name? What was my name? Was I Mrs. Tony Van Ingen? Elizabeth G. Van Ingen? Mrs. H.A. Van Ingen? Liz...? Ms....?

The summer of 1981, an attractive woman whose pink name badge read "Mary Beth" stood smiling and handing out lipstick samples at a cosmetics booth. Her blond hair fluffed glamorously around her face and her eyes sparkled beneath intense blue eyelids. In her dark blue business skirt, jacket, and heels she looked pleasantly out of place in this dusty farmers' environment. I registered for a free facial, using without hesitation the name Liz Van Ingen.

A week later, Mary Beth was at my door. "I'm on my way to deliver a load of green peppers," she explained, as she hefted her pink bags of cosmetic tubes and jars over her shoulder and slammed the door of her pickup. "But I have an hour to let you try the products yourself, right here in your own kitchen!" So she was a farmer's wife *and* a consultant. I loved the pampering from the facial as well as how my face felt after using the products, so I agreed to talk with Mary Beth's leader the following day about becoming a beauty consultant myself.

"It would be a great career for you, Liz," the young woman named Tawnya said over breakfast at a local coffee shop. *Career? For me?* I thought. She sat across from me in a purple ultra-suede business suit, and her brown eyes shone with enthusiasm as she opened her three-ring binder. "You can make money on your own time, be your own boss, and meet a lot of people." She turned the pages of her notebook, and her magenta fingernails clicked on each page as she pointed out the benefits of the business. Her broad smile and a confident chuckle carried me along, and I found myself laughing and thinking that selling and demonstrating cosmetics would be the most fun and lucrative *career* in the world. Maybe this would be my "something."

"Give it a try," Tony said, when I told him about it that evening. "You'll be great and it will keep you busy when I'm out of town. I'll bet you'll be driving a pink Cadillac in six months."

So I began a career with Mary Kay Cosmetics that did turn

out to be fun and lucrative, and that lasted more than twenty-five years. It was perfect for me because it didn't matter who my husband was, where I went to college, how well my kids did at school, or what exotic places I'd lived. I would succeed only because of how well I was able to do the work. I now had my own goals, and all I needed from Tony was his confidence in me and his encouragement. "Go ahead and do your own things, Sweetiepie. Don't worry about me," he said.

At first, the job fit perfectly into our accepted roles in the household, with me working part time around Tony's and the girls' schedules. As the years went by I earned the position of Independent Sales Director and the privilege of driving a pink Buick Regal for free. Tony always drove a company car. Now it was my turn! When the girls were out of the house and on their way to adulthood, my confidence soared as I drove that pink car to teach and train as far as North Carolina in the east and California in the west. I missed Tony, of course, but I basked in his pride in me and I was certain we'd have lots of time together when we retired.

PART THREE

Don't Send Me in Dark Despair...

CHAPTER 12

The End and the Beginning

Iowa and China, 1995–98

"WHY ARE WE STANDING HERE?" Tony asked. "You got up to go to the bathroom and woke me to come and look at the moon. I'm glad you did. It *is* beautiful."

"Oh. Yes."

With Tony's arm around my shoulders we stood at the long window by the front door, looking across the driveway. It was three o'clock in the morning. I took Tony's hand and led him back to bed, where he slept immediately. I lay on my back, staring at the dark, torturing myself with thoughts of Tony's out-of-character behaviors over the past couple of years.

We had moved into this house in August 1978. Now, twenty years later, in August 1998, we were alone, our three girls having left years ago to create lives of their own. I was gaining freedom and energy from the in-home sales business with Mary Kay Cosmetics that I had started in 1981, but Tony was winding down from decades of work in international business.

"I'm just stalling now," he had said one evening in 1995 as we sat on the deck with a glass of wine, both of us realizing our years were going by swiftly. "I don't ever want to retire. I don't even want to think about it, but I know I'm halfway out to pasture now." I, too, wondered how he would use forty years of experience in the international tire business and all his foreign language ability once he retired.

A few days later, he came home with brochures from several organizations soliciting retired businessmen to donate their time abroad assisting new businesses. "Possibilities," he said, and tossed the applications on his desk. Soon after that comment, in 1995, just before his sixty-fourth birthday, Tony had come home from work early and as he had done many times in the past, and had "News!"

I heard the quick toot of the horn in the garage before he came bursting into the kitchen. "Lizzie! They want me to go to China! Bandag is starting a business in China!" he grabbed me and lifted me off my feet. "I thought they were through with me, but I know I can do it! Maybe you'll come with me sometime!"

He enrolled in the Berlitz Language School in Chicago for a three-week crash course in Mandarin Chinese. He called me from Chicago and poured out Chinese phrases, chuckling and repeating some sentences he had learned. On the phone, he sounded Chinese! But when he came home and those same words came out of a tall, blond Dutchman, I could only laugh. I caught his excitement and found books about Chinese history, culture, and politics, so this enormous world opened up for me, too.

He organized his passport and visas, checked and rechecked his papers, and in October of 1995 left for three weeks in China. During the next two years, he averaged four long trips a year, pushing his energy and his habitual enthusiasm to keep up the pace. When he was home, he was irritable, but I didn't make an issue of it and understood that switching from China to Iowa every few weeks was difficult at his age. When he forgot a date we had made, or ignored things I said to him, I assumed he was distracted by his work and tired from travel. I noticed that his agenda–date book had become sloppy, with thick red felt-tip check marks and underlines all through it—not his usual style.

In the fall of 1996, Tony bought tickets for both of us for a three-week trip to China and we started packing. He had always been meticulous, but now he was obsessive, counting underwear, putting his toiletries in and out of his bag again and again.

Once in China, he took one morning off to go with me to see the Terracotta Warriors in Xian, but almost as soon as we had arrived he said, "Let's go back to the hotel. I have to get back. I have work to do." And later, "No! We can't stop here! Lizzie, we don't have time. I have to get back!" His attitude disturbed me—annoyed me actually—but it was his trip; I was lucky to be there at all. I hired a guide for myself and saw attractions that I found culturally interesting but Tony didn't have time for.

One day over lunch of noodles and shrimp, Gary, the Chinese business contact and guide, explained the afternoon's schedule. As we got up to leave, Tony put his hand on his friend's shoulder. "Well, Gary, what's on for this afternoon?" Gary and I glanced at each other with eyebrows raised, and Gary repeated what he had just said. I laughed away the wave of dread that filled me, but made no comment. Maybe Gary hadn't noticed. Maybe I was making it up. That evening, instead of going out on the town as we usually did when we traveled, I sat quietly in the hotel room and watched Tony write down word for word what had gone on that day. "I always do this," he snapped at me, "I have to be on my toes in the morning. Now where did I put my..."

"Your briefcase?"

"I can't find my, my..."

"Your briefcase. Here it is."

Back home in Muscatine, I expected routine and rest would relieve some of the pressure of travel and that he would be his old self again. But that was not the case. One Saturday when we were delivering meals-on-wheels, as we had done for years, he barked at me, "Don't tell me! I know the way!" and took a wrong turn while leaving the hospital with the meals. I realized with a start that it wasn't the first time he'd mixed up something that was routine, or forgotten where he was. His recent slip-ups came flooding back to me. Dread rolled through my body. *Please, be making this up,* I thought. *I don't want you to be forgetful! That's not like you!*

Then for several months I didn't notice any incidents, and I was sure I had imagined it all.

That fall of 1996, after we returned from China, our middle daughter, Linda, was married in California, and she and her husband, Jeff, came to Muscatine at Christmastime for a family celebration. It was a lovely time, with the two families getting to know each other around two long tables in our living room and dining room.

"Should Dad be drinking?" Linda said to me in the kitchen as he continued to pour wine and Champagne. When she was still living at home, I had gone to ALANON and Tony to AA for a while and he had stopped drinking. "Oh, Linda, he's fine. That was years ago. Now we often have a glass of wine or two with dinner. It's okay. This is a celebration! His brothers and sisters are here from all over the country, and we are all so very happy for you!"

Still, I was aware that Tony disrupted the evening somewhat. He kept rearranging chairs, and counting people, and then interrupting conversation by escaping to play the piano. I decided I was the only one to notice his strange behavior, and the next day I put it out of my mind.

Tony made three more arduous trips to China the next year, during which I worried whether he would find his way back home. At last he was talking about retiring and we went together to a financial advisor. The possibility of Alzheimer's floated through my thoughts like a wafting feather, but I refused to admit it even to myself; so how could I say to a stranger, "I think my husband here is losing his mind?" The advisor and Tony decided long-term healthcare insurance was not needed. I said nothing.

Tony's official retirement date was set, and in January of 1998, he was feted royally as an honored retiree at the Bandag International Business Conference held at a luxurious resort in Palm Springs. He stood under an enormous photograph-poster of himself, his smiling, confident face overlooking the reception hall, while people from the many Asian countries where he had worked came up to him with warmth in their eyes, saying they would miss him. Men and women from Central and South America shook his hand and thanked him. The Canadians presented him with a rugby shirt with a red maple leaf on the front, and "VAN INGEN #1" on the back. I stood next to him, fielding questions and covering for him when he was confused. He glowed as he greeted the people he had worked with. I wondered if he understood what was happening.

CHAPTER 13

Duct Tape and an Appointment

Iowa, 1998

"WE HAVE TO CLEAN UP around here. This place is a mess," Tony announced at the breakfast table one day in June 1998, the first summer of his retirement. "I'll start in the garage and tackle the basement later."

He moved the cars out of the garage and tore into his task. He pulled half-used cans of wasp spray and weed-killer and plant food off the shelf and tossed them, clanking and clinking, into an old cardboard box and closed it and sealed it with duct tape. "This, over here with nails and things, is just a nuisance," he said, tossing a plastic divider box crashing into a black garbage bag on the concrete garage floor. "If I need a nail again, I'll buy one."

The next moment, he looked over at the cardboard box he had just sealed and ripped into it, yanking at the duct tape. "What's all this stuff doing in here? We have to get rid of it."

"Tony," I said as I looked in, "you just filled this box with those cans."

"No. I didn't. Don't tell me that. Now what's in this suitcase? Oh, your old oil paints. Throw it out. You haven't painted in years. And these canning jars. You won't need them. We're going to rip up the vegetable garden and replace it with lawn. It's all too much, too much work and confusion."

I had reached my arms out towards him, not knowing how to respond. No more garden? What would he do without the vegetable garden? No more tomatoes? Dripping, sweet tomatoes in the summer? Or zucchini? For his favorite zucchini bread? I, who hadn't known a green bean from a soy bean, had become proud at the end of the summer to see the jars of red tomatoes lined up on the basement shelves alongside clear, currant jelly, from our own bushes.

"Tony, I'm not ready to stop living yet. What are you doing?"

"We've got to keep our chain saw so I can cut down the dead trees and limbs. Where's the axe?"

"The axe?"

"Hand me the broom so I can get at this corner."

I couldn't tell him I had taken the axe to the neighbor for safe-keeping. Tony had already had episodes of irrational temper and I was afraid. I decided to take the chain saw to the same neighbor as soon as possible. They were too dangerous to have within reach of Tony's slipping mind, though the last time he had tried to use the chain saw, he couldn't figure out how to start it and threw it in a corner.

Inside the house, he cleaned out his dresser drawers, keeping only a few pairs of navy socks and counting eight sets of underwear, throwing out the rest. He kept three pairs of identical khaki shorts that he wore year round and threw out ties, trinkets, and handkerchiefs. The two bottom drawers were empty. Somewhere in the depth of him, he knew he couldn't cope with clutter and choices.

"Look at this mess," he said, sitting at his desk. "All the paperwork I have to go through, and all these files I have to sort out. I can't find anything anymore. I don't know where I am. I can't focus. I put something over here and don't remember what I was doing. There's just too much stuff."

"I know, honey, it's not easy. You like things organized."

"It's just that since my retirement I don't have a direction. I was so stupid. I never planned. I never wanted to retire. If I was still working, I'd be sharp. I used to get up and know what I was going to do. Now I don't know what day it is." He dropped his head into his hands. "I knew I couldn't handle work anymore. I didn't want to quit and yet I knew it was time. All that traveling. It was time."

In the midst of his "paper work," he often jumped up and went to the piano and played for an hour or so. It seemed to calm him as he put himself in a private world with no one telling him what to do or reminding him that he was confused.

He's fine, I'd think one day. *I'm making it up.*

Then something would happen.

"It's six o'clock. Where are you going so early in the morning?" His head peeked at me from under his pillow.

"To the Y."

"What's there? Why are you going there?"

"I go to aerobics."

"Since when do you do that?"

"Tony, I've been going to aerobics every Monday, Wednesday, and Friday for four years."

"Oh, I know. Just kidding."

I tied my gym shoes and tried to brush aside a similar conversation from the night before.

"I sold my McDonald stock yesterday," I had said, holding out the annual report.

"Why do they send you the report if you sold it?"

"I only sold it yesterday."

"It's a good stock. Do you own McDonald's stock?"

"Tony, I just said…"

"I'm not so sure what you mean." He looked at me with his brow wrinkled in confusion.

Increasingly, when he spoke, I just listened; my responses only confused him. What he said was often absurd. "Who put those signals here? They are in the wrong place!"

"Look at that man there. He is so stupid! He's mowing his lawn crooked! How stupid can you get?"

"Whose pencil is this? Did you leave it here? Where does it belong? I'll just throw it out!"

I tried to reason away the change in him. *He's bored*, I thought. *He has nothing to focus on. Is it Alzheimer's? No, no. Impossible! I couldn't think that!*

One evening he walked into the kitchen where I was getting dinner ready and snapped off the TV. "What's all that noise?"

"I'm listening to the news."

"Well," he yelled, waving his arms in the air, "I'll just move out! Go on a trip for three months! You never listen to me!"

"Tony..." I turned to see his eyes round and red with anger. I held my breath and couldn't reply. I put the pot of rice back on the stove, turned to face him and stuffed my annoyance way down deep inside me, where it simmered. Instead of the gleeful bubble that used to float inside in me, I felt a lump of growing anxiety. It hurt. My anxiety was building up from an episode the previous weekend.

"Leave me alone!" he had shouted. "Everyone forgets names once in a while. It's just part of getting older. Leave me alone!" He couldn't remember and his frustration boiled over.

"I know, Honey, I'm sorry. Forget it. You're right, it's nothing." I was standing at the mirror waving an open tube of lipstick with one hand. "The people we invited to Sunday brunch at the club this morning are Ralph and Alicia, you know, Ralph and Alicia from across town. Oh, and Jenny, I forgot about Jenny. I'll bet they bring their ten-year-old daughter with them. I made reservations for four and there will probably be five of us."

"You what? Lizzie, you are so God damned stupid! I'm not going! You are so incompetent! You're not capable of doing anything right! You're always doing this to me! You're trying to ruin my life! You are the worst kind of person! Now I know the kind of woman I married! You've been doing this to me for years!" He was screaming now as he ripped off his tie and threw it and his jacket across the bed. "Get out of here! Just get out! I never want to see you again! You're ruining my life! I'll leave and go to Alaska and never come back!"

Then he stormed into his office and slammed the door.

I clung to the bathroom sink in front of me to keep from

slipping to the floor. My chest felt the blow as though the attack were physical. My insides were quivering. I gasped for breath and waited for a moment in the deadly silence.

I walked stealthily into the hall "Tony? Honey? Sweetheart? Are you okay?" I put my ear to the closed door and turned the knob. He was sitting at his desk, his head in his hands. I stepped in, touched his shoulder, and put my arms around him as a mother would hold a hurt child. But I also stood ready to jump back, anticipating more rage. I could feel tightness in my chest as I struggled to breathe deeply and calm my fear.

"What happened?" he whispered. "I don't know what happened."

"I don't know. Forget it. It's all right," I said, slowly patting his back. "Come on. Let's go."

Tony stood up, shuffled over to the bed, tied his tie, picked up his jacket to go to the club, where the hostess easily set another place for Jenny. Tony apparently forgot about his outburst, and I, still unnerved, faked a pleasant visit with our friends.

The following Thursday I spilled out this story and my heartache at the kitchen table of our daughter, Marianne, in Des Moines, a two-and-a-half hours' drive from Muscatine. Reaching for my hand, she said, "You can't live like this, Mom."

"Last Sunday," I continued, "I was cleaning up from breakfast when Dad walked into the kitchen and asked if we had eaten yet. When I reminded him of the waffles and bacon and eggs, he said, 'Oh, yes,' but I knew he didn't remember."

"Mom, we both know what the possibility is. Let's call the Alzheimer's Association and see what they say."

"I'm probably making it up, Marianne. Most of the time, he's fine. I'm just not sure."

Marianne made the call while I sat with a nervous stomach and fear creeping into my soul. The phone call was a cop-out, really, stalling because I knew what was in the brochures, and I knew it all applied to Tony. I couldn't think of any other explanation for his weird behavior and our strained relationship.

Since our trip to China two years before, I had been alert for indications of forgetfulness. My husband, the meticulous organizer, the one who never forgot a name, who easily switched from one language to another, who was cheerful and accepting of all people, was changing into someone I didn't know. Was he aware of what was happening to him? Was he as afraid as I was? I had tried to talk to him about it but neither of us wanted to make our fears concrete by verbalizing them. In March, 1998, I had written a note to Tony's doctor, Dr. B., an old-time internist, semi-retired now, who kept only his patients who weren't sick. In the note, which Tony took with him to his annual check up, I couched my concern about memory loss among such things as indigestion and cracked dry fingers. Dr. B. did not respond to my note.

Now, after looking over the information from the Alzheimer's Association with Marianne the following week, I called the University of Iowa Hospital and made an appointment for Tony. But then I was afraid to tell him, afraid of his anger at my organizing his life. Most of all, I was afraid to find out for a fact that he was really losing his mind.

Two days before the appointment, I blurted out that I was concerned about his slipping memory and his confusion and that I had scheduled him to see a neurologist. I held my breath.

"Oh," he said, "I'm a little concerned myself." I exhaled. *Why was I so afraid?* "But if I'm going to see someone special, I'll go through my own doctor. Do it myself."

I cancelled the appointment I had made and forced myself to be patient, waiting for Tony to follow up with Dr. B., which he did with this letter.

> Dear Dr. B.,
> My wife (Liz) continues to have some concern regarding my forgetfulness and "tiny bit" of confusion. I am aware of this condition although I feel comfortable about my daily activities. We have talked about this and thinking that medical attention may be beneficial if needed. My March 17 neurological examination with you scored 27 out of 30. However, are other testing means available? Would a neurologist be needed?

I have been very relaxed since my retirement last January, which is a major change after my strenuous activities I had to deal with in the past. Could the resulting "condition" have slowed me down mentally?

Liz and I would appreciate your comment and advice.

Thank you.

Sincerely,

Tony Van Ingen

Dr. B. made an appointment with a neurologist, Dr. N., for November 11th, 1998.

Three days before the appointment, Tony and I were invited to a party, a company awards night dinner at the country club. I expected the lively social time we usually had with people we had known for years. The evening's entertainer was a psychic. He was too good. He pattered on in an entertaining way and told personal details about people in the group. We each had written on a 3x5 card our name, any number that was meaningful, and one question. We each put our own card in its own small brown envelope and sealed it with glue stick. The psychic gathered up the envelopes and without opening them he held them up one by one and started his show. He told a lady her microwave was broken. It was. He told another woman about the time she cut off the tip of her finger. True. Then, never having seen Tony before that night, he tossed a brown envelope on the table in front of him and said, "Tony, this is yours, isn't it?"

Tony opened it up and said, "It's my handwriting."

The psychic said, "You're a very strange man. I'm not messing with *your* mind!"

The audience laughed but I felt an eerie chill. My heart pounding, I glanced around the table at his colleagues. Had they noticed Tony's strangeness and told the entertainer? Or was this man truly psychic?

That night I dreamt that Tony and I were in an empty, fenced-in arena like a corral. There were three of us: Tony, another indistinct but evil man, and me. Tony and the evil man were fighting. The man was trying to hurt me, but I wasn't really involved. I think he had a knife. Tony beat him to the ground and he was out, but not finished off. Then Tony and I were together again, but the man rose up and Tony said it was okay. Tony walked away and I screamed, "You can't leave me with him!" Tony said, "Yes, I have to, he's okay. I subdued him."

Was the evil man the *Disease*? Tony would struggle with this demon, but he would not be able to finish him off. I was going to be left alone, without Tony to help me with *his* illness. Was the knife there to sever the human connection Tony and I had? It was too horrible to contemplate. There still was no diagnosis, but in my heart, I *knew*. Tony had Alzheimer's.

I was disturbed enough by the dream to get out of bed and go into the living room, my heart pounding, and sit in the dark and think. Moonlight streaked through a gap in the curtains and glanced off a spot on the Iranian copper tray-table, a wedding gift from Jaleh, our maid of honor. My bare feet squirmed around the pattern on the red and blue Persian carpet. The silver samovar on the buffet stood as a sentinel watching me. The spirit of our early days together remained present in our lives through these and other treasures that we now took for granted, hardly noticing them. Even the plain gold band I was twisting around on my finger hardly registered in my conscience. It was just a part of me, a twin to the one Tony used to wear but now left in his trinket box on the dresser. In more halcyon days, we had purchased the rings in a small shop on Lalazar Street, a specialty area with luxury jewelry merchants in downtown Tehran.

CHAPTER 14

Doubt and Diagnosis

Iowa City, 1998

ALL THROUGH OUR MARRIED LIFE, Tony was the organizer, the detail person, and when everything was in order, he invited me along. I thought it would be that way forever. So when we went to the neurologist appointment I was slightly anxious, not knowing who was in charge.

I had seen this doctor two years previously for my own headaches, likely the result of tension I experienced as I struggled to live with the bewildering personality changes in my husband—his forgetfulness, disorientation, and tempers.

We sat in Dr. N.'s consulting room in chrome-armed chairs, looking at bare walls, no clutter. Tony sat as quietly as a child whose mother had noticed a mysterious rash. I tried to think how I would explain my concerns without embarrassing Tony. His forgetfulness was not as difficult to live with as was his frustration and anger over his forgetfulness. Could I say that? I was learning to be patient with his repeated questions and stories, but his outbursts of verbal abuse and unreasonable anger aimed at me were difficult to cope with. I felt like I was worth nothing, zero. I wanted an explanation, needed to know Tony's behavior was not capricious but had a cause, something we could fix.

The doctor came in and introduced himself. He was a small man, head shaved, with a wiry runner's physique. "What is the problem, here?" he asked me, looking at Tony. My voice shook as I told of his forgetting, confusion, and tempers. The doctor then looked at the ceiling, nodded, and did a basic neurological work-up, examining Tony's eyes, testing reflexes and asking questions.

"No problem neurologically," the doctor stated. "Could be chemical, but not neurological."

"But Doctor," I said, barely holding myself together, "*something* is wrong! What about his disconnect from me? He is unresponsive. He gets lost. He doesn't seem to hear me. Something is wrong!"

Tony sat in his chair with a pleasant, passive smile, apparently oblivious to my anxiety. I looked from one to the other as though the two of them had an understanding between them and I was the one with the problem.

The phone rang and Dr. N. picked it up, listened, and spoke. He had much more challenging and interesting problems to handle than a wife whose husband was ignoring her and shouting at her, but I persisted. "Can't we test his memory or his brain? This is not normal behavior for him."

"Well," the doctor said finally, "I see that Liz is still concerned, so we could send him to my friend Dr. G., a psychologist, a shrink, for psycho-topic tests. That would be about four hours of pencil tests, including I.Q. Tony would have to agree. Tony what do you think?"

"Yes, that's all right," Tony said. "Fine." We set an appointment with the psychologist, Dr. G., for three weeks away.

That day, I started early to make sure we were on time.

"What are we doing today?" Tony asked, getting out of bed.

"We have a doctor's appointment in Iowa City."

We went into the kitchen for coffee. "Are we going someplace today?"

"We have a doctor's appointment in Iowa City."

After breakfast, he sat down to play the piano. "Shower, Tony, we have a doctor's appointment in Iowa City."

He went to the bedroom, pulled open his socks drawer, lifted up handfuls of navy blue socks, chose one, unrolled it and put the two socks parallel to each other on the bed. He opened the underwear drawer. He took out one pair of undershorts, unfolded it and laid it next to the socks. He held up an undershirt from the drawer, shook it out and put it next to the shorts, smoothing out the wrinkles, then took one step back, hands on hips, and studied his work.

"What are we doing today?"

"We have a doctor's appointment in Iowa City."

During the forty-five minute trip to Iowa City, sitting silently next to Tony as he drove, I shifted my mind from a patient, passive mode into an assertive, get-it-handled mode. I shoved back the unreasonable stigma I felt at having to go to a "shrink" and braced myself to ask the right questions to get the answers I needed. I had to look honestly at what was happening to Tony, and therefore, to me. We were no longer on the privileged, healthy, easy side of life. We were slipping into a troubled new world where uncertainty ruled and no amount of money, education, past history, or even common sense or love would keep us out. I was desperate for help.

At the appointed time, we walked into a building of psychologists and psychiatrists, prepared to stay for four hours of testing. I gave our name to the receptionist and we sat down in dark brown easy chairs. The beige walls and the faded print of Monet's foggy "Houses of Parliament," perhaps meant to calm anxious nerves, did not. The shadow of the single lamp on the corner table dimly lit the outdated *Time* magazine that I picked up and leafed through. Dr. G. appeared and introduced himself with a humble nod and led us into his consulting room.

He seated us in chairs at right angles to each other, not near enough to reach over to hold hands, and pulled his own chair from behind the desk and scooted toward us for more intimacy. I didn't need any prompting. I blurted out my concerns, Tony's failing memory, his temper, his disconnect from me.

When I stopped, the doctor said nothing but turned to face Tony, who leaned back in his chair and began a casual, one-sided conversation. He had traveled to sixty-three countries, he said, spoke five different languages fluently, had held several executive positions, and was now trying to come to terms with his retirement full of long days with no goals. I had heard the same speech, the same words, over and over again, but this was the first time for the doctor. It all sounded so plausible and impressive. People, doctors, were always impressed with Tony's résumé and his easy, confident manner.

"He's confused. He forgets what he is doing. He doesn't hear me," I blurted. "He gets lost. He shouts uncharacteristically. He throws chairs. We have no conversation. He forgets what he's just said. He tells me the same story over and over and over again. He doesn't answer me. He's not right in the head!"

"Well, now, Liz, Tony's just retired and that's not easy for any man, especially one as active as Tony here. Give him some space to adjust. Maybe what you need is a marriage counselor."

"A marriage counselor! You mean it's all my fault?"

"It's probably neither one's fault. You both need to work on this relationship together."

I felt my face flush red with anger and embarrassment. I thought I might be sick. *He doesn't believe me. But what if he's right? Am I a controlling wife, just an interfering, pushy wife? What is happening to my world?*

Dr. G. continued, "I see you're distressed, Liz, so we'll go ahead and do the tests. You can make an appointment on the way out." So we weren't there for the four-hour tests, only for a fifteen minute interview to see if the testing was necessary. I yanked out my agenda and scribbled the next appointment date in my book. Tony was no longer able to make his own appointments and I covered for him. I strode out of the building, head down, holding back my anger and disappointment. *There's nothing wrong with him but depression,* I thought, *maybe he's just strange and disconnected from everyone.* Maybe for these thirty-five years of marriage I never knew him. He'd traveled a lot. I'd lived my own life, so to speak, when he was gone and I spoiled him when he was home. Maybe I had invented him. Now that he was home all the time, was I seeing the real Tony? The one with a furious temper? Was I the one disrupting our home, making an issue over nothing? I felt responsible for our getting along, but out loud I said, "Honey, if there's nothing wrong with you physically, you'd better shape up and be nice. No more tempers, no more throwing chairs or screaming bad things at me."

"Sure," he said.

What I didn't realize, of course, was that he didn't remember the tempers, the throwing of chairs, or the verbal abuse.

A week later, we were back in Iowa City at Dr. G's office. I sat in a different waiting room this time, doing a crossword puzzle during the several hours Tony was taking his "pencil" tests. This room had a children's corner and I wondered if the toys were for child-patients or for children while their parent was with the doctor. I felt sad for the children either way. I wondered how many people had been in this room seeking help from unbearable pain, from a life just too difficult to cope with on their own. I felt sad for all those people and I felt sad for us. But I felt hope, too. We were here and we were asking for help.

At the sound of the door opening, I looked up. Dr. G. stood over me with his apologetic nod, his brows knit together.

"Liz...well, your husband *does* have memory loss."

"Yes." I whispered, "I know." Was there a tinge of sarcasm in my voice? Certainly not joy at being proven right, but some small satisfaction in having my suspicions validated. I stood up on weak knees to follow him.

He led me into the room where Tony sat at a small round table, pleased at being the center of attention for such a long period of time, answering the questions. His eyes twinkled as he looked up at me. "I got them all right!"

"That's great," I said leaning over and giving him a hug.

Dr. G. seated me next to Tony and sat down across from us at the table. He shuffled and tapped his papers. "Liz," he said, dipping his head and avoiding my eyes. "Tony tested in the ninety-first percentile for intelligence."

So I wasn't wrong, I thought. *He is smart.*

"But," he continued, "his working memory is in the first per-centile. Pretty significant. It could be the start of something."

"Something?" I said, "I've been afraid of Alzheimer's all along. Is that what it is?"

"It's one possibility. We can't diagnose without further test-ing. I will send a report to Dr. N. He will schedule an EEG/MRI scan and various laboratory studies."

I couldn't stop the tears from spilling out of my eyes and down my cheeks. It was fear and relief, terror of the future and vindication of my suspicions all at once.

I couldn't speak.

We stood up to go. Dr. G. looked at us both and took my hand in two of his. "I'm sorry to be the bearer of bad news."

Tony smiled. "What bad news?"

Though the "bad news" was not definitive, and certainly not the start of Tony's disease, I accept this appointment, December 15, 1998, as the date of his diagnosis of probable Alzheimer's Disease (A.D.).

CHAPTER 15

Facts and Fears

Iowa, 1998

I STOOD ON THE DECK of our house, arms crossed, looking into space. The acre of lawn that Tony loved going over with his riding mower spread beneath me, and beyond that the narrow creek and our neighbor's rolling, oak-filled pasture. I don't believe I was thinking anything. I was just there. Waiting. The discovery that I was right about the Alzheimer's diagnosis did not bring the conclusion I thought it would; the diagnosis was not the end, or any kind of solution. What lay ahead was more mystery, and an unknowable and unpredictable future.

Alzheimer's. I couldn't think the word without tears running over and down my cheeks, not really sobbing but dropping my arms to my sides, letting the tears spill out from inside me of their own accord. My chest was thick and I found it hard to take a deep breath. I had lived with a lot of uncertainty in my life, and I even prided myself that I was able to cope with change and adapt to anything. But this?

Over the years, I had sometimes imagined sudden death, abrupt widowhood from a plane crash. Or disaster. What would I do? Where would I go? Where did I belong without him? But this! Losing him bit by bit! How did I do that? Did I have a choice? Ahead of me were huge decisions that I'd have to make by myself, about the house, retirement plans, health insurance, wills, finances, nursing home, the logistics of life. Best not to think; not now, just wait.

I went into the house and slumped down on the living room couch, aching with overwhelming sadness, feeling no blame or anger, only heavy, thick sadness, lost in this new world with no one to guide me.

"What's next? What should I do? What's going to happen?" I had blurted out at the neurologist, who had finally agreed that Tony probably had the start of Alzheimer's.

"I'm sorry I can't help."

"But who can I see who will tell me what to do?"

"I'm sorry. There are no answers, but Tony might do better if he lost a little weight. You cook too much good food, Liz," he joked.

"I don't make the bowls of ice cream he eats every night," I snapped.

Can't help. No answers. No help. No answers circled around in my head, along with *Now I'm responsible for his weight?* This man was a neurologist, after all. A brain surgeon, not a social worker.

When I got my emotions somewhat under control, I picked up the phone and dialed Tony's sister Hannie, a physical therapist in Milwaukee, who had dealt with Alzheimer's patients and was concerned about her brother. I told her what we had learned and how desperate the future looked. I explained what she already knew about me, that I wasn't the nurse type, that I didn't know if I could do this, and that I felt stuck, my life out of my control. She heard my desperation.

"Liz," she said, "you don't have to take care of him. There are resources and all kinds of agencies and people ready to help. You don't have to do it alone; in fact, you don't have to do it at all." I was silent and she added, "You can leave him and hire someone else to care for him." Again silence. "You'll have help." And then, "Some people even divorce."

I gasped, emotion welling up in my chest. "Oh, Hannie! No! I couldn't! I'm his wife! He is my husband. I feel so sad for him. I have loved him so much. I could never leave him."

When we hung up, I sat stunned, staring at the floor, letting the tears flow. Hannie in her wisdom had given me options, and permission to make my own decision. Nobody would *make* me do anything. If I stayed with Tony, it would be my own choice. If in the years to come I felt trapped, I would remember it was my choice to be where I was. Now I needed to *do* something, take some sort of action, get busy. Where would I find the directions for the rest of my life?

I called the Alzheimer's Association in Davenport, thirty miles from Muscatine, and attended the next support group meeting two weeks later. I went to our small bookstore and bought the book they recommended, *The 36-Hour Day*, and began my education.

In 1906 the German neurologist, Alois Alzheimer, published a paper describing the case of a fifty-five-year-old woman with dementia. In the article, Alzheimer described the plaques and tangles in the brain that have become the markers for Alzheimer's disease but which can be conclusively recognized only by autopsy. The disease causes gradual breakdown in the nerve cells of the brain so the brain changes and no longer works as it used to. As a result, people with Alzheimer's disease become less and less able to make sense of information from the outside world and to send messages to their bodies. They, meaning Tony, will become unable to think, remember, understand, and make decisions as before. He will have trouble with everyday activities such as getting dressed, cooking a meal, or washing the car. My heart beat frantically, my palms sweaty with anxiety as I read. Eventually, he will become unable to look after himself but will develop some other illness such as pneumonia, which will cause death. Horrifying words describing Tony's disease, words like progressive, degenerative, and irreversible swam in and around my mind, swamping my emotions like a bad song.

I picked up another book, *Mayo Clinic on Alzheimer's Disease*, and began to read. I knew nothing about the brain, and on these pages were maps, so to speak, of the brain. Seeing colorful diagrams of healthy brains versus diseased brains and reading words like beta-amyloid plaques and neurofibrillary tangles gave me comfort in knowing that people were working to find causes and cures. I would never be an expert on the intricacies of the brain, or this disease, but I would refer to these diagrams and definitions over and over again for many years looking for explanations and predictions.

What I wanted most was concreteness and certainty, but found that though there are predictable patterns in this disease, they are so nebulous as to be *unpredictable*. How long would the illness last? Anywhere from three to twenty years, or longer. There were three stages, no seven, or rather five, depending whose scale you used, all cautioning that symptoms were mixed up so no definite lines could be drawn. Periodically, almost daily, I evaluated Tony's behavior, trying to determine what stage he had reached, trying to fit him into a category and guess what might happen next; but I only frustrated myself by trying to make order out of a chaos of indefinites. I had the same feeling of sand being washed out from under my feet that I had had in Saudi Arabia when I discovered that time, once so dependable, was not concrete at all. Each technical book had a chapter exhorting me to get our finances in order, that is, our wills, power of attorney, and titles to the cars and the house while Tony was cognizant enough to understand something of what we were doing and to cooperate. Accordingly, I made an appointment with our lawyer, hesitating over the word Alzheimer's as though it were something shameful and could be helped. As it happened, the lawyer's father-in-law had had the disease, so he knew what was going on, and he helped me to sort things out and get our affairs in place for the time when I would be in charge.

I found companionship and comfort by reading books in which caretakers shared their stories. One story told of a daughter choosing to be reunited with her estranged father, assuming his care when no one else in the family would. Another story told of a woman who moved her mother from Boston to Berkeley, disorienting the mother and totally disrupting her own family. One woman, a single mother of a three-year-old, brought her father to live with her and watched the two pass each other on the scale of life, one going up and one going down. A loving husband refused to accept help with his ill wife, until his home and his wife and he, himself, were a shambles. Then there was the opposite story of a wife who left her husband because she couldn't live with a man who couldn't carry on a decent conversation. An ill professor kept forgetting where he parked his bicycle, so his wife became a regular at the second-hand bike shop, buying replacements. The books had titles like *There's Still a Person in There*, *The Long Road Called Good-Bye*, *Death in Slow Motion*, *He Used to Be Somebody*, *Alzheimer's: A Love Story*, and *A Curious Kind of Widow*. An autobiography, *Losing My Mind*, was written by a man who himself suffered with the disease and who, for a while, was able to recognize what was happening to him and articulate it. Until, of course, the confusion and loss of memory, even of what he had just written, won out. Every case was unique; every caretaker's way of handling it was individual, and I tried to read without judging.

We were entering new territory, as foreign as any Tony and I had ever experienced as a newly wed couple years ago. I would need to learn a new vocabulary, and to develop new sensibilities, and to make my own map. I would come to know new communities, those with the disease and those who cared for them. I had a new role to play in life, maybe the final one, and I wanted to do it well.

When the day came for me to go to Davenport to the Alzheimer's support group, I dressed as I did for business: in a suit, heels, and makeup. I think I was also trying to distance myself from the real-life situations I was bound to find at the meeting. Maybe by dressing up, the disease wouldn't touch me.

The group met in the board room of a day-care facility for older people, only some of whom had dementia. I remembered walking into the teachers' lounge in Tehran many years before, not knowing what to expect, whom I would meet there, or where I would fit in. I took a deep breath, braced myself and entered the room. Several women and a couple of men, all apparently older than I, sat in hushed conversation around a long oak table.

A blondish middle-aged woman, a nurse, Marilyn, according to the name tag pinned to her green sweater, looked up when I opened the door. "Hello, please come in."

I burst out crying.

"Is it a parent? Your mother? Your father?" she asked, pulling out a chair for me. Conversation stopped and searching eyes turned my way.

I shook my head, unable to speak at first. "No, it's my husband. My husband has been diagnosed with probable Alzheimer's and I don't know what to do."

Now their eyes avoided mine, and I heard, "Oh, your husband. So young. Oh, no. I'm sorry."

"We can only tell you our experience," Marilyn said. "Every case is different, but there are many common threads and problems where we can help each other." Then, one by one, they went around the table and quietly shared their stories and what had happened in the disease process since their last meeting a month before.

I look back now with some horror at my reactions to what I heard. I couldn't believe that this was the world I was entering. I felt raw, defensive, and achingly sad.

"My husband is lying in his bed in the nursing home, eyes closed," the gray-haired woman at the end of the table began. Age and stress lined her face, though she had put some effort into her appearance with face powder and lipstick. "The nurses turn him often to prevent bedsores. His hands are in a type of stiff brace-mitten to keep his fingers from curling up and stiffening there. I visit every day and feed him. Of course, he doesn't know me, or know I'm there."

"Why do you go?" I whispered.

"I go there for me," she said quietly. At the time, I didn't understand.

The next lady, well into her eighties and cheerfully chubby, said, "My husband is in the day-care program in the next room, so I can come to this meeting. I don't leave him alone anymore. He and I went to the supermarket yesterday and he wanted to take brown paper bags at the check-out instead of plastic. I kept telling him, we have enough of those! We have lots of brown paper bags. We don't need any more brown paper bags! But he wouldn't listen and took more brown paper bags! I think I'll go mad. He just doesn't listen! We have too many brown paper bags."

I thought, *What's a few more bags if it keeps the peace?*

Next was a gentleman, with wispy, white hair, who wore a tie and a jacket, frayed at the cuffs. His eyes roamed from one of us to the other with a smile, but he started to weep before he could speak. "We've slept together every night for over fifty years," he said, his eyes reddening. "Never been apart. I don't know what I'll do. It's so hard. I do everything for her. I'm exhausted. Maybe it's time to place her. Maybe it's time." The room was silent, but there were nods all around. It was a decision only he could make and I learned that the euphemistic term for "putting her in a nursing home" was to "place her." Would I ever have to make a decision like that?

The lady to his right rested on her arms stretched in front of her on the table. One hand balled up a handkerchief, dabbed at her eyes, then passed it to the other hand, back and forth. Her husband was still at home. "I have to be careful not to leave the cellar door open," she said. "He might fall down the stairs and break his neck!"

I am ashamed that my immediate thought was, *Leave the cellar door open! This is too horrible!*

The last woman to speak was thin and pale, with dark circles under her eyes, and we learned that indeed she was not well, having been in the hospital herself during the last week, I assumed from fatigue and stress. In the month since the last support group meeting, she had placed her husband in a facility.

"How did you know it was time?" I asked.

"He fell apart in a Frosty Freeze ice cream store." She said, handkerchief to her eyes. "He started hitting and attacking people. We called 911."

I was shaken when I left the group that day. Stunned. I borrowed several books from their library, hoping to learn from reading, so I would not feel the need to return to the group soon. I knew I had a place to go where I would be supported with understanding when I reached desperation, as I surely would. Many people get strength from their faith and real practical help from their church community, but I didn't belong to a church and didn't want to join one now just because I needed help.

Now my friends were no longer women like me, who dressed up and went to work. Suddenly my associates were older husbands and wives and grown children whose only commonality was a loved one with Alzheimer's. Just as in the teacher's lounge in Tehran, a camaraderie developed among these disparate people.

I was not yet ready to tell our friends. First of all, I couldn't mention the "A" word without breaking down. Second, I didn't want people to treat Tony any differently from how they always had. And third, by telling, I would be confirming the diagnosis. Social skills are the last to go in the Alzheimer's patient, I learned, and I thought Tony appeared the same as ever to our casual acquaintances. I wanted to put off the separation from our friends as long as possible. I protected Tony as I always had from hurt and embarrassment, but I was also protecting myself from facing the inevitable and both of us from assuming the new identities people were bound to give us when they knew:

"Have you heard? He's the one with Alzheimer's."
"Did you know? Her husband has Alzheimer's."
"They say it's harder on the spouse."
"I've heard the spouse often dies first from stress."

We continued to go out with friends and stop in at the country club occasionally for dinner. I was on edge all the time, trying to make sure Tony presented himself well and wasn't rude.

"Tony, Honey, listen to Joe. He's also been to China," I said one night when Tony was monopolizing the conversation at dinner.

"You stay out of it, Lizzie." He was desperately trying to keep his connection with people, but as table conversation confused him, he did all the talking.

"You know what I like, Lizzie," he said when he could no

longer comprehend the menu. "Just order me something." Later it was, "I don't have my glasses, Lizzie. You sign the bill."

I was tense, calculating every move I made and every word I said so Tony would not get upset or blow up in a rage.

Most days he went about tasks he set for himself, sorting the newspapers, stacking them perfectly, then sorting them again. He folded the laundry, or worked a jumbo-size jigsaw puzzle. He was resourceful, as always, and kept himself occupied. He still drove alone to the grocery store for pastries and apples, and there he visited with everybody, the clerks, the shoppers, and their children, putting great effort into being cheerful and holding himself together.

Some days, around three or four o'clock in the afternoon, the strain was too much, and he became anxious and demanding, the palm of his hand slapping down on the kitchen table. I would jump, then smile as though it was normal for him to slam a chair up and down and yell at me to stop what I was doing and listen to him. The term for this uncontrollable physical and mental angst is "sundowning." The behavior could be set off by the dimness of evening light, or confusing noise from a radio, TV, or conversation. Some people cover mirrors and remove photographs in the house because the person he sees is unrecognizable. Because of all of Tony's world travel, I was interested in the theory that his circadian rhythms had been upset. I would never know for sure the cause, but I knew that by late afternoon, Tony was often overly tired and unable to cope with the simplest things. But I was tired, too, by that time of day and may have unconsciously communicated fatigue and stress. I was always looking for something I could control, and I think the agitation was his way of telling me what he couldn't say with words: that he was afraid, confused, and angry. "Sundowning" sounds poetic and could have had a lovely meaning—like sunset, or sun porch—but it didn't.

For Tony, sundowning often expressed itself as incessant and urgent talking until he worked himself into a frenzy. He paced and rushed around the house demanding that we go somewhere *immediately*. The clever mind he was always so proud of was betraying him and, though he couldn't allow himself to talk to me about it, I knew his interior terror was unbearable.

Some people with Alzheimer's become docile and cooperative, never showing symptoms of sundowning, but instead they may wander and get lost. Tony did not wander, but I wasn't sure he never would. I registered him in a Safe Return Program and received ID bracelets for us each to wear with a national identification number in case he would get lost. The system required a Good Samaritan to recognize that he was a confused, lost person and call the hot line. I couldn't imagine Tony would wear a bracelet, and I was afraid even to ask him. I didn't want to embarrass him, to tell him that he had Alzheimer's. He had never needed my help with anything and I just didn't know how to handle it. So I kept the bracelets in a drawer for a later time when I might intuit his wandering and make him wear it. I did, however, make two wallet-sized cards with a picture of both of us on one side and contact information on the other, along with the Alzheimer's logo. I put one in his shirt pocket every day, and I kept one in my wallet, so if I was in an accident someone would know I was a caretaker for Tony and find him. There is a better system now called Project Lifesaver, where the ill person wears a locked-on bracelet with a chip in it so he can be found within a few minutes when someone is looking for him and doesn't depend on a stranger recognizing him as lost and calling in.

Often "shadowing" accompanies sundowning. Tony trailed me around the house, so neither of us had space of our own. Fortunately, Tony found his haven in the piano, where he could shut out conversation and thoughts of his illness. The part of his brain that controlled this physical ability was intact for a long time. Once while playing the piano he stopped and turned around and laughed. "A fella was just in here and wanted to buy my brain. I sold it to him, but I fooled him! There was nothing in it!"

He must have known he had Alzheimer's. I thought I wanted him to admit it so we could share the burden, but at the same time whenever he said things like, "My brain is just not working," I comforted him so he wouldn't feel bad, instead of letting him

talk. I still wanted him to be a strong and okay person for
for himself. We each reached our own level of acceptance
lowed us to survive in our own way. One day sitting at the kitchen
table he said, "I feel like I'm a kite flying away up in the sky, going
this way and that with no one holding the string." I wanted to be
his anchor, to hold the string.

My books told me that when he had a breakdown I should
look for something that had triggered it. The books said that I
was not responsible for the blow-up, but something I did might
have started it. One night during those first months after the diagnosis, I lay in bed, the bedside light still on. My ears were alert
to the slightest sound and my heart beat with apprehension. Tony
had gone, stomped out of the house, twice that evening. Would
he come back? I was angry and afraid at the same time.

"I'm through with you!" he had shouted earlier, slamming the
door on his way to the car. "It's over!"

I had been looking through the newspaper at the kitchen
table when Tony walked in and put his binder under my nose,
opened to a page with columns of numbers. Small, neat columns
of meaningless, penciled numbers. Then he started talking.

"For heaven's sake, Tony." I laughed to hide my irritation that
he could interrupt me as though what I was doing had no importance, that *I* had no importance. I was discountable. That was
the trigger that set off the temper. He scooped up his binder and
slammed it into the floor, the pages flying all over the place.

"You're constantly putting me down! I'm through. That's it!
I'll just leave! Get out of here!" He grabbed the car keys. "I'll go
a hundred miles an hour and see what happens!"

My immediate reaction as he left was to sit stock-still for
several minutes, as if moving would cause more shouting, even
though he wasn't there. His shouting stabbed me to my core. I
took a deep breath, got up, and started picking up the papers. He
burst through the door, snatched at the papers, and stomped into
his office. I followed. He erupted like a volcano.

"I don't want these papers!" He threw them on his desk,
crashing the pencil cup and knocking over the desk lamp, and

turned to me, shaking both fists in fury. "Get out! Just get out of here!"

His eyes were very round and very blue. I could see the whole of the iris, just round and furious. It suddenly struck me that he was, in fact, *demented! That's what a demented person looked like!* He slammed the door behind me, and I stood in the hall as the box covering the doorbell clattered to the floor. Then silence. I tip-toed around and got into bed. I listened, heart beating, eyes wide, wondering what he was doing in there, so quiet.

He stomped out of his office, the temper still boiling over in waves. He was helpless to stop it and so was I. He went downstairs and the house was quiet. I lay still, thinking he might be asleep. Finally, he came up the stairs, grabbed his keys and left again, saying, "I don't know where I'm going. I just have to get out. I need some peace. You're driving me crazy with your constant put-downs."

I went to bed. I waited with my head on the pillow, staring up into the darkness, heart pounding, eyes and ears alert. He was gone about fifteen minutes this time, then stormed back.

He rushed in. "I'm going crazy! You're driving me crazy! Always putting me down! Controlling everything! You don't appreciate all I do for you! I help in the house, do the taxes. You'll have to get someone else to do your taxes! I'm leaving! It'll cost you probably a thousand dollars to get someone to do your taxes! You can have the house. but not one penny! I'll change everything into my name and leave! Go to Alaska for a couple of months! Peaceful without you constantly driving me crazy! I'm afraid to get in bed with you! I might push you right out!" This came out in bursts, punctuated by his fists shaking in the air.

I thought it was over but it spewed out again. Rants about Alaska and his fists shoved in my face. "Are you afraid you'll hit me?" I asked.

"No, I don't ever hit women," he reassured himself as he got into bed. I allowed his answer to reassure me, too. He had never hit me or the kids or the dogs or anything I could think of.

I quietly said, "Let's talk about Alaska tomorrow, not tonight."

"Not you! You're not going!"

"Right," I said. I reached over and rubbed his back a little. He calmed down.

"I'm exhausted," he said and was immediately asleep.

I was exhausted, too. But I didn't sleep. I was so sad for him and for me. So sad. I thought of the other comments I had made in the last few days, looking for something in myself that I could fix. What could be construed as nagging, putting him down? I had told him that I'd rather spend money on a new deck than go to Europe. Was that nagging? Putting him down? It was so difficult for me always to be aware and careful of what I said. By keeping my thoughts and opinions to myself, I was beginning to think I *had* no opinions, no thoughts, nothing important. I lay there imagining how we'd be if he weren't ill. With him as his old encouraging self, we would be, could be, both of us, energized, enthusiastic, doing, experiencing new things.

I had imagined after forty years busily raising children and being separated so much we might finally spend time together, just us. I imagined other couples had spent private time with each other during longer courtship periods than we had and perhaps waited a few years before having children. Our time together was now.

Tony had thought of going overseas with a non-profit organization when he retired and donating his business expertise to an underdeveloped country, but he couldn't even complete the application. I would have loved that, but if not, I envisioned him helping me build my own business. Now he didn't know, care or acknowledge any of my efforts or activities. He couldn't. He was sick. Rather, he saw whatever I did only as diverting attention from him.

I lay there knowing that nothing I said or thought or did was important to him; nor did it matter to anyone, really, in the long run. Nothing was worth arguing about or persisting in, or repeating. I didn't need to emphasize a point or make sure I was understood. I was no longer witty or clever or interesting or wise. I was nothing. If Tony couldn't see me or acknowledge me, was I even there? Maybe this total negation of myself was my way of coping. Was I just going to disappear? Both of us, just fade away? Sometimes life looks better in the morning, so when I got up the next day, and sat in the kitchen smelling the freshly brewed Arabian coffee, tangible reminders of our vibrant life surrounded me. The five-foot-tall brass candlestick from Morocco stood askew in the corner by the dining room. The wicker basket I had carried over my arm to the *marché* every day for four years hung on a nail by the garage door reminding me of good times. The blue and white filigree birdcage hung silently in its custom-made arch between the living room and dining room, daring me to forget.

CHAPTER 16

The Days, the Nights

Muscatine, Iowa, 1999

I *AM WAITING. IT IS SATURDAY. Again. Another week gone by, one day and then one day again. I get up in the morning and go to bed at night. Another day, another week, another year gone. It seems more progress—yes, progress—would have been made in this disease. It is insidious and so slow that it inches along without my realizing the changes in me as well as in him.*

My mind continued to wander. *I attempt to see a future but can see none; nothing is there. Alzheimer's runs an average of six to ten years or more, 2100 to 3500 days or more. I'll be sixty-eight or older if I outlive him. I want the disease to be over.*

"What does he do all day?" his brother, Martin, asked me when he called from his home in Virginia one morning. After a few pleasantries, I handed the phone to Tony. "It's Martin," I said, and went into the living room.

I could hear Tony talking as I lay back on the couch and thought about Martin's question. What *does* he do all day?

He brings me coffee in bed in the morning. I set up the coffee maker each night and next to it, put out our two mugs, each on its own white paper napkin. His is blue with a B-17 on the side; mine has Van Gogh's sunflowers. When Tony wakes up, he sits on his side of the bed, reaches over to pull open the curtains, wiggles his feet into his slippers and shuffles to the kitchen. He pushes the "on" button, and comes back to the bedroom, and standing with one hand on the chest of drawers for balance, he pulls on his khaki shorts and buttons on a plaid, short-sleeved shirt with a left breast pocket and button-down collar. He tucks in the shirt, threads his belt through the loops on the shorts, pulls twice on the end of the belt with the holes, and fastens the buckle. He walks to the kitchen, then pads slowly back down the hall with the napkins and our mugs full of hot coffee. I take a napkin from his hand and put it on my nightstand and he places my cup there.

"I didn't put sugar in yours," he says every morning. "Do you take sugar?"

"No thanks," I say every day.

"There are too many things on your table. You have to get a bigger table," he repeats. I don't answer.

Every morning he sits on his side of the bed facing the window, his back to me and coffee in hand, and starts to talk. Some people with Alzheimer's lose their ability to talk. Not Tony. Once he starts, he goes on and on, struggling to remember and stay connected to me and to the world. He wanders on about his childhood, his parents, his years in the army in Korea, about each sister and each brother, about each aunt and each uncle, about the war years in Holland, about the rented garden plot where his father taught him to grow carrots and endive, and about his schooling. All of this I have long ago transcribed into a book for the grandchildren. Each story stays in his head for a week or two, repeated throughout the day and evening, but always, in the morning, with coffee.

When the dawn sky is a bright and exciting red, he repeats a rhyme in Dutch about the *"morge rood,"* the same one I know in English, "Red sky at night, sailors' delight, Red sky at morning, sailors take warning." I thought I would never forget the Dutch words, but I have.

When I finish my coffee, I start to get up.

"Oh, no," he says. "You stay there. I'll get you more coffee. I'll get the paper."

So I stay in bed, hating my laziness, reluctantly accepting the peace. In the past, I loved to get up in the morning with places to go, people to see, and work to do. Then, I was in the process of developing my own business as an Independent Sales Director with Mary Kay Cosmetics, and I relished the action, the purpose, and the people.

Now I am just lazy and disgusted with myself.

"I'll get the paper," he says. He turns and marches out the front door and down to the end of the driveway, where the *Wall Street Journal* waits in the garish orange plastic tube attached to our country mailbox. He marches as he did in the army, arms in a rifle-holding position, turning a sharp corner and marching two steps in place before going on. If our neighbor Paul is out, Tony stops, marches in place and salutes him with a grin, always a happy grin. Paul spends a minute joking with him before they both go inside with their papers.

Every morning Tony sits on the end of the bed, takes the blue or red plastic cover off the paper, blows up the bag and ties a knot on the end like a balloon. He stands up, puts the bag on the bed behind him and with a leap in the air, he sits on it. Bang! We both laugh. Every morning. He sorts through the paper, will not share it, but reads something aloud from the front page, and then haltingly, reads it again. "How was that?" he asks. "Did I read it right?" I decide the world will create news whether I know it or not, so I relax and let the world take care of itself.

Soon we are in the kitchen at the table with more coffee. Tony reaches for a banana. He peels the banana. "Watch this, Lizzie." He tosses the banana peel from his end, the far end, of the table into the sink, or near the sink, or on the window ledge above the sink. Sometimes he laughs and puts the peel on his head before the toss. Every morning the banana, the peel, the toss, my applause. Next he eats apple pie, or pastry, while I have my cereal. I put the dishes in the dishwasher and he wipes the kitchen counters with a thoroughness I don't seem to possess.

Still on the couch, with this litany going through my head, I suddenly realized Tony was no longer talking on the phone.

"Who was that?" he asked as he put the receiver down.

"That was Martin," I said.

"Martin who? There are so many Martins."

"That was your brother Martin."

"Oh, yes, of course."

He could still sit on his riding mower and take care of the lawn in the summer, but when the snow came, the sequential steps to start the snow blower were too much for him so he said he preferred to shovel. And in truth he did love to bundle up in a stocking cap, sweaters, a windbreaker, and warm gloves and get after that snow, always moving in an orderly pattern and calling me, as a small boy would, to see what he had done. The cold, the exercise and the sense of accomplishment invigorated him.

He wanted to help me with my Mary Kay business by putting product on the shelves, until he began putting it in the wrong room or the wrong shelf or even putting it back in the carton it came in. I gave him a roll of stamps to affix to forty addressed envelopes and he carefully stuck them on the wrong corner. The post office accepted them but I recognized it as one more thing he couldn't do.

I no longer dressed for work. I wasn't going anywhere, so I wore jeans and a sweatshirt, whatever was at hand, comfortable and sloppy. Most days I put on my makeup so when I passed myself in a mirror during the day I could wave and say, "Oh, hello! It's you! You are still there!"

Usually I woke full of love and respect for Tony, awed by the courage he had to get up every morning, and with his habitual resourcefulness, cheerfully occupy himself. The garbage concerned him, and the kitchen which he cleaned and shined, calling me urgently after every move he made. "Look how neat!" or "How's that?" He adjusted the central heating thermostat and opened and closed the curtains incessantly. He stacked wood in the fireplace, rearranging it for hours before it was just right. He filled the bird-feeders and handled the pictures of the grandchildren, repeating their names over and over, "Garret and Ellen, Nicholas and Elizabeth." His own three daughters he could name only in sequence, "Caroline, Linda, and Marianne."

In his office room he sat at his executive teak desk and listed columns of figures. For years he dialed an 800 number and entered his PIN to hear and record daily the amount of his 401K, but now he had no idea what the numbers meant. Trying to find a purpose for his days, he had filled several three-ring binders with pages of columns of random numbers that he copied over and over. "Lizzie, come and see my work," he called from his office repeatedly throughout the day, or when he adjusted the thermostat, or fiddled with the curtains. He tried so hard to be useful and responsible, and it was driving me crazy. Friends asked me why I didn't ask him to wait, to tell him I was busy, to tell him to please leave the curtains or the thermostat alone. I had told him, of course, but he couldn't remember; he just couldn't remember. Even for ten seconds, he couldn't remember.

"I know I'm slipping a little, but *don't* call it a disease," he said that morning. "I'm still smarter than most. I don't want to be one of those dumb people. I don't want to think about it. I'm not a worrier; worry just makes you sick and miserable." He stood up and stretched his fists above his head. "It's going to be a great day!"

The piano was a blessing for both of us. He hid himself in the playing of the music and his troubling world dropped away. People and noise and issues were gone, no thoughts, no one reminding him he was losing his mind. Once he started playing, he played and played, starting at the beginning of his song book and going through, flipping pages back and forth, song after song. Then I would hear, "Lizzie? Did you hear that one? Shall I play it again? Lizzie? Lizzie?" and I knew my quiet time was up, too. He always finished with "La Mer" and "The Third Man Theme." "Look at me," he'd say now. "No papers! I'm playing with no papers in front of me!"

"Good for you," I'd answer.

During the year of 1999, I observed changes in Tony but couldn't accept that he was as sick as he was. I took his missteps as simple mistakes, assuming they wouldn't happen again and that he would be okay and do it right next time. When he put the postage stamps on the wrong corner of the envelopes for my business, I laughed and said anybody could make a mistake. I adapted, covered up, and protected him and myself from facing reality, though what do you do with *reality* when you do face it? Anybody can make a mistake, right?

I was at a loss as to how to deal with the future, knowing it was now up to me to make sense of what was left of our lives. I could no longer expect to communicate with Tony. I had waited too long. Over the last few years, when Tony returned from a trip I thought we'd spend time together and really connect, but something—like dinner with friends, or gardening—always got in the way. Next time, I thought. Later. Now it was too late. Meaningful conversation was finished.

My urge was to *do* something. We could take walks, but Tony tired quickly or had an achy leg, and sat on a bench while I walked the river front on the path and hurried back to him, fearful that he would panic and wander off. We did not watch much TV because the noise confused him and he couldn't follow a story. Sometimes a news or sports program triggered a memory, so he turned off the sound and started to talk and I was left without the punch line. It didn't really matter, after all. Nothing really mattered anymore. My new philosophy was that nothing in life has any value intrinsically, just the value we choose to give it. If you give it no value, it has none and doesn't matter. My life was disappearing from me as surely as his was from him. My sense of myself depended in large part on Tony's response to me, and now his response was fading fast, approaching the time when I could expect none.

Our mail was full of the brochures that retired people get, advertising tours and cruises. Tony liked the ones that had pictures of China or South Africa. I tossed the rest, but one sponsored by the University of California caught my eye. It advertised a short cruise, just five days in September, through the Inland Passage from Seattle, Washington, up to Alert Bay and back to Vancouver. Tony was traditionally the initiator of our trips. Now if we were going to do anything, *I* would be the planner. It was a small ship, just seventy passengers, with stops for hiking and nature study along the way; it was not a dressy cruise, just an informal, camping-type adventure on a rugged boat. We could manage that and visit my mother in California while we were on the West Coast. In May, I sent off the deposit for the September cruise. In June I made the plane and hotel reservations. I really wanted to go on this trip, because I had spent high school summers in the Pacific Northwest and was eager to see it all again. Most of all, I needed something to look forward to.

The first week in August our daughter Caroline, her husband, Stuart, and their two kids, Garret, eight, and Ellen, six, visited us from Arizona for a week. Tony was confused by the activity in the house and was jealous of my attention toward the kids; at one point he yelled at the grandson whom he adored, just the way he yelled at me. We could all see he was out of his mind, demented. Eight-year-old Garret stood, not moving, his eyes wide with incomprehension. His dad, Stuart, face flushed with anger and incredulity, took his son by the shoulder and guided him away, far out into the yard to the bench under the willow tree. As far as I know, Stuart never spoke to Tony again. On the surface, to someone who doesn't understand the disease, Tony's behavior would appear to be that of a grouchy old man. Misunderstandings and hurt feelings can cause a lot of family discord. Fortunately, Tony's disease brought our daughters and me closer together, which is not always the case in families dealing with Alzheimer's. Their dad became a focal point for care and concern.

One day during their visit, the family had respectfully tossed their shoes by the back door when they entered the house. Tony came into the living room where I sat with a crossword puzzle and said, "I'll show those kids to leave their shoes every which way! I took one shoe from each pair and threw them out!"

"Oh, Tony," I laughed at his joke, "for heaven's sake!"

At one o'clock the next morning, I was asleep and he was still up roaming around. He woke me with, "Lizzie, Lizzie, you've got to help me. I'm in real trouble now. I can't find the shoes!"

"The shoes? Did you look in the garage? The car? The garbage can?"

I got up and we searched the house. "I found them, Tony!" I called and pointed to the dining room. On his hands and knees, Tony pulled them out from under the dining room table and arranged them neatly with their mates, then climbed, contented, into bed next to me.

Heavy sadness hit me when Caroline's family went back to Phoenix and our life returned to "normal." The tension and uncertainty during their visit meant our home was no longer a haven for our own children. Alzheimer's was horrible. Certainly, my life as caregiver was permanently altered, but whole families become upset, estranged, torn apart by this disease. *Will Caroline and her family ever come back*, I wondered?

The week after the children left, Tony and I shopped for daypacks and hiking boots for our trip to the Pacific Northwest. It was a pleasant day because I was totally with Tony, one hundred percent focused on him. I thought that was all I needed to do keep him calm and in control on our upcoming trip. Our daughters warned me that this cruise was not a good idea. What if he had a catastrophic reaction when we were at sea? Was there a doctor on board? Did I have a plan for an emergency?

CHAPTER 17

A Lost Car and a Cruise

Muscatine and Canada, 1999

ONE QUIET EVENING, August 19, 1999, a year and a half after diagnosis, and just three weeks before we were to leave for the Northwest Cruise, Tony slammed out the kitchen door and was gone.

Frankly, I was glad, glad for five minutes of peace in the house alone. The car screeched out of the garage and I heard the door roll shut. Sinking into a chair at the kitchen table, I hid my head in my hands and in the stillness of the kitchen, reminded myself that nobody was making me stay there. My choice. That very morning he had sat on the edge of the bed holding his head and had said, "My brain isn't working, my brain just isn't working." I ached to gain control.

Gripping the edges of the kitchen table, I pushed myself up from the chair, shuffled to the wall switch, turned out a few lights, and, shivering, stumbled down the hall and got myself into bed, wearing my bathrobe and socks. I lay on my back staring into the dimness, wondering if I should do something. What? Call the sheriff? No, he'd be back. Give him ten minutes. He'd be back. What had I done to set him off like that? My whole body ached as I lay there remembering.

Tony had come downstairs to my office where I was working at my desk, his calendar in his hand. He stretched out on the couch and said, "Next week we have to get our tickets to Europe to see my mother, make arrangements for our trip to Holland. Are you with me on this?"

"Trip to Europe?" That was new! We could hardly negotiate the grocery store. "No, not really. Our next trip is a cruise to the Pacific Northwest. I don't know if we can manage Europe, too."

He leaped off the couch, fists in the air. "You're always crossing me! I'll go without you! I can find some lady to go with me! You stay here by yourself! I'm going to do what *I* want! I have to get out of here. I'm leaving."

"It's not the money...."

He charged at me, red-faced, finger pointing, fury and madness spewing out of him.

"I can't take it! I can't take *you*! I'll do what *I* want! I want to see *my* mother. I'll just get out! I'm leaving!"

He raged up the stairs to the kitchen. I sat still for a moment, to get my breath and regain control. I shut down my computer and started quietly up the stairs. Tony was at the kitchen door, open to the garage, slamming around, briefcase in hand.

"I've already called and checked in at the Holiday Inn." he yelled, "I'm going."

"Sweetheart..." I started, and he slammed the door behind him.

Gone.

"Sweetheart..." I doubted that he had called the Holiday Inn. If he went there at all, it would be to the bar.

Full of self-recrimination, I tried to figure out what had happened. Should I have said, yes, we'll go to Europe? Did I have to agree to everything to keep the peace? I drifted into a tense, fragile sleep while I waited for him to come home. I woke with a start. Loud banging came from the front hall. I threw off the covers and ran to front the door. I yanked it open and gasped in horror. Tony was on his knees, head down, arms up, fists pounding the door so hard that when I opened the door, he literally toppled in and rolled onto his back, arms and legs flailing uncontrollably.

"I'm going crazy! I don't know where I am! Where am I? I'm going totally crazy! Just kill me! There's no reason to live! You're driving me out of my mind!" His head whipped from side to side. His arms and legs stabbed at the air. Unearthly sounds came from his throat.

I backed away, terrified, afraid to go near him, but when he relaxed, I got down on my hands and knees and held him tight, whimpering, sobbing. "You're home. It's your home. You're safe. I'm here. I'll never leave you. It's okay. I love you. I love you."

Then fury struck again, and I jumped back, avoiding his thrashing limbs.

"Just kill me! I'm going crazy!" He grabbed at the railing that divided the hall from the living room and tried to pull himself up. Then he let go, falling back into my arms and whispering, "Just kill me. I'm going crazy." We sat like that for many minutes. I don't know how long—a long time. Suddenly, he jerked himself to a sitting position and said, "Where's the car? I don't know where the car is!"

I opened the door. No car. "Just leave it," I said. "We'll find it later."

"*No!* Where is the car? We have to find the car! Is it in a ditch? I could have killed someone! I've got to find the car! Look behind the house."

I left him and went outside and saw the car on the lawn that separated our house from the neighbors'. "I see it," I said, coming back inside. "I'll take care of it."

He struggled to his feet and leaned on me and shuffled to the bedroom. I took off his clothes and shoes and got him into bed. He lay back, then sat up, eyes wide. "The keys! I don't know where the keys are!"

"I'll find them in the morning," I said.

"*No!* We have to find them now! Put the car away now!"

I went outside with a flashlight, thinking the keys could be on the lawn, in the driveway, or in the dirt. Too logically, I found them on the dashboard. The driver's seat was in the almost horizontal position, so he must have pushed all the buttons and then had trouble getting out of the car. I pictured him stumbling around panicking, his shoes were wet and muddy, not knowing where he was, *terrified*, crawling up to the front door.

I hesitated, telling myself he was still more responsible than I, demanding that the car be found and put away. Clinging to denial and illusion, I put the key in the ignition and the engine roared to life in the quiet night. I turned the car toward the garage and rolled it in. I sat for a moment, preparing myself for re-entry. In a daze, on automatic pilot, I got out and walked slowly around the car to the kitchen door, reached up, and pushed the garage door button. I tiptoed into the house, hoping he was asleep and wouldn't hear me.

But there he was, sitting up on his side of the bed shaking his head.

"Why did I leave? What made me leave the house?"

"Just relax," I said. "It's over now and you can rest." I thought he wouldn't remember.

But he did.

Like a volcano, the rage came again, spewing out the fear, the panic, the anger, his arms and legs jabbing like spears of lightning. "You wouldn't let me go to see my mother! She's dying and you don't care! You talk to your mother every day and I can't ever talk to mine. You don't care about my feelings! You won't go with me and you said it in such a mean way! I love your mother and I don't understand how she could have such a terrible daughter as you! It makes me so mad!"

I stood at a safe distance until he finally flopped onto his back and slept.

I did not sleep.

I looked at the green numbers on the bedside clock: 5:30. Still dark.

I threw on jeans and a sweatshirt and huddled at my desk with the phone and the Yellow Pages. I needed assistance.

I was afraid.

Tony was helpless.

I was not.

As I remember that horrific night, I realize that I would have been justified in calling 911 while Tony was on the floor, frightened, frightening, and out of control. He would have been carted off in a straitjacket and our subsequent lives would surely have been different. There are no rules here. Another twist of fate; it never occurred to me to call 911. Just the day before, I had thought I was postponing my life to care for him, but now, with a surge of adrenalin, I knew this *was* my life. I was postponing nothing. I had made choices—first to marry him, and then, in Casablanca, to stay married, and finally, after his diagnosis, to be by his side as he struggled with losing his mind. I breathed deeply and shifted from a state of fear to a "take control" mode. Not waiting for offices to open, I picked up the phone and left messages with doctors, a realtor, and organizations that might give me some help.

By nine o'clock that morning, I had an appointment with a local physician for Tony, and with a therapist for me. I called and talked with our neurologist. When I described the incident to him he asked, "Had Tony been drinking?"

"No," I answered. No? I wasn't thinking.

In my panic for help, I had called our friend and realtor, Don Sturms, and by nine-thirty, he was at the house to appraise our property. I met him outside by the front door and blurted out the truth, which I hadn't yet told any of our friends.

"Tony has Alzheimer's, Don. He is going crazy. We both are. I'll have to sell the house." I shaded my eyes in the sunshine and stared at the spirea hedge losing its bloom, and the berm of sleeping, dried, perennials, our home.... I backpedaled. "Not immediately, Don," I said, "but someday. Someday soon this place will be too much for us." As we stood in the driveway talking, I told him about Tony's illness and the frightening episode of the night before.

Fifteen minutes later Tony came out into the sunshine, dressed, shaved, hair combed, smiling and greeting Don as though nothing had happened. As I looked across the driveway at my husband, straight and tall and handsome, I was overcome with love and compassion for him. From looking at him, no one would guess he had a terrible, mind-destroying disease. He hid it well. Seeing him like that, I lied to myself, or fooled myself, that he wasn't so bad. My desire for the old Tony was so strong that my imagination made excuses for him, and I believed them.

The rest of the day was a soft day, a tender, careful day, as though there were balloons of air between Tony and me, gently separating us. He talked, I listened.

"I was so angry, Lizzie, that you wouldn't let me go to Europe. I can't go *alone*. I could feel it building up and I just snapped. I didn't check in at the Holiday Inn. I sat at the bar for a while. Then I had to get away. I decided to drive to Davenport or Chicago where you'd never find me. Lizzie, I could have killed myself on the highway and you'd never know where I was."

He had no recollection of his terrifying seizure on the floor by the front door. I thought I needed to tell him so he would know why I was uneasy, to say the least, about traveling to Europe.

"Sweetheart," I began, "last night..." I looked at his blank, round blue eyes and knew there would be no comprehension. He made no comment when I stopped in the middle of the sentence.

Sitting in the therapist's waiting room the next day, I wondered if this was the right place to go for help. Did he know anything about Alzheimer's? I was shown into his consultation room and had barely introduced myself to Ira, when I gushed out my story, pausing only to grab another Kleenex and take a breath.

"You're not dealing with Alzheimer's," he said. "You're dealing with alcoholism!"

"No, I'm not," I sobbed.

"Yes, you are!"

"No, he's got Alzheimer's."

"You're in total denial."

I sank deeper into his brown leather couch, clutching the Kleenex box. "No," I had told the doctor. Tony had been gone for five hours. Where could he have been but the bar at the Holiday Inn down the road? The place closed at midnight. Then where did he go? What was I thinking? *Was* I thinking? Alzheimer's books said to be careful with alcohol, but I hadn't taken charge and stopped him. How could I do that? I had thought life was over anyway—what difference would a glass or two of wine make?

Twenty years before, Tony had taken himself to an alcohol treatment center for three weeks and had stopped drinking for a number of years. In time a glass or two of wine with a meal had crept back into his life. I had been the co-alcoholic, covering for him, protecting him from taking responsibility. Now here I was doing the same thing for Alzheimer's, or—alcoholism?—again. The neurologist had asked me if Tony had been drinking when he had the seizure. No, I had said. No. Total denial.

But if this were true, it was good news. All Tony had to do was stop drinking and he would be the old fun, intelligent, person who loved me. "Not quite," Ira explained. "He might have Alzheimer's, but we can only tell after he has stopped drinking."

Tony did not understand, but he did agree to stop all alcohol for four months so we could go on the cruise I had planned.

His own appointment with the doctor resulted in an antipsychotic drug I could administer as needed.

That was good enough for me. I felt secure that there would be no more seizures and we could go safely on our five-day cruise and visit my mother in San Francisco on the same trip.

It was a real vacation for me, and Tony enjoyed it too. Tony could tell the same stories over and over at dinner because we had different people at our table each night. He was happy with a non-alcoholic beer in the evenings and proved that what I had heard was true: with Alzheimer's social skills were the last to go. I was able to relax some and enjoy the nature walks with Tony's arm around me and felt actual companionship with him.

The ship docked in Vancouver and we flew from there to San Francisco, where we stayed in a hotel for two days before flying back to Iowa. At one point, I forgot my credit card at a restaurant and had to leave Tony in the hotel room to go back and get it. I worried as I left him, and I worried on the way back. What could I tell him so he wouldn't blow up at me for being so stupid forgetting my credit card? I racked my brain for an acceptable excuse and just couldn't think of anything plausible.

I returned to the hotel room and entered quietly. He opened his arms in delight at seeing me and said, "How was it, Sweet-iepie?"

"Fine," I answered, and waited. That was it. No questions, nothing. He stood, smiling. He hadn't a clue. He was no longer interested in me or what I did. He didn't care. He *couldn't* care. He couldn't manage it.

I felt the loss, even the loss of his anger, as loneliness.

CHAPTER 18

Mothers and Mourning

Holland, 1999–2003

BACK HOME IN IOWA from the Northwest and after four months of non-alcoholic drinking, Tony had forgotten that he had ever been a drinker. "I never have liked Scotch or wine, never cared for the stuff," he said. We cannot know how much brain damage was caused by alcohol, or if the Alzheimer's was precipitated by alcohol, but it doesn't matter anymore. *The 36-Hour Day* suggests if the caretaker suspects alcohol abuse, the Alzheimer's patient should avoid alcohol for nutritional reasons and because he may become "nasty, stubborn or hostile." I know it's worse than that. The caretaker may herself be so blinded by the tragedy of watching her partner disappear into the nothingness of Alzheimer's that she may not be capable of seeing the treachery of "a glass or two of wine with dinner."

In November, I felt confident enough in Tony's stability to plan a trip to Holland. I couldn't deny him the chance to see his mother. The problem for me, as I see it now, was that in raising my children I had expected *prog*ression, that is, what they knew today, they would retain tomorrow and add to it. With Alzheimer's it is *reg*ression, and I had a difficult time realizing that Tony might very well *not* know tomorrow what he knew today. I had no reason to be "confident in his stability." Nevertheless, I planned the trip.

In Amsterdam, in between visits to his mother in a nursing

home, we strolled along the canals, holding hands and stopping to eat Dutch pancakes rolled up with bacon and cinnamon and lots of butter. "Oh, Tony, we have to have *outsmiter*," and we stepped out of the damp, chill air into a small restaurant and ordered this delicious specialty of fried eggs on top of rare roast beef sliced paper thin on fresh white bread. The Dutch language came automatically to him, as did French and German, and I laughed, never knowing which one he would come out with. At night, we held tight to each other under a fluffy down comforter, but our sleep was interrupted by his hallucinations. "Lizzie!" He sat straight up in bed. "Look at the bicycle on your table!" Or, "See the flowers climbing up the wall!" I felt him slipping away from me, and sadly, two weeks after our return to Iowa, he'd forgotten that he'd seen his mother.

We returned to Iowa from the trip only to be notified a month later that his mother was now dying and the whole family was gathering at her side. It would be the first time since his father's death thirty years before that all six of the brothers and sisters would be together. So we made the trip again, confused and arduous, spending the millennium New Year's Eve in bed in a hotel in Haarlem, Holland, listening to the reveling and fireworks in the streets.

Tony's brothers and sisters *knew* he had Alzheimer's. I had told Hannie first, and she had told the others some time ago. But when Tony laughed and teased with his siblings as he always had, they didn't fully understand that he was truly confused and wasn't joking when he said, "Why are we here? Where are we going?" They laughed with him. We sat through a short church service in Dutch, then stood in the gray drizzle while their mother's casket was lowered into the green plot next to that of their father. "Who died?" Tony asked as we left the cemetery in a parade of black umbrellas. When we gathered for dinner that night, I looked around at the family and knew it was the last time we would all be together.

When we returned once again to Iowa, I tried to establish

some kind of routine, knowing a predictable environment was best for those with Alzheimer's. But there was no predictability in Tony. He seemed so sane for a day or two as we gardened side by side as we always had. I became complacent and took him with me to the hardware store to buy a garbage can.

"We're not buying that," he shouted suddenly at the checkout counter.

"Yes, we need this to put the black bag in, Honey." I paid for it and dragged the clanging metal container out to the car.

"No!" he said, yanking it out of my grasp and hauling it back into the store. I reversed the sale and we drove home.

Little by little he was losing his grasp and I had to catch up, never quite believing he couldn't do today what had been easy for him yesterday.

I continued to look for some way to gain control of the chaos and protect him.

At breakfast, I faked a laugh at Tony's childishness, pathetic and sad. Sometimes he wiggled his nose and twitched his head, saying, "This is how a rabbit eats." Quite good, actually. Now he put everything on his head, the banana peel, his coffee cup, the empty cereal box, laughing and enjoying himself. He presented himself to my book group in the living room, with his hands on his hips and a tower of eight or ten baseball caps on his head. He laughed and said, "Go get the camera, Lizzie!" and laughed some more. Fortunately, my friends laughed, too.

I no longer told him where I was going or what I was doing and didn't expect a response from him when I did. The simplest, "I got the car washed," or "Guess who I saw today," elicited no appropriate response. For several years, I had been able to go to Des Moines for Thursdays with the grandchildren, leaving Tony at home on his own.

But one evening when I got back from my day in Des Moines, I found him wandering through the house. When he saw me he shouted, "I'm leaving! I'll just go to Alaska for three months!" I coaxed him to the couch where he began to sob, literal tears. Sitting beside him, I stroked the back of his hand, and as he spoke, put my arms around him.

"I can't leave you. I can't live without you. I don't know what's happening. I have to get control. You can't tell me what to do. I have to control myself. I know I can. I haven't been well these past few weeks. Just not myself. I have no purpose, I start one thing and then, big deal, put it away, and walk around the yard and come in. You don't know. When you're gone, I just sit there doing nothing, nothing in my head. It's like I focus down a tunnel, cut everything out so I'm not confused. Then what's left in my head? Nothing! Nothing is there! I don't know what to do. What can I possibly do? You are busy with your business. I have nothing. I have to go away and be by myself for a few months, go to the beach and sit and look out...and do? What? Nothing. I have to go away. I don't want to leave you! I haven't been feeling well. For a few weeks, months I've been trying, pretending to be up, that everything is fine, but it isn't."

What could I do but weep? I realize now that when I tried to imagine what was or wasn't in Tony's mind, I was so unbearably disturbed that I responded to what he tried to present to me on the surface rather than the terror that was overtaking him.

I saw no end to it. Alzheimer's was a condition, progressive in symptoms, but a condition, nevertheless, that is not itself immediately life threatening. We would live with it always, he and I, not through it, but with it, probably forever. We were both physically healthy and came from families of longevity. He would not be released quickly, nor would I. I saw no recovery, no hope for tomorrow. Just the day, hope of having one pleasant day.

In one sense, I had a new kind of freedom. Someday in the future I would have to be with Tony around the clock, but not yet. At present, I could still leave him for short periods of time and I was discovering strengths I'd never needed before.

In September, I left Tony alone so I could be by my own mother's side as she neared death. The neighbors, Paul and Ellie, checked on Tony and he seemed all right, but when I phoned him, I heard him say, "You have to come home! *Come home now!*"

"Yes," I answered, "I'm coming." But I stayed a few more days after Mother had passed away to help my sister with affairs. Then I flew back to Iowa to get Tony and take him back to California for the interment in the small town of Sutter Creek, where Mother had grown up.

From Mother's childhood home, now a bed and breakfast, we walked under a blue sky up to the cemetery on an unmanicured country hillside. The sun warmed us on that fall day as we stood in a circle around the grave we had dug ourselves, just big enough for the container of ashes, the size of a See's candy box, we said. I looked at Katie, her children and mine, and at our grandchildren and breathed in the familiar California dry air. Being with family in a place of my childhood under such circumstances, I felt the loneliness and apartness that Alzheimer's had brought into my life. Tony stood by with his warm arm around me, comforting me with little squeezes as I cried and for a moment, I was able to pretend he knew what was happening and that he still cared about me. I had to face the possibility that the next time we gathered here would be to bury Tony.

My mother's services coincided with my forty-fifth high school reunion in Berkeley. I never imagined I could be with Mother at the end, or ever be able attend this high school reunion. Tony behaved so well at the reunion dinner that no one knew he had Alzheimer's. His physical appearance gave nothing away and his social skills while meeting new people and repeating the same story over and over were quite appropriate.

Back in Muscatine, we fell once again into our slow struggle with life. By April 2001, I developed severe bursitis and couldn't lift my arms above my shoulders, or behind my back. I left the house only to go to a physical therapist, and to a chiropractor for lower back pain. I was on medication for migraines and arthritis. I was in tears much of the time. I struggled to get to aerobics. Tony was still driving himself to the YMCA to walk around the track with a friend, refusing to go with me in the same car because he would have to wait half an hour for me to finish my aerobics class. He wanted to maintain his independence, never mind that he got lost and once didn't get home from the YMCA for two hours.

I went back to the therapist who referred me to a psychiatrist for antidepressant medication. "Oh, no," the doctor informed me. "You have situational depression, not clinical depression. You'll get over it. You don't need an antidepressant." So I continued to carry Kleenex in my pockets and suffer almost constant tears and headaches.

One evening Tony and I went to dinner at the club with friends who were understanding and patient. I laughed and relaxed with a little wine and felt safe. Unfortunately, my guard was down and I didn't notice or care that Tony was also drinking wine.

I got in the driver's seat to go home. Tony sat next to me and started screaming, "You're ruining my car! Don't touch the buttons! I'm not riding with you! Let me out! Stop the car right now! Stop the car! I'm getting out!" *Bang, bang, thump, bump* he pounded on the dashboard, *wham* on the door! I checked to make sure we were locked in, and backed out of the parking place with his arms flailing and grabbing at the steering wheel. My heart was hammering, but I intentionally took deep breaths to calm myself and focused on getting us home safely.

When I pulled into the garage, he stormed out of the car and with furious strides marched away from the house and up the road in the cold without a jacket. I threw my hands up in the air, no longer amazed at this behavior, and watched him disappear into the dark. At the top of our road, about half a city block away, he turned and charged back to the house, ignoring me as he banged through the kitchen doorway with his head down. He stomped down the hall, where he swung open the bedroom door several times hard against the wall, shattering a full-length mirror all over the floor. He thumped his fists on the walls in his office, knocking off pictures and the cover of the doorbell in the hall, which hit the thermostat and knocked it open, upsetting the timer. Then he turned around and disappeared downstairs into the basement.

Silence.

I was afraid to go down there in the dark, thinking he might jump out at me. I stood at the top of the stairs listening, eyes wide, peering into the dimness. I heard him crying, *"Aaaaahhh! Help me!"* I crept down the stairs with a padded coat hanger in my raised hand to protect myself if needed. He was lying on the couch, arms and legs thrashing, calling out, "Help me! Oh, help me!"

I took the stairs up two at a time and found an antipsychotic tranquilizer pill left over from that other awful time. He took it and reached for the glass of water like a man dying of thirst. Soon the panic subsided and I was able to get him to bed. He slept hard.

How could I have let that happen, again? Alcohol! What was wrong with me? I *had* to be more responsible, more than I had ever needed to be, certainly more than I wanted to be.

When he woke in the morning, he assumed his usual cheerfulness. He saw the shattered mirror and looked at me questioningly.

"You broke it," I said. "Here's the broom and dust pan."

He swept up the sharp pieces and funneled them carefully into a paper bag. When he finished, he sat again on the edge of the bed staring at the floor, his forehead wrinkled in puzzlement.

Finally he said, "It's frustration at having nothing to do, no purpose. I didn't plan my retirement right. I thought it would be easy. But I have no purpose."

I told him, "Sure, it's frustration, but the alcohol last night was like putting a match to tinder. No more real stuff! I don't want to fall into that trap again. It is insidious, creeps up. Done!" I was speaking to myself, of course. He had no idea what I was talking about. *I* was the one who had to take charge of his drinking.

After five years of living with my increasingly demented husband and accommodating my life to his, I needed a break, so in May of 2003, our middle daughter, Linda, volunteered to help out. She was by then a professor of history at the University of Nebraska in Kearney, and the proud new mother of Mary Emily, our sixth grandchild. She came with her baby to stay with Tony for a few days to give me a much-needed respite. While I was in

Vermont on an Elderhostel trip with my sister, Linda experienced first hand what she knew in her mind to be true. Tony didn't know who she was and wouldn't let her bring the baby upstairs. He drove himself to Applebee's every night for dinner and didn't want a stranger in the house. She was shocked and upset and hurt. She cried over his personal "to-do" list—mail a letter, get garbage ready for Thursday, take a shower. She was still emotionally attached to him, remembering how capable and masterful he had been on our home-leave trips. Now she saw what I saw, and felt what I felt. She cried as I cried. But she was also able to look at us objectively, and when I returned, she made me aware of changes in the two of us that had subtly developed unnoticed by me even as I watched for them.

"Your relationship has shifted, Mom," she said. "You take charge now, and treat Dad like a child, praising good behavior, and you pat him on the shoulder and make excuses for him and fill in words for him and tell him what to do. And, Mom," she continued choking with tears, "we talk about him as though he was an object, a piece of furniture, as though he's not there."

I took her hand and cried with her. She was right about all that. We had changed. She wrote when she was back home again, boosting my morale considerably.

> Mom,
> You are really great and—ironically—are rising to the challenge that Dad's once again set before you. I think about all the ways you've met new situations—all our moves, new people, cultures, different phases of our family life—and you've always come through. You have such a great attitude and approach to things—life—you're really great Mom. It's funny but I know Dad's really proud of you for doing such a great job. Love, Linda

That letter gave me courage and somehow, the understanding that maybe Tony *would* have been proud of me, in spite of his giving no indication that he was aware of me or my struggles. I wandered through the house, the letter in one hand, aimlessly searching for something to give me a grip. Tea. Yes, it was time for a cup of tea. When we left our last overseas assignment, South Africa, I swore I would continue the tea ritual every afternoon. I hadn't done it, but now was the time. The kettle whistled and I sat in the kitchen with my hands around a comforting mug of tea. I re-read the letter and pictured Linda, six years old on her first day of school in South Africa, in her blue-and-white checked school uniform and navy felt hat with the elastic under the chin, the little girl who was now an adult and was encouraging me through a difficult time.

CHAPTER 19

A Hundred Scattered Pins and a Decision

Iowa, 2003

B ACK AND FORTH, back and forth, Tony passed in front of me on the riding mower, his eyes focused on a raspberry bush in front of him so the rows would be straight. I stretched my legs out in front of me and rested my head on the back of the lawn chair, so that my straw hat fell over half of my face and my eyes became slits behind my dark glasses. My hands drooped languidly off the arms of the chair. My nose twitched with the scent of newly cut grass and I was vaguely conscious of the repetitive crescendo and diminuendo of the mower's engine as it passed in front of me, back and forth, back and forth. How soon would I be the one mowing the lawn? The snow blower with its sequential start-up had been too much for Tony last winter. Was this the last summer for the lawn? Fatigue swamped me. I couldn't do it. I didn't want to do it. We'd have to sell the house and go somewhere else. I didn't want to think about it. This was Iowa in the middle of July, five years after diagnosis. Underneath the lassitude, I felt the stirring of adrenalin that had surged through me the last time I really took action and called the doctors and real estate broker. Was I waiting for another crisis? A swift kick?

This house had our footprints on it, literally stamped on the living room ceiling by a misstep while the boards, wet with stain, were still on the ground. For twenty-five years Tony had taken care of this place, but today he could finish the lawn and then get back on the mower and mow it again, forgetting he had just done it. He would be no help with a move. I couldn't imagine him agreeing to leave the place. If I did decide it was the right thing to do, I'd have to do it all myself.

When Marianne lived two hours away in Des Moines, she had wanted us to move there, near her so she could help us and so we would know her children as they grew up. My weekly Thursday jaunts to visit her had ended when I no longer felt comfortable leaving Tony alone for a whole day. When he was throwing things out in the garage a few years ago, I had said, "I'm not ready to stop living." Was I ready now? Maybe a big change would revive me. Maybe not.

The girls tried to carry on phone conversations with their father, but he did all the talking in jumbled, rambling words. "Mom, be careful," they said. "You need to be near one of us. We've already lost our father. We don't want to lose you, too." I saw three choices: Phoenix, near Caroline; Kearney, Nebraska, near Linda; or Des Moines, near Marianne. Or was there somewhere else?

Suddenly, that summer, Marianne and her family moved away to Colorado for her husband's job and I was left alone in the middle of the Iowa cornfields with an increasingly demented husband and no family nearby. Where were all the agencies and resources Hannie had referred to years ago? They were in Milwaukee and other large metropolitan areas. Though I was in touch with the outreach person for the Quad Cities Alzheimer's Association, hands-on help was a good distance away. Muscatine was a small town just beginning to address the needs of caregiver families, and Tony, my problem solver, had himself become the problem.

Tony spent his days at his desk in the office we had fixed up for him in an unused bedroom. He opened and closed file folders, stacked papers in neat piles on the left of him, then moved them to the right, then gathered them up, sorted them again, and called me in to reassure himself that he was working on something important. Crumpled papers surrounded the wastebasket and torn bits of paper filled it. He called me again and again. "Look at this, Lizzie. See all that I have to do."

Every time I went into his office, he gave me the grand tour. "Let me show you something," he said, gripping my wrist as he guided me to the framed certificates on the wall. "This is from Holland, where I grew up. See these signatures? All the professors signed it and it says here that I can go on to study jurisprudence or medicine at a higher university. And this one here, see all the signatures? I don't exactly…but…it is a very important one, very important."

He pulled me toward the wall map with hundreds of black pins marking the places around the world where he had worked. Europe was black with pins, as were the Middle East and Persian Gulf. Central America was solid black. Every state in the U.S. had at least one pin, as did the provinces of Canada. The countries of northern Africa and southern Africa were well dotted and a hefty sprinkling of black dots covered Asia. *I suppose this is comparable to my charm bracelet*, I thought. *Black pins and gold charms, a journal of our lives.*

"No, don't pull away. I'm not finished," he insisted, renewing his grasp on my wrist. "Those are little black dots, sticks, all over. See that? And here we have a very beautiful…. I'm not so sure…." Moving away from the map, he indicated our framed Persian marriage certificate, three pages of delicate Arabic script with our signatures inserted, surrounded by borders of blue, red, and gold arabesques. He stared briefly at the picture of us in the droshky on our wedding day, but turned toward something more immediate in his mind. "Now, *this*," he continued, taking a step back to admire a glossy, framed color photo, "is my car."

His new car. I hated that picture. I had implored our friend at the car dealership, "Please don't sell him that car. Please. Tony's sick. He has Alzheimer's disease. We don't need this high-end, brand-new 2000 Buick Park Avenue Ultra. He can't handle a car like that. He doesn't need all that power. We're not going on any trips. You can help me. Please don't sell him that car." To no avail, as evidenced by this glossy, framed photo of Tony standing with his hand caressing his navy blue (with subtle metallic undertone) brand-new car. A tattered but cherished two-by-three-inch black-and-white photo was wedged into the frame, showing Tony fifty years earlier, in the same pose, with his hand lovingly resting on the fender of his first car, a '48 Chevy.

Everyone who came to our house got this tour, no matter how often they came. Refrigerator repairman included. It seemed that every repetition helped Tony remember who he was. I knew that and stood there beside him again and again, thankful that he wasn't using a wastebasket or footstool for a toilet or wandering off as some Alzheimer's patients did. How long could I continue to watch this without going crazy myself?

One evening early that summer, we sat comfortably eating cookies in the living room after dinner. "Now, listen, Lizzie," he began, and then proceeded to tell me what I had heard over and over and over again.

"Sweetheart. Stop. Take a breath." I took a deep breath myself. "Why are you telling me that same story again? I know your brothers and sisters. I know all about your schooldays. I know about your army days and Korea."

"I have to, Lizzie; I have to tell you so I won't forget. I don't want to forget."

I thought, and silently scolded myself once again for my impatience. I listened. No television. No music. No two-way conversation. He kept up a constant patter, his words needing no response, giving him the illusion that we were having a conversation as he desperately tried to hang on to that part of his life that gave him his identity. Without that, he would lose himself.

As I squirmed with impatience, grateful I hadn't forgotten how to knit after putting it aside for twenty-five or thirty years, Tony sprawled on the chair opposite me, legs straight out, crossed at the ankle, one heel twitching back and forth on the Persian carpet. I watched for a hole to appear under his heel. He continued his monologue.

"Look at this space," he said, surveying the living room. "This is the best house."

I looked up. He continued, "The light fixtures are wonderful, don't you think? Where did they come from?"

"Iran, Honey, we got them in...."

He looked at me with those vacant blue eyes. 'This is a very nice um, *thing* to sit on. We have the best one. We're lucky to have that place there for, you know, the uh, *things*, the pieces of tree, hot, but be careful. I'll handle it. We don't want to, you know. See the yellow the fish, er, the um, the birds? They are getting food from that...there, hanging there. Look at them all! I'll have another one of these, delicious, but you'll have to give me a, a, a little white paper. They're, you know, on my hands. I want to stay here forever. It's, you know, don't you think? I am so happy here. What a great place! I always wanted, you know."

"Oops! You dropped your napkin."

"There you go again! Don't interrupt me! You're always do-ing that! You made me lose my train of thought! You're not lis-tening! I'll just leave, go to Canada for a few weeks, just get out! Throw the whole thing out! You can get yourself a new husband!" His arms flew up and his legs kicked out at the coffee table, jos-tling it and dumping the magazines. "Get rid of all this trash!" he said with anguish, and grabbed his head in his hands.

I controlled my breathing, stood, and slowly pushed my knit-ting firmly down into its basket. One step in slow motion took me over to the couch where I sat down and circled his slumped shoul-ders with my arms and tucked my head under his chin. "Shhhhh," I whispered. "It's all right. I'm sorry, shhhhh." His arm reached around me and we sat, head to head, for a moment in blessed silence.

"I'm living with a nut," I told Marianne on the phone the next day when she called. "Sometimes he seems so normal that I forget that he is sick and react as I would to a well person who does silly things. Yesterday he took a light bulb outside to change the floodlight and put it down while he climbed the stepladder to take out the old one, which broke in the socket. A minute later he was in the kitchen with the new bulb in his hand, telling me, 'I found this under the bush. It must have been there for ages.' I laughed and told him, 'That's the one you took out, the new one.' He squinched his eyebrows together in that bewildered look that makes me so sad and then yelled, 'No! Where does this belong? Why was it outside?' Then he slammed the light bulb on the counter and pounded his fist on the table.

"Why don't I learn?" I continued. "He's sick and won't get it. Maybe I should have just said, 'Oh,' and left it at that, or said nothing at all. Those are our conversations, Marianne. Tonight he said not to fix him dinner. He wanted to fix his own egg and toast. Then five minutes later he asked when dinner would be ready."

I went on. "It's not really too bad. I just throw up my hands and let it go. There is nowhere I have to be and nothing I have to do for myself anymore. I don't need to snap at him. The problem is that one little comment from me or one small item left out of place, even a pencil on the table or a magazine left open, can set him in a rage where he throws things and lashes out at me. I am afraid and tense all the time."

"Oh, Mom," Marianne cried. "Oh, Mom!" What could she do?

I was falling apart physically from the stress. Ferocious headaches often kept me quiet or even in bed. The bursitis turned into tendonitis and I couldn't lift my arms. Pain shot down my right leg and it often tingled with numbness. I felt a lump inside my chest and had difficulty breathing. Was something going on in my body that I wasn't aware of? Cancer somewhere? Was I getting ready to have a stroke? A heart attack? All my emotions were stuffed-down, unexpressed stress. Tony was not aware that I was upset, would never have known why, never be sorry, never show empathy at all. I became a zero. Tears spilled from my eyes without provocation, just because I couldn't contain all the sadness. I filled time dozing on the couch, knitting, doing crossword puzzles, watching baseball on television and waiting for the Cubs to score.

"Mom!" Marianne called from Denver the end of July 2003, soon after they were settled. "You'll never believe this. Less than three miles from our new house is a Memory Care Facility. You have to come and see it. You have to move here. This is too perfect, and I have found an area nearby where they are building small patio homes. You have to come and see!" Her words took no more than a second to register, and when they did, a leadenness lifted from me and I felt a rush of encouragement and possibility.

I put the phone down, grabbed my notebook and a pen, and started making lists: Reasons To Move and Reasons Not To. Everyone in the professional business of taking care of Alzheimer's patients knows the ill person does best in familiar surroundings. Keep everything the same. The same chair to sit in, the same daily routine, certainly the same house. How could I even think of moving Tony? But, previously, professionals had also advised me, "Take care of yourself." *How many times do I need to hear that often the caregiver dies first and stress can kill you? What does it mean, "take care of yourself"? When you are using up your life for someone else's, how do you take care of yourself?* I was beginning to realize that getting a massage every two weeks wasn't enough. To take care of myself meant I needed to start making decisions for my own benefit and not just for Tony's.

By the end of that week, the first of August, I put my "Reasons to Move" list in my purse and met my friend Denise for lunch at Applebee's in Muscatine. Denise was the Quad Cities outreach person for the Alzheimer's Association and had become my friend. She was a little younger than I, with a few gray strands in her hair, and overly concerned with others. She met me with a warm hug and we sat down. She looked at me from across the table with her eyebrows knit in concern.

"Where is Tony?" she asked.

"Home," I said.

"Alone?"

"Yes."

"Are you sure that's okay?"

"No."

"Oh."

"I'm thinking of moving to Colorado to be near my daughter," I blurted out, "What do you think about that?"

"Oh, Liz. Good for you! If you are really serious, you need to talk to Geri at the University of Iowa Hospitals. She is a nurse practitioner and works exclusively with the families of patients with Alzheimer's disease. She doesn't even see the person who actually has the disease at all. She will help you."

Overwhelmed with emotion, I felt a plan was forming. I had something to *do*.

"How is your family?" I asked Denise, hesitant to hear her answer. Her husband had died of Alzheimer's at the age of forty-seven. His father and his brother, as well as his uncles, had also died in their forties of Alzheimer's. She had six children, grown now, and she was terrified for them and their families. Alzheimer's is not generally hereditary, though there is a familial tendency. The type of disease that strikes very young people, as in Denise's husband's family, does have an inherited gene. Her children and their cousins had volunteered to be part of a study in the search for a cure. The researchers knew which if any of the children had inherited the gene, but the children had chosen not to know who had it and who didn't. What could they do about it if they knew?

Her eyes reddened as she said, "Well, yes. One of the nieces is showing first signs." We held each other's hands across the table, unable to begin to understand what we had to accept.

A few days later, on a Thursday, Tony had an appointment for a check-up with his general practitioner, a man who had taken the place of his former doctor. Thursday was garbage day, and he had awakened a half-hour before the alarm, which was set for five-thirty. At five, he hopped out of bed, turned on the lights, put his shorts on, and strode out to the garage. The night before, he had prepared the two black garbage bags and put them in the trunk of his car so animals wouldn't get them. He had tied them tightly with clothes line cord, bought at the hardware store specifically for this purpose, which he had cut into measured lengths and hung over a nail, handy for Wednesday-night garbage bag preparation. As a Boy Scout in Holland, he had learned to tie knots, and he did an amazing job on those black bags, double-bagging them and tying twice as many knots. In the morning, he drove the thirty or so yards to the end of the driveway, opened the trunk and carefully placed the two bags just so on the road. I had to admit that he was resourceful in keeping himself busy. He kept me busy, too. "You have to watch me tie these knots. Don't go away! If I'm not here you'll have to know how to do it. Watch carefully! Lizzie, don't laugh! You're not watching!" Again, I marveled at the physical dexterity he maintained doing something he had known how to do since childhood. I had learned that verbal memory and physical memory are in different parts of the brain. How could I be annoyed when he was trying so hard to be helpful and necessary? The hour of the morning we spent with our coffee routine and waiting for the garbage man to come was our time together, pleasant but not what I expected our retirement togetherness to be. When Tony heard the truck approaching, he ran outside, waved his arms and stopped the man before he picked up our bags. "Good job!" he called out. "Thank you so much! Good job!" Only then could we get ready for the forty-five minute trip to Iowa City for his doctor appointment. I sat next to him in the car, assuring myself that he was a good driver, as long as I pointed out where to turn.

This doctor had a full gray beard and the gentle, soft manner of the Mennonites, the Amish group to which he belonged. His own wife had died of Alzheimer's. Tony seemed fine during his exam, knew how old he was, talked lucidly and impressed the doctor with his well-being. His blood pressure was 100 over 60, his heart strong, and cholesterol under control. Privately I was able to describe to the doctor Tony's behavior at home and my own disintegration.

"It's not unusual for him to open a big envelope and put it on his head like a hat, but I can't laugh with him anymore. He sits for hours on the couch cutting out articles from the paper that he cannot read and stapling them together importantly. He gets angry and throws things. I try not to react but I don't know how long I can last. I squelch my irritation when he zips thru the channels on the TV, silent and flashing by. He doesn't know what a channel is. He can't remember how to do it. With each ability he loses, I die a little bit, too.

"The worst of it is, Doctor," I continued, silently weeping, "that when he forgets where he is or what he is doing, he is afraid and lashes out at me. I think he is terrified and I am, too."

The doctor took my hand in both of his and said, "Yes, I understand. Some people with dementia are more combative than others." He gave me a prescription for Atavan for Tony, to calm his anxiety. "Keep him safe and take care of yourself." *Thanks,* I thought as we returned to the car. *Take care of myself? How?*

During the trip home, I drove and Tony slept, and when we got home he curled up on the couch for another two hours. He had put so much effort into being normal at the doctor's office that he was exhausted. It had been a long day for him, with two activities. He had gotten up early to handle the garbage before going to the doctor's.

Three weeks later, on September 11th, 2003, having left Tony home alone, I sat in an anteroom at the University Hospital in Iowa City, waiting to see Geri, studying again the list of things I wanted to tell her and ask about. I didn't want to waste this appointment and nervously tapped my pencil on my notebook.

I looked up when I heard my name and followed a nurse who opened a door to a little cubicle with a desk-table pushed into one corner and two straight chairs. Geri walked gently into the room, shook my hand, and I burst into tears. I was so desperate for help that my voice caught with emotion and uncertainty. I was filled with anxiety. She was comfortably round, with a warm smile, rosy cheeks, and a calm confidence. The pages I had written rested on my lap unread as Geri knew the minute she saw me what was going on. Tears streamed down my cheeks onto my notebook as I let her take charge, asking me questions and giving me answers. When I left an hour later, I almost skipped to the car. I had to adjust the rear view mirror because I was sitting a little taller.

Geri had listened to me! She hadn't dismissed me; she had taken *my* life seriously and *told me what to do!* I had a guide and a plan.

She said, "Number one: call your doctor and get on an antidepressant, Zoloft or Prozac, before you fall completely apart." *Yes!* I thought.

She made an appointment at the Neurological Clinic there at the University Hospital for a complete evaluation for Tony. Ah! I wanted to know what was *really* going on and where in the disease process he was. She recognized Tony's symptoms, like seeing weird things in the night and the quick flare-ups, and named the probable cause for each and the part of the brain that was affected. The symptoms all had names and were related to parts of the brain that could be treated. I was so relieved to learn that somebody knew what was going on with the disease that I didn't think to write down the specifics. I didn't need to. What good would knowing scientific terms do me? What I was concerned with was behavior, his and mine, living day to day, feeling some control. I had tried to pretend that Tony wasn't sick so I wouldn't have to deal with it, so life would be the same. I didn't know *how* to deal with it. I wanted something like steel wool to stuff in the cracks so everything would be all right again.

"He should be on medication stronger than Prozac, with some antipsychotic component," she said when she heard about his behavior. "It is better to treat in order to *prevent* violent behavior than to wait for it to happen and then try to treat it. The doctor will handle the new medication after the neurological appointment. And Liz," she continued, "keep a charged cell phone with you at all times, and think ahead of a safe place in your home where you can lock yourself in." That gave me a chill, but I understood what she was implying. In fact, I had known all along.

"Thirdly," she continued, "he must stop driving—the sooner the better."

"But, he's still a good driver," I said. "He drives slowly and carefully. I'm not afraid of his driving, especially when I am with him to keep him from getting lost. I know he would be angry if I told him he couldn't drive anymore."

"Liz," she gently urged, "think about this. His judgment is severely impaired. He could hurt someone else, or himself, badly. If he got in an accident, even if it was not his fault, he has Alzheimer's and you know it. You could be sued for everything you have. Stronger medication will make it easier for him, and for you, to get this done."

"Okay. I see. Of course. And Geri?" I ventured. "I am thinking about moving to Colorado to be near my daughter and her family. Should I do that? Would it be terrible for Tony? Am I being selfish?"

Her answer was unequivocal. "*Go!* Move as soon as possible. Tony may still be able to cooperate somewhat and he probably has enough cognition left to adjust. If you wait longer, he will be more difficult. Alzheimer's is taking your husband," she stated bluntly. "Don't let it make you a victim, too."

I got in the car and adjusted the rear view mirror, but I was looking forward now. I could see a future. But first things first. I called my long-time personal friend who was a doctor and told her of my situation and of Geri's recommendation that I have some kind of antidepressant "...before I fall completely apart." I made an appointment with her and she prescribed Zoloft, with the admonition that I shouldn't take it for an extended period of time.

My exuberance and certainty about moving to Colorado waxed and waned in the next few weeks, but I was taking hold, sure we would move, even though reasons to stay put in Iowa popped up daily. The major one, of course, was Tony himself. He constantly raved about our wonderful house. How could I take him away from all that he loved—his lawn, the birds, the fireplace, and the neighbors, the garbage, the newspapers, and the space? And I? How could I leave the friends who had been a constant emotional support for me and start over where I knew no one?

This move had to be right for both of us. Was it?

Muscatine held no future for us, with no family nearby and professional, trained help for Alzheimer's care just developing. What would happen to Tony if I became ill or incapacitated?

One evening when Tony was at the piano and I had finished cleaning up the kitchen, I pushed open the swinging kitchen door that had never stayed put and walked through the living room, seeing with new eyes the drooping, dull ochre curtains that I had put up twenty-five years before. The copper tray was dull and stacked with old magazines and papers. I looked down at my feet as I made my way to our bedroom on the grayish path in the center of the matted carpet in the hall. The bedroom had been many colors over the years, and could use some perking up again. The house looked tired and my closet was small. How had I lived with such a small closet? I didn't like the house anymore. Tension filled every room. Would it be different elsewhere?

A small home in Colorado might give me a new perspective, new energy, and professional help for Tony.

I booked a flight to go to Denver for one day to see what Marianne was excited about. I had to trust that Tony would be all right by himself for one day.

I sat at the gate in the Quad City Airport in Illinois, waiting to board the seven-thirty A.M. flight to Denver, when the loudspeaker announced a one-hour delay. I stood up, angrily looking around ready to *do* something. Then I sat down. I would wait. An hour went by, and then another, while I fidgeted and wondered if it would be worth it to fly to Denver for so few hours. Maybe this was a sign that the move was not a good idea. Ridiculous. Stick with the plan. Marianne and I would need to do everything we had to do in just a few hours. I waited. I could do it.

And I did do it. I took the shuttle from the Denver airport and found Marianne waiting on her porch steps with Katherine, as Nicholas and Elizabeth were in school. We all climbed into her SUV and were off to look at the model patio homes under construction in Highland Walk, a section of Highlands Ranch, a planned community of 80,000 people on the south side of Denver.

As we walked through each one, I chose the smallest one, as it was plenty big, with the living area downstairs and three bedrooms and two full baths upstairs. Finally, on advice, I changed my selection to the model with one bedroom downstairs so if one day Tony couldn't make the stairs we, or he, could sleep there. The homes were free-standing houses arranged in groups of four, facing different directions to ensure privacy. The Association took care of the outside of the house and landscaping. No mowing. It couldn't be better. A decision made. Done. I was taking control.

In the SUV again, we scooted the three miles to the Alterra Memory Care Facility on University Avenue. We rang the bell and a buzzer let us in. The soft green decor was pleasing, and the thirty or so chairs arranged in a semicircle in front of us told me that there were activities planned. Ugh! I couldn't picture Tony sitting in a semicircle with old people for group activities.

Kathy, the marketing director, was expecting us. She was dressed in a flowing skirt of bright green, with red hair rolling freely over her shoulders, intense blue eyes, and a voice that spoke slowly as though to kindergarteners. In her office, she gave me forms to fill out and explained the procedures.

"We'll save a spot for him," she said. "I know how hard it is for you, but we will take good care of your husband. The best thing to do is to start him right away with day care at least three days a week so it becomes his routine. You might consider five days while you are unpacking and moving in. Now, I know you are not ready for him to live here, but would you like to see the rooms? Meet some of the residents?"

"No. No, thank you. Not now. We, umm, we don't have much time."

I did not want to see what was behind those locked doors. Locked doors! I just wasn't ready. Not even for a small glimpse.

"It was cheerful in there," I said to Marianne when we left. "The part we saw. Kathy was knowledgeable and compassionate."

"It didn't smell," Marianne said.

"Right. I can't believe he's ready for this. It would be a new life for me, too."

202   *Elizabeth Gibbons Van Ingen*

"It's perfect, Mom."

"Yes. Maybe."

We had a quick, late lunch at Noodles and Company, then picked up Nicholas and Elizabeth from school and took them home. I sat on the floor with the three children climbing all over me.

"Opa and I are going to move here to Colorado to be near you," I ventured.

"For real?" Nicholas said, crashing into my lap with hugs and kisses. There. I had said it out loud, made a commitment to my grandson that I couldn't back out of.

"Yes, for real."

On the quick two-hour flight home, my mind wandered through the patio home I had selected, upstairs and down. I mentally put the piano in the dining area with the table, and the couch, first one way and then another, under the window, trying to picture the fit. *Plenty of room, if I get rid of half of our furniture. Simple, easy to take care of…. in a virtual sea of homes, all alike. Will Tony be miserable living so close to neighbors? What will I do with the two Persian carpets that had been the center of our living space all over the world for forty years? Well,* I thought, *get on with it.*

As I got into my car at the airport in Moline, Illinois, I turned the ignition key, and soon was crossing the Mississippi River into Iowa. My thoughts turned toward what was awaiting me there. I didn't want our home to be a place I dreaded to go but I realized that I was always tense there now, careful of every word I said and every move I made. I wanted a home where we could both be comfortable, take our shoes off, sprawl, laugh, cry and be comforted, dump worries outside. I thought of my friend Rena, who wore a wig when cancer treatments caused her hair to fall out. She said she loved going home so she could take off her wig. *That's what I want, a place to "take off my wig."*

I drove slowly along the two-lane road through the little town of Blue Grass, the dry cornfields on my right, ready for harvest, and the Mississippi on my left. *I will miss all this,* I thought. I had come to love Iowa.

"Brace yourself," I whispered under my breath as I pulled into the garage. Before I could get out of the car, Tony opened the kitchen door wide with a grin to match. I stepped into our kitchen and into his open arms at eight o'clock in the evening. I let out a sigh as I snuggled into the familiar warmth of his body. Nice fit.

"How was it?" Tony asked, hugging me tightly.

"Fine," I said, hugging him back, thinking I *am* glad to be home. Abruptly, he dropped his arms, turned away from me and walked over to the piano and began to play.

Suddenly, loneliness overcame me, followed quickly by anger. *He doesn't care about me*, I thought, slamming the pot onto the stove to boil water for spaghetti. *He just doesn't care. I am of no account. I don't matter. I am alone, but I still have to fix him dinner. No one is here with me! Don't leave me, Tony!* I opened a jar of spaghetti sauce and slopped it into a pan. I grabbed a paper towel to wipe up the spill. *Clean as you go, clean as you go.* His words never would leave me even if he did.

"Come and eat something," I snapped. "Come and eat. Dinner. It's time to eat."

No response.

I walked over to the piano and seeing his expectant, confused eyes look up at me I softened and took his face in my hands and gave him a kiss. "Come for dinner, Honey. It's time to eat."

We ate, cleaned up and went to bed, where he fell quickly asleep. But I, lying next to him with my hand in his, our feet touching, was alert with new thoughts. *I feel like a sneak*, I thought. *No, I am a sneak. Can I really sell Tony's house out from under him? The house he personally designed?* My mind's eye remembered the paper model he had meticulously made to scale on graph paper, Scotch-taped together, and positioned on the dining room table at the farmhouse. *If we move, where will we put the Tunisian birdcage now hanging in its own custom-cut arch? Will we have enough room for our books?*

But I had decided. Sell the house. Buy another one, and go. *I'll tell Tony a little later*, I thought. No need to upset him so soon.

I pushed that particular scene to the far back of my mind. I recognized the familiar push-pull emotions that had come over me with all the other big moves of our lives.

Big moves. I had done it before—Iran, Casablanca, South Africa, California, Iowa—and now Colorado. But this time I was alone. Lying next to Tony, my mind drifted from Casablanca to dreams of the Rocky Mountains and the vibrant city of Denver. *But wait. You're not moving yet, Lizzie*, I told myself. *There is another issue you have to face.*

Tony was still driving. I cowered under the covers knowing I had to be the one to stop him.

CHAPTER 20

"*Lizzie, Where's My Ticket?*"

Muscatine, October 2003

TONY BEHIND THE WHEEL was insanity. *"If he had an accident, even one that was not his fault, we could be sued for everything we have."* Geri's warning repeated in my mind. Killing someone, or getting lost in sub-zero weather didn't seem remotely possible to me, but the financial risk did. We would need money, and lots of it for his care as the illness developed. He had been diagnosed with Alzheimer's disease. I knew it and would be liable. Guilty.

"My God, Mom! You've got to stop him from driving." The words of my children repeated in my mind every time he went out. I *knew* one day he wouldn't be driving, but I did not want to think about how that day would come about.

I was not so much in denial, as my girls suggested. I simply lacked the emotional energy to do what had to be done to keep him off the road. I was drifting along on semi-smooth water, looking up at the clouds, ignoring the undercurrent that propelled us toward the edge. We were headed for a gigantic drop over the falls, into a churning froth below, to be tossed in the turbulence, out of control. I paralyzed myself into inaction, anticipating Tony's anger and bewilderment, remembering instances when I was driving and he grabbed the wheel, or shouted and slammed the palms of his hands on the dashboard.

People who knew told me, "Let the doctor take the blame, then you won't be the bad guy. Then you can be on Tony's side." These wise words *sounded* simple, but I decided to think about it later. It was easier for me to be a passenger in this trip and be quiet. I didn't like being in the driver's seat in any sense of the word. Not yet. I was comfortable fooling myself, thinking and hoping that he was still the capable, responsible man I had married, taking care of me, and yet I was smart enough to keep a physical distance from the strong arms that could lash out at me.

In the five or so years since the diagnosis I had grown strong enough to buy a house but lacked the courage take Tony's driver's license away. Why? Because I hadn't *told* him about the house and the driver's license issue demanded direct confrontation.

One morning, Tony spread all of the cards from his wallet on the kitchen table. "Look, Lizzie, my driving 'ticket' expires next month on my birthday. I have to get it renewed."

How can he be so aware of that when he can't remember that he mowed the lawn? I wondered. *Maybe he also knows that he shouldn't be driving, so getting him to give it up won't be so difficult.* I saw my chance and called for an appointment with his doctor for the purpose of getting a signed form stating that, in the doctor's opinion, Tony should not be driving. Then, I'd take it to the Department of Motor Vehicles.

Tony drove us both to Iowa City to the appointment, where I asked to speak to the doctor privately before he saw Tony, my heart thumping as I whispered my mission to him. I didn't want Tony blaming me, hating me, yelling at me. I wanted him to blame the doctor.

I showed Tony where to write his name, the date, and his birthday on the registration before we were shown into the doctor's office, where we sat together facing this gray-haired man with the kind eyes, whose own wife had died of Alzheimer's two years before.

"Tony, you can't drive anymore." The doctor tried to hold Tony's gaze. "You have to stop driving."

"Oh?" Tony said, "Why is that?"

"Your reactions aren't good. You could get lost. You could have a bad accident and hurt someone. You have Alzheimer's disease."

"Oh, I don't think so," Tony said, and stood up to go.

So much for taking the doctor's word, I thought, but I did leave with the signed affidavit stating Tony should not have his license renewed.

At breakfast a few days later, Tony reminded me again that his license, his "ticket," would expire in two weeks. I jumped in, like diving off a high board, and said, "Let's do it today. I have a quick errand to do first. I'll be right back and we'll go together."

"Okay, but I can go by myself."

"Fine," I said, thinking he wouldn't be able to find the DMV by himself. My plan was to dash to the Department of Motor Vehicles with the doctor's form so when we went in together they would know not to issue a license to him.

With a rush of adrenalin, I hopped into the car on my sneaky mission. I had a lump in my chest and sweaty palms as I walked into the DMV and made myself step up to the woman behind the counter, who greeted me with a red lipstick smile. Her nametag read "Mary," and her bangle bracelets clattered as she reached out for the form I pushed across to her. "I have an unusual request," I stammered. "I don't want my husband to have his driver's license renewed. He can't be allowed to drive." Her penciled eyebrows shot up as she glanced at the page.

"Your husband has to sign the form to show he's read it," she snapped.

"But I don't want him to read it. I don't want him to know I am the one who brought it in."

"It's the law," she said. "He has his civil rights, just like anyone. He has the right to know who says he can't drive. Oh. This form is not valid anyway. The doctor didn't fill in his medical license number."

I snatched the papers from her outstretched hand and ran to the car where I had one of those new car phones in a bag. I called the doctor's office and asked the nurse for his license number.

"Oh, the doctor is out and I have no idea what it is." My heart sank. "Please! Can't you look it up and call me back? I need it right now."

I went home to get Tony, as I had promised, and turned into the garage. No car! Did he go to the DMV by himself? For one brief moment, I allowed myself to slump on the steering wheel and cry. Then I turned around and drove the five miles back to the DMV. I rushed in and Mary stepped aside from the person she was serving and told me, "Your husband *was* here. I stalled and told him he didn't pass the vision test and needed a note from his eye doctor, and he left." I found out later that he had then driven the two blocks to our dentist instead of the optometrist, walked in and said hello, and left.

"Thanks, Mary." I turned and ran out past the line of people, all eyes on me. In the car again, I called the nurse and got the information I needed to validate the form, then drove home slowly, not knowing what to do next. Seeing the opportunity vanish, I turned into our drive. Still no car. As I opened the door to the kitchen, the phone was ringing. "This is Mary. Tony's here right now."

I slammed the door behind me, and raced back to the DMV. Tony turned around when he heard me bursting into the little office, now crowded with people. "What are *you* doing here?"

"Mary called to see if I had a letter from the doctor. I do and you have to sign it."

"What does it say?" he asked.

"It is from Dr. Martin and it says you can't drive. Sign here."

He did. I felt sick. He didn't understand and *he trusted me.* I turned the paper over to the second blank line. "Here. Sign again here." He did.

With his head high, shoulders back, he handed the form to Mary. She took his picture. He laughed. We waited. We chatted. I was sure Mary could see my heart thumping in my chest. Poor Tony! He stood and walked over to Mary when she called his name. She handed him a plastic card with his new picture, home address, weight, and height on it. Across the top in red was written NON-DRIVER'S IDENTIFICATION. We walked outside to our separate cars; Tony smiling, happy at having accomplished this task, stopped and looked at his new card. His "ticket."

"Lizzie, what's this?"

"It is your identification, Tony. Honey, it is not a driver's license. You are not allowed to drive anymore. The doctor had said you can't drive because you have Alzheimer's disease. He is legally required to do that."

"But I just wanted my ticket. Why haven't they given me my ticket? They have stolen my ticket." My chest tightened to see him so confused.

He turned abruptly and stormed back into the office, shouting and pushing his way past the other people there.

"Yes, you can appeal," Mary said and she gave him a thirty-day permit allowing him to drive pending the appeal. "Just bring in a letter within thirty days from a neurologist saying you do not have Alzheimer's disease."

We drove home in our separate cars. Inside, we sat at the kitchen table to begin the weeks and months of futile explanation.

"Why? Who says? Since when? I am *not* sick." He slammed his hands flat on the table and I jumped, feeling the now familiar jolt of fear run through me.

Pent-up words and emotion poured out of me. "You were diagnosed five years ago, Sweetheart. You have *Alzheimer's disease!* I've never pushed you to understand because I didn't want you to be self-conscious, or to feel bad, or to worry over your future. Instead, *I* have been self-conscious and felt bad and *I* do the worrying. It's like *I* have the disease, but it's *yours*, not mine. You are *sick* and *you're not allowed to drive!* You can't drive anymore! You have to face that yourself. I cannot do it for you."

Amazed, I heard each and every word pour out of my mouth.

His blue eyes stared, unblinking, back at me.

"Well, that's okay. Fine. We'll go together everywhere. You drive. Now, goddamn it, who can we see to get this straightened out? They've stolen my car! They've stolen my ticket! You've got to call someone, *do* something! I want my ticket!"

"We'll work it out, Honey. We'll do the best we can."

A week later he was still totally bewildered. We read and re-read page forty-six in *Alzheimer's: The Answers You Need*, the chapter titled "Why Won't They Let Me Drive?" Tony took a pink and then a yellow highlighter to the page, then a black ink pen and underlined, drew arrows, and wrote these notes in the margin, trying to understand:

"This needs to be checked properly!!! Alzheimer's disease is a bad driver if not controlled by the driver and checked!!!"

He affixed his return address stickers all over the page. I don't know why I thought he would grasp what was happening to him. He was sick, very sick, and I watched helplessly while he tried and tried to understand. He couldn't.

"They can have my car. I'll just buy another one and drive that." He pleaded with me, "Lizzie, you have to *do* something. Find a doctor to help me."

From then on when we went out, we took my car, not his. Sometimes he was compliant. Often he was anxious, and would slam his fists on the dashboard, yelling at me, "Where are you going?" or "Don't turn here!" or "What do you think you are doing?" I quivered inside but rarely reacted, just ignored his ranting and kept my eyes on the road. I felt like my life was leaking out of me and what was left was an inert lump, like bread dough that doesn't rise, bread dough that's been punched down—*pfffft*. And Tony was deflated, too. I seemed to be hitting him with one thing after another.

The week after he lost his driver's license, I prepared to deliver another blow and listed the house with the realtor.

CHAPTER 21

Curb Appeal

Muscatine, October 2003

I SAT ON THE EDGE OF an easy chair in the Sturms' living room, my calendar on my lap, pen in hand, and faced Don, our realtor. He was a short, compact man, with strong, dark eyebrows that somehow inspired confidence. He was well respected for his years of experience selling homes in Muscatine.

"It's time, Don," I said. "What do I have to do to sell the house?"

"You'll want to do a few repairs before we show it and hold an Open House."

"Oh, an Open House. Yes, I understand," I said. "But we have to wait. I can't tell Tony yet. I'll get the things fixed up and then tell him. He wouldn't understand and would be anxious and fearful and very angry. I'll wait on that. I want to sell the house, but I can't tell anybody. Doesn't make much sense, does it? But that's the way it has to be for now. So what do I have to do to the house?"

"Well, the first thing I'd do is fix the garage floor. It's cracked and unsightly, a bad first impression for a prospective buyer. I suggest you tear it out put in a new one." I went home, made some calls and started that project immediately.

"Wonderful, wonderful!" Tony said, when work had begun, applauding the jackhammers at work. He stood grinning and clapping as the concrete dust whirled around him and seeped through cracks and into the house. He chuckled and laughed with the workmen as though he had orchestrated the project, and indeed, he had wanted to fix up the garage for a long time.

"You need a new septic tank," Don told me after the inspectors had come out to the house. "The codes have changed in the last twenty-five years. You can't sell the house with an out-of-date septic tank."

Looking over our three-quarter-acre lawn, the inspector told me, "We can't put the new tank in the same place. It won't fit. We have to tear out the old one, and then dig up another part of your yard for the new one." I groaned at the expense and the mess. Tony was delighted when the trucks rolled over his lawn to suck out the contents of the septic tank and dig it up. He waved and cheered from the deck like a child and watched the hole get deeper and the pile of dirt and mud get higher.

Tony followed Kurt, the house painter, around the house as he touched up trim and chipped places on the siding. Kurt, with a twinkle in his eye and a chuckle behind his graying mustache, was an entertainer in the evenings, accompanying his German songs with the accordion and delighting anyone who would listen to his silly jokes. "Here's a good one," he said, hesitating in his work to visit with Tony. Tony laughed appropriately somewhere around the punch line without any comprehension. Kurt sang as he drifted around the corners and climbed up his ladder in his white, paint-splattered overalls, swinging a paint can and his portable radio, forever blaring Rush Limbaugh. He had been at our house many times. Tony and Kurt had shared a camaraderie, both being immigrants from Europe.

Kurt called from downstairs, "There's a leak somewhere causing those spots on the downstairs ceiling. Shall I paint them over?"

"Yes," I said, "but I'd better call the plumber first." I did and he fixed the leak from the upstairs bathroom.

I shuddered at all that was being done and would have to be paid for. I wondered if I would have enough money left from the sale of this big house and property to buy the small patio home in Colorado I had put a deposit on.

Tony was oblivious, not to the work, but to the meaning of the work. By now, October 2003, he was unable to remember from day to day, so what was going on each day was a new and thrilling surprise of activity.

I'll tell him why we are doing all this a little later, I reasoned. *Selling the house just wouldn't be an option for him, not a possibility, but he's enjoying the activity. No use upsetting him yet. Later, maybe with the doctor's help.* I was afraid of him and his temper, but I still thought he was rational enough to need a plausible explanation if we had an open house. Wouldn't he have questioned why people were snooping through his house? I put Don off a while longer. No advertising, no sign in the yard, no Open House. Later.

"I'll tell all my customers," I'd tell Don. "Someone will know someone who will buy my house. We can tell people just as long as Tony doesn't find out we are selling it."

One morning our neighbor, Paul, came over holding something in his hands behind his back. "Look at this, Liz. You lost some shingles in the windstorm last night. You'll want to have the roof repaired." I called the roofer. He came and Tony held the ladder for him. Another bill.

The concrete dust from the jack-hammer, the trucks carting in equipment for the septic tank and digging up the lawn, the men on the roof, the plumber, the painter, the noise of the workmen's radios blasting, and total confusion did not ruffle Tony. He didn't question a thing. He chatted with the workmen and had a fine time.

Small pieces of furniture left the house surreptitiously with friends who promised not to mention the move to Tony. Tony himself helped me cart bundles and bulging boxes to the Salvation Army. Linda came from Nebraska with a U-Haul and took the rec room table and chairs and the sleeper-couch. When I sent the dining room rug we had bought forty years before in Isfahan to Caroline in Arizona, I told him it was at the cleaners. Marianne was on the spot in Colorado to select the countertops and fixtures for the new house being built there.

The disorder and chaos of getting the house ready to put on

the market, the decisions about the new house, and organizing the move itself were good reasons for not involving Tony until really necessary. I was sure that there would be no cooperation from him. He had by now lost all power to reason.

Occasionally, I stopped to think about what I was doing. One morning in early March of 2004, after Tony had brought me coffee and asked if there was anything he could do for me, we sat companionably on the edge of the bed and watched the brilliant yellow goldfinches at our feeders. There must have been twenty or thirty fluttering around. We both loved them. I would miss them. Would Tony? Would he remember them? I had been preparing the move since October and now it was March. As of yet, no signs in the yard, no open house. Would he ever understand? Was there any reason to tell him?

I was constantly learning and relearning to be patient. I would repeat a saying from Jon Kabat Zinn to myself often, "*Impatience* is the strong energy of not wanting things to be the way they are." I didn't have any extra energy to waste on being impatient. I was exhausted. "*Patience* is remembering that things unfold in their own time. The grass grows by itself." Our move to Colorado was unfolding. When people asked me for specifics, the date we were leaving, the day I'd tell Tony, what I was going to tell him, and were we going to fly or drive, I had no answers. I just didn't know. I was waiting for answers to appear, unfold.

I got up from the bed where we were sitting with our coffee, walked into the kitchen, and stood looking through the picture window over the sink. I saw the first haze of spring, buds breaking open on the giant oak trees that filled the view. Below, green shoots of the daffodils that we had planted years ago were spiking up from the still brown lawn. We would be gone when spring burst out in the Iowa cornfields. The blossoms on the magnolia tree on Mulberry Street would come and go this year without me.

Early in the week, I had revisited my twenty-nine years in Muscatine at a three-hour goodbye gathering. Two long-time friends had brought my past to my present with elegant, splendid hospitality, by assembling women I had known and grown to love over the last twenty-nine years. I took the time to reflect on how long, how much, how varied, how deep, how warm, how fulfilling, and how rich my life in Iowa had been. We women had supported each other through growth and crisis, through calm and upheaval, through the core of our lives. I was not leaving Muscatine without sadness and loss. I lowered my head and understood Tony would not have the same opportunity to say goodbye. Without my antidepressants I'm sure I would have wept constantly and been in a great turmoil about the logistics of leaving. As it was, I learned that I could make decisions and get things handled, not as Tony would have done them, with perfect organization, but handled nevertheless.

I thought we would drive the fourteen hours to Colorado in my car, stopping in Nebraska with Linda for one night.

"Mom, are you crazy? You can't drive with Dad for two whole days. You are asking for trouble." All three girls said the same thing, in pretty much the same words. "Don't drive. Fly. It will be difficult, but only for two hours."

Tony's outbursts on a recent half-hour drive to Davenport came to mind. "Don't touch those buttons! You're ruining the car! Where do you think you are going? Turn here! Turn here! I'm not driving with you! Stop the car! I'm getting out!" accompanied by thumping and pounding on the dashboard. *Right. We would fly.* I purchased the air tickets. The date was set. March 23, 2004.

We had one more doctor's appointment before we moved. The ideal time to tell Tony we were moving would be in the doctor's office, with the doctor's support and assurances. I wrote a note explaining the situation to give to the doctor when we met with him. Then I tore it up. Did I really think Tony would understand and cooperate? Would he remember the next day? If he did remember, how would he react? How would I calm him? Better to wait until right before we left, maybe a day or two.

The logistics were complicated, but unfolded as friends and relatives stepped up and gave support and overwhelming practical help. On the twenty-first of March, my beige Buick went to "be serviced," as my friend Micki and her husband, Dennis, picked it up to drive it to Colorado for us while they went to visit their own daughter who lived there. I sold Tony's blue 2000 Park Avenue Ultra, which I had always resented, to a friend who would pick it up the day we left for Colorado.

Tony's sister, Hannie, and her husband George, came from Wisconsin on the twenty-first to help. The night before we were to leave, Hannie and I looked across the dinner table at each other. I had planned to tell Tony then, while she was there to support me, that he and I were leaving Muscatine forever and moving to Colorado. I couldn't do it. The evening was too pleasant. I was too nervous. I said nothing. After dinner, I packed his suitcase and hid it in my closet.

Early on the twenty-third, we managed to get Tony up and dressed, the suitcases in the car. I still couldn't tell Tony where we were going. It was much easier to put off upsetting him and me, too, and just go.

"Have a nice time, Tony," Hannie said, as she and George drove us to the airport for our early-morning flight. "Have a nice vacation." She told me later that she had held her breath until we were actually on the plane, she was so afraid that he would balk at the last minute.

I will never know how much Tony understood of what was happening. I do know now I gave him credit for much more awareness than he actually had at the time. I was so afraid of his anger, his temper, his physical strength, his disappointment at losing his house, and his resentment of me, that I stopped lying to myself and began lying to him.

CHAPTER 22

"Welcome Home, Honey!"

Denver, Colorado, March 2004

TONY IN THE AISLE seat and I next to him, with his big Dutch hand covering mine, heard the familiar roar of the engines. This was to be our last trip together—short, and several worlds and a lifetime away from our first flight together from Beirut to Tehran. We were on another adventure, forty-four years later. "Let's not discuss it now," he had said then when he asked me to marry him. "I love you enough for both of us." Now it was my turn not to talk about the future. It was *my* love this time that would be enough for both of us.

"Where are we going?"

"On vacation, Sweetheart. On vacation."

Our longest previous flights had been from Berkeley to Port Elizabeth, South Africa. Then I had felt like I was going down into a pit, to the bottom of the world. Now, this short flight was taking us to wide spaces, and deep breaths of what I hoped would be a new life for both of us. In the old days, we traveled with three children and, at least once, with thirteen pieces of checked luggage. Now it was just the two of us with one checked bag each and carry-ons, and barely time to a enjoy cup of coffee in a cardboard cup before we landed at the Denver Airport.

I spotted Marianne striding toward us from the luggage carousel. "You made it! You're here!" she cried and gathered us in her arms. "Dad! Oh, Dad!" She organized us in the car, with Tony next to her in the front seat, luggage tossed in the back.

Then suddenly, the Rocky Mountains!

"Watch now as we go over this hill, Mom, Dad," Marianne said as she drove us from the Denver airport, her eyes sparkling, her pony tail bobbing with her enthusiasm. "There's Longs Peak and Mount Evans, and in the haze over there you can make out Pike's Peak." The Rocky Mountains filled the view before us in the morning sun, sharp and clear, uncompromising. A few thin veils of clouds, virtually transparent, wafted in the dips between snow-covered peaks. Dark streaks of shadow textured the pure whiteness of the snow and below the snow line, like carelessly placed lines of rickrack. The front range and the foothills rolled towards us, layered in ever-darker shades where the morning sun hadn't yet reached. The mountains were so dominant and spectacular to our newcomers' eyes and minds, that we could ignore the housing developments in the foreground and see the mountain range's magnificence above all else.

Tony, in the front seat next to Marianne, leaned forward, his hands on his knees. "Look at that!" he said. "Just look at that!" His eyes were wide and his head turned from side to side as he stared out the window at the abrupt change in scenery from the deceptively barren late-winter fallow fields of Iowa. He lifted his hand and rubbed his chin and then his eyes. "Just look at that."

Marianne's big black vehicle, which she used to transport her three children and all their gear to activities, now held her parents and their gear, as it zipped south on E-470, circumventing the city of Denver, to the Marriott Hotel, just off Interstate 25, in Highlands Ranch, less than an hour's drive. She circled the hotel parking lot and turned to me with raised eyebrows when we spotted my beige Buick parked in the second row.

Marianne came with us to check into the hotel. I handed Tony a key-card, wrote the room number on a piece of paper, and put it in his shirt pocket. The desk clerk slipped an envelope over the counter to me with my name on it. I opened it, took out the key to my car, and dropped it into my purse. Sneaky. I had learned to be devious. We took the elevator up and followed the hall to our room.

"I'll do it," Tony said, holding out his key-card. He turned it over in his hand and slid it into the slot, took it out, and flicked it up and down over the slot until it slid in again, this time the right way. The green light blinked and he opened the door. He beamed as he looked around. "Very nice. No connecting door. Just the way I like it," he said, going over to the curtains. He pulled them open and we looked out on the parking lot. I scanned the area and zeroed in on my car.

Marianne, almost as tall as her dad, hugged him tight. "Welcome, Dad." She hesitated. Then, with a quick "I'll call you later, Mom," she left.

Tony turned to face me. "What are we doing here?"

"We're on vacation, Honey. We're here to see Marianne and the kids. We'll have a good time. You'll love it. Let's put our things away. You're going to love it. This is a vacation," I lied.

Tony opened his suitcase, took out his shaving kit and went into the bathroom, where he unzipped the bag, took his toiletries out one by one, and lined them up on the left side of the sink exactly as he had in all his hotel rooms for the last fifty years. While he busied himself with his clothes, I stood and stared out the east-facing window, looking beyond the parking lot to the expanse of flat land we had left behind us.

Turning, I saw that Tony was hanging up his trousers. He lined up the seams, tucked the cuffed end under his chin, folded them in half at the knee and put them through the hanger. He gave them a little shake and hooked the hanger over the bar in the closet, on the left side, his side. The same routine every night of his life. Some bit of the Tony I knew was still around. It was early Sunday morning, March 23rd, 2004. We were in Denver with a week to wait for the furniture to arrive. So far, so good.

We had settled into our hotel room, come down for breakfast, and then walked out of the hotel to the parking lot and over to the car. My insides were shaky again. When was Tony going to ask about the car? He got into the passenger side without comment.

I let out a breath of relief but braced for a reaction. I drove, finding my way on roads and freeways new to me, to the Denver Zoo, where Marianne was waiting for us with her children, Nicholas, Elizabeth, and Katherine. Tony got out of the car and strode off ahead of us, chin tipped up in the air, scanning the area.

Marianne turned to me and asked, "Where is Dad going?" Then she turned to her son. "Nicholas, go after Opa."

I had learned to keep my eye on Tony the same way I had kept track of a toddler, so I understood her concern. I looked beyond the giraffes, and there came Nicholas skipping along beside his Opa. "Here's my boy!" Tony called out. We picked up hot dogs for lunch and sat at a picnic table to eat.

"Look at Opa, Mom," Nicholas said. "Why is he sitting over there with those people? Does he know them?" Tony had joined an older couple at their table and was chatting away. "Oh, well," I sighed, glancing over but not moving from my seat, "leave him alone. Those people will understand something is not quite right. He's not harming anyone. And he's smart. There's more shade at that table." The children had been told Opa was ill but they were too young to realize his strange behavior was a part of it.

As we wandered through the Zoo, Tony led the way, marching ahead with the little girls, Elizabeth and Katherine, dancing around him. "Oh, Marianne," I said as I put my arm around her shoulder, "this is so right for us to be here. We're going to be okay."

On the drive back to the hotel, Tony began asking questions. "Whose car is this? Where are we going? Whose car is this? Where are we going? Whose car is this?"

"It's my car, our car. Micki and Dennis drove it here for us. We flew here and they drove the car here for us. Isn't that nice? It's our car."

"Yes, but whose car is this? Where are we going?"

"It's our car. We're going to the hotel." It was meaningless to answer, but I couldn't help myself.

When the waiter came to our table on Monday morning, I handed him a small card that said, "My husband is memory impaired and will not understand you. Please be patient." I was hoping to avoid awkwardness in restaurants for the next week. My mind, however, was on the movers back in Muscatine. At that moment I pictured them going through all of my things, packing and wrapping all of our possessions into boxes, lifting and carting our household goods into a van.

After breakfast, I took Tony to Alterra, to register him and gauge his reaction to the place. "We can't have him here for one minute until he has a TB test," the director, Christine told us. We had time to get the test before Friday and Saturday, when I wanted him to stay all day so I could go to the new house without him for the telephone and cable installation.

Tony stayed close to me during that visit to Alterra. "Who are all these old people?" he asked. I tried to visualize him blending in with this population nodding in chairs, or pacing up and down the hall, heads lowered, mumbling.

"Mom, Dad looks just like those people," Marianne assured me. "See that man over there? Just like Dad." I couldn't see it.

"We're here on vacation, Tony," I repeated when he became agitated. Following up with, "Here take this, you will feel better," as I handed him a sedative, Lorazepam, and a glass of water. Medicate and lie. Lie and medicate. My right eyelid twitched nonstop now. In spite of the Zoloft I was taking, I was having a hard time sitting in the hotel knowing I was about to thrust Tony into a new environment without having prepared him. Meanwhile, Hannie and George were in Muscatine supervising the packers, filling nail holes, patching paint, exchanging light fixtures, painting the deck and getting the house ready to show.

Wednesday, when we had been in the hotel four days, my cell phone rang while Tony and I were at breakfast. Hannie was calling from Iowa to tell me that the replacement carpet had been delivered but that it was the wrong size. The floor under that blue Isfahan carpet in the dining room was just plywood. When we built the house we had economized by not putting expensive hardwood flooring in that large space that would always be covered by the carpet. I had a store cut a remnant to size to replace it so the house would be more presentable to sell. It didn't fit.

"Okay," I said, "go ahead and get one that fits. Send me the bill."

The bug exterminator was to do a last "search and destroy" visit to the house in Muscatine, followed by the Merry Maids coming in for a final cleaning at the same time.

The end of repairs and expenses came with a sudden solid offer on the house. Gone was the dream house, no longer a part of our lives. Tony's grand design, it contained parts of all the places we had lived and had provided a home for our children's growing-up years. The house had done just what it was supposed to do, but now was obsolete, used up, ready for another family.

"Turn to the side," the X-Ray technician said. "Your left side. Turn. No, this way. Turn your body this way. Hold your hand up, no, your hand, your left hand, up, up." Tony laughed raising his arms and kicking out with one leg and then the other. The young woman sighed and turned to where I sat in the chair waiting. "Can you help?"

I jumped up and took Tony's shoulders and turned him, and held him, and wept inside myself for his confusion. "This way, Honey," I whispered to him. I knew the truck was to leave Muscatine that day with our accumulation of goods gathered over a lifetime. Our home was never a decorator's dream but rather a collection of things we loved that triggered memories of our life together. Would their familiarity bring comfort to Tony? Was that possible?

Thursday was a waiting day, waiting for the van and waiting for the results of the TB test. Caroline flew in from Phoenix, and my sister, Katie, came from California to help with the unpacking, but I didn't see them. I stayed with Tony because I was still afraid of upsetting him and didn't know how to explain what was going on without telling him the whole truth that we were moving.

Friday, the moving truck arrived. My family unpacked and placed the furniture according to my plan and the pictures I had meticulously taken of every corner of our house in Muscatine.

Tony's office was replicated as perfectly as possible with his desk on the left as it had been in Muscatine, the wall map on the right. All the accessories were on the desk and the pictures hung on the walls exactly as he had known them. The bed was made, clothes put in closets and dishes in cupboards, all carefully pre-visualized, somewhat like Tony's paper mockup of the house, thoroughly planned.

Saturday was day zero.

By late afternoon, Marianne called me at the hotel. The house was ready. I checked out of the hotel and Tony helped put our suitcases in the car. Nervous anticipation gripped me as I drove the five miles to our new home in the housing development still under construction. I was aware of my heart beating and my eyelid twitching. My senses were alert. I should have told him. How could I have not told him? I had given him a pill two hours ago to calm him. I needed something, too.

I parked the car on the street in front of number 3973.

"Here we are, Honey," I said. "Let's get out and go in."

Tony and I each carried a suitcase up the walkway to the three front steps. I set my suitcase down outside and took Tony's hand in mine as we approached our front door. It was painted green. My childhood home had had a green front door. Good omen. Marianne opened it wide with arms outstretched. "Welcome home!" she said, and we stepped inside. Caroline stood beside her, and my sister, Katie, next to her.

"Oh, it's beautiful!" I cried, "Tony, Honey, look how beautiful! They've done such a good job! We live here now! See? All our things! This is where we live now."

Tony stared at our beige couch and loveseat framing the copper tray table carefully placed in the center of the Persian carpet from Isfahan. He recognized our oak kitchen table and cane-seated chairs in the dining area. He reached out and touched his upright piano pushed against the wall. His clock, a retirement gift from his company, hung on the wall above the table, its tick noticeable in the silence following my exuberant exclamation. Directly in front of us, over the fireplace, was a reminder of our twenty-nine years in Iowa, a vivid collage of Iowa corn—a brilliant, warm yellow.

"Look, look!" I put my arm on his back and turned him to the left, walking the few steps down the short hallway. "Here is your office. See? Your office!" We both stared at his desk to the left of the door, and on it the pencil cup with the American Flag that I had given him to celebrate the fiftieth anniversary of his arriving in the States. The calculator was plugged in, green light flashing just as he had left it, his chair turned toward us, ready for him to sit down and go to work. On the wall to the right of the door, just as he had left it in Muscatine, hung his map, his personal map, covered with black pins.

Caroline, Marianne, Katie and I had stopped breathing as we watched him for a reaction. Suddenly, it came.

"What's going on around here?" Tony bellowed. "This is all my stuff! They've stolen my things! My children have stolen everything! That's okay. That's okay. Let them have it. You can take everything! I don't care! Let me out of here! Keep it all! I'm going back! I'm getting out of here! Get out of the way! Let me out!"

He snatched up his suitcase and strode out the front door into the darkness. "Dad, Dad!" Caroline called as she raced outside to stop him. She grabbed his arm and he twisted away. "Dad! Stop! Stay here!"

"Don't push him, Caroline," I reminded her. "He will push back! No force! Gentle, gentle." Tony walked quickly out of sight and disappeared in the darkness.

Marianne darted for the phone and called 911. "My dad has Alzheimer's disease and has just walked out of the house and it's dark and he doesn't know where he is!" She gave them the particulars, hung up and waited. Caroline ran out of the house, spotted her dad some distance away and hurried after him. "Dad, Dad!"

"I should have told him, should have prepared him," I said, as I sank into a cane-seated chair, my hands covering my eyes. "Why didn't I at least tell him *today*?"

"Because you never would have gotten him here, Liz." Katie said, her hand gently touching my shoulder. We looked up at a sound by the door.

Caroline and Tony came slowly up the walk, arm in arm. Tony was breathing heavily, his brows knitted together. I hugged him, then fumbled in my purse for the pill container. "Here, Honey, take this," I said and reached into the cupboard where I knew the glasses would be and got him some water. Marianne handled the call-back from 911.

Tony became drowsy from the medication and the girls left after I assured them we would be all right. He and I walked up the stairs and into our new bedroom, with the familiar old bedspread, his bureau, mine, the Van Gogh print on the wall of a man and a woman sleeping under a haystack. Home. I helped him get into bed.

Tony slept. I did, too, but woke intermittently. *We made it*, I thought. *We're here. It's done. All the planning, all the secrecy, the lying and sneakiness are over.*

The next few days were unimaginably easy. Tony followed me everywhere, bewildered but cheerful. "Ha! Ha! Wrong door! Where's the bathroom?" He would sit on the living room couch and repeat, "We have the best place. Aren't those the best, you know, over there? Look at this." He never mentioned the old house. It had vanished from his mind until one evening while looking at a photo album he saw it and he knew he had some connection with it.

"Those people had to leave that house. My *parents* used to live there but they had to leave. We have to go see my mother. She died? Nobody told me!" Then he got up, and went to the piano and began to play his songs. He was home.

After two weeks, attending only two mornings a week, it was clear that the Day Program at Alterra was not working out. Tony had a "manic" component to his disease and the facility couldn't cope. Christine, the director, called me into her office when I went to pick him up on Friday of the second week.

"This environment is too stimulating for him, Liz. He needs

lots of one-on-one attention and it's not possible in a group set-ting. He had an "altercation" with one of the staff who wouldn't let him go through the door into the kitchen. And today he swirled out his belt and whipped it around like a sword, scaring people! We can't have the residents or the staff frightened. He's a big man. We can't keep him here unless he has a significant medication change."

I swallowed hard, like a mother being told her preschool child is a bully. I was used to people being charmed by my husband, laughing and enjoying his jokes.

"He is happy here most of the time," she continued. "He en-joys the group programs and activities, eats the lunch well, but does *not* like to be in the living room areas when the doors are locked."

Well, who would, I thought, and said, "He is much better at home now, less anxious, since he has started on Seroquel, the an-tipsychotic, and Namenda, the new Alzheimer's drug, as well as Aricept. I thought he would also be better here, too."

"That's good, but not good enough to be in our Day Pro-gram. He is too unpredictable." She suggested I ask Dr. D., an elder-care specialist who attended the residents at Alterra, about a higher dose of Seroquel to calm him.

"I'll be okay with him at home for a little while," I said, and went to find Tony.

He was in the hallway badgering an aide with conversation. She was laughing and he was animated. That's good, I thought, but it's that one-on-one care that they can't provide. I can under-stand that. But I was sad watching them. He saw me and opened his arms wide for a hug and called out, "Well! How did *you* get here?"

"Come on, Honey," I said, "let's go."

So, I kept Tony home and spent all my time with him. Time together. That's what I had yearned for, and this was it. But now, under these circumstances, I was more alone than I had ever been when he traveled. I was learning to defuse his explosions—so far—and the medication helped. I was still under the delusion that he knew me and loved me. Intellectually I knew it was not so, but I also knew he couldn't live without me, or *someone like me*. In the support group, we laughed and decided *any woman would do*, but I was not ready to accept that for myself.

We took walks together in our new neighborhood and to the grocery store. I had worried that he would miss his friends in our old grocery in Muscatine, but he didn't know one store from another. He went up to every child or baby in a grocery cart, and if there was no child, he spoke to the mother with laughter and a twinkle in his eyes. "Oh, you have blue eyes! I have blue eyes! Well! Blue eyes! See? We both have blue eyes!" His finger pointed back and forth from his eyes to the other's. Again and again. I went on with my shopping and left the targeted mother to cope. Generally, mothers glowed at the attention he paid to their children, and the service people soon got to know him. "Oh, he is so friendly," they said. In the longer aisle across the back of the store, he step-hopped and skipped beside me. I looked the other way. We bought bananas. Every day. And the same package of raspberry pastries. Every day. "Tony, we have enough bananas. We don't need more bananas. Put the bananas down." He threw them on the table and grabbed more. "I *will* get bananas! Don't tell me what to do! Leave me alone!" I remembered the woman years ago who was so upset that her husband wanted more brown paper bags. "Yes, sweetheart, we need bananas." *This is not hard*, I thought. *I can do this.* I was not ready to "dispose" of him yet by over medicating him.

The second Saturday in April, after we had been in Colorado for just three weeks and Tony had been kicked out of daycare for one week, I left him at home alone while I attended the Alzheimer's support group at Alterra. I listened and learned with less hysterical emotion than I had at the first support group I had attended in Davenport five years earlier. I came home with the *Senior Blue Book* and a list of recommended agencies that provided care in the home.

I kept a Calvin and Hobbes cartoon taped to my desk that stuck me as particularly pertinent right then.

*Calvin: "They say the world is a stage. But obviously the play is
unrehearsed and everybody is ad-libbing his lines."*
*Hobbes: "Maybe that's why it's hard to tell if we're in a tragedy
or a farce."*
Calvin: "We need more special effects and dance numbers."

I needed the dance numbers, so I began looking for pamphlets
and news articles about my own interests. I collected information about classes at the Arapahoe Community College, University of Denver, the Lighthouse Writers Workshop, the Colorado
Symphony Orchestra, the Art Students League, and the Denver
Botanic Gardens. I didn't have to do it all right away, but I could
see fullness in the future. Nature and geology were everywhere,
all new to me. Maybe I wouldn't have to spend all of my days on
the couch doing crossword puzzles.

I drove with Tony to Dinosaur Ridge one day to see footprints from an incomprehensible 200 million years ago. On Mt.
Falcon Lookout, we wandered among the scented pines and spotted a doe and her fawn leaving their own footprints, like ours,
temporarily in the dust.

I was no longer lying to Tony and so had fewer headaches and
less tension, and the bursitis in my shoulder began to ease. Our
evening stroll took us through our under-construction neighborhood, Highland Walk. The patio homes and the three-story con-
dominiums a couple of streets away showed changes daily. As early evening darkness crept in, I felt the eeriness of empty streets,
homes with no light in the window, and not a soul or sound but
our own soft steps around the unoccupied buildings. The view
of the mountains would diminish as the buildings went up, but it
would always be there, somewhere, around some corner.

"This is going to look like New York City with these three-
story condos on both sides of the street," I said to Tony one evening. There was no comprehension but I did feel companionship as we strolled through the dusk hand in hand, in spite of the
aloneness that was to come, looming in the shadows of the vacant
buildings. Then he said, "Rotterdam was bombed so badly. They
have to build fast."

The next day we walked to the lookout ridge behind our house. From there on a clear evening we could see an open vista of 360 degrees, including Longs Peak, Mount Evans, Devil's Head Mountain, Pike's Peak, the plains of Highlands Ranch, the Denver Tech Center, and when the sun was just right, the glint of the gold dome from the capital building in downtown Denver, twenty-two miles away.

"We have to go back," Tony said, looking out over the vastness. "We have to go back to the States."

"We *are* in the States, Honey. We're in Colorado. See? There's Denver in the distance."

"Oh, they have a Denver here in Germany just like the one in the States?"

"Um, yes," I answered.

Back at the house, we sat in the living room. I knitted, Tony talked.

"Do you have a husband?" he asked.

"Yes."

"Really? Who is that?"

"It's you, Tony. My husband is you."

"Really! Are you sure? Do you have children?"

"Yes. I have three daughters, and so do you!"

"No, I have six children. I am the oldest. Then there's Nellie, then a boy and another boy...." He recounted his brothers and sisters. "Are you male or female?"

"I am female. I am your wife."

"Where are you going to sleep tonight?"

"I'm going to sleep upstairs in bed with you just like I always do."

"Well, no. I don't think you can do that. You see I'm male and you're...."

Another night during that first month of settling in, Tony suddenly put on his jacket and demanded, "We have to go back home! Now! Why aren't you ready! Oh! You make me so mad! Let's go! Lizzie, *now!*" slamming his fist on the kitchen counter. "We have to leave! We have to go back!"

I grabbed my coat and keys, thinking, where should I go? We

got in the car and I headed for Interstate 25 towards Colorado Springs. It was dusk. I didn't know where I was going. After ten or fifteen minutes I thought I would turn around and go back and he wouldn't notice, but I saw a spectacular sight and blurted out, "Oh, Tony, look at that big rock up there. It does look like a castle doesn't it? No wonder this town is called Castle Rock." Now I've done it, I thought. I can't turn around because he'll see the rock again and know I am going in circles.

I kept going south, waiting for darkness, then used the off-on ramps to head back north, afraid of his blow-up any minute. Fortunately, it never came. He didn't have any idea where we were and wouldn't have recognized the rock if he had seen it. Back at the house, he opened the door and walked in. 'Well! It's so good to be back home!"

Sometimes we walked the mile over to Marianne's house and saw the grandkids for fifteen minutes, finding that quick, short visits were best. The joy of frequently being with the children swept me with warmth. Marianne shared with me the day-to-day challenges I had with her dad. She saw and could sympathize with me about the little things that came up frequently, constantly, too numerous and petty to talk about, but ever annoying, frustrating, exhausting. Like a kink in your leg. You go along a few steps and you think you're okay, but, bing! There it is again, and you have to be careful, watchful not to have it happen again…but it does, and sometimes those "bings" get very close together! I was constantly on my guard. Just knowing that another person was aware of these details was comforting, making life less heavy.

My first trip with Tony to downtown Denver, twenty-two miles north, was during rush hour. I had suggested that Tony go with me to the nearby bookstore for coffee and pastry just to get out of the house. It was four-fifteen. When we got in the car, he shouted to *"Go to Denver! Now!"*

"Honey, we're going to the bookstore for pastries.…"

"You are so stupid! You never listen to me! All right, I'll just get out and walk! You'll never see me again!" He pounded his knees and the dashboard.

My temper boiled and I slammed on the brakes in traffic and shouted back, "Okay! Just get out! Go! Walk!"

"That's right! Kill me!"

I regained my composure and explained rush-hour traffic, and my original intention for our drive, not to deaf ears, but to a non-comprehending mind. I drove straight up Broadway to 20th Street stopping at a hundred stoplights, turned around and came straight back. Two and a half hours driving nowhere with a demented person next to me, my introduction to the city of Denver.

At that moment, I did not feel like a loving caretaker. I was simply living with a severely impaired person who didn't require physical nursing. I was feeding his ego, excusing his little-boy antics, tolerating his volatile personality and abuse, and trying to keep the peace. I felt guilty knowing he was doing the best he could to cope but I also felt fear, dread, anxiety, sadness, loss, loneliness, anger, and disintegration. It was easier to give in than to argue or take a stand, to just let go, like drowning in very deep water. Relax and become nothing. I had moved to Denver because I knew there was professional help. It was time to use the resources that must be available.

A woman at the support group encouraged me to investigate agencies listed in the *Senior Blue Book*, which provided qualified professional caretakers. The result was that I hired Nadine, a retired nurse, Tony's age, seventy-two. I found her personable and competent. She started on May first, coming three hours twice a week, so I could leave the house and have some time to myself. When I came home, I found Nadine and Tony working on a jigsaw puzzle for six-year-olds, or Tony playing the piano while she listened with attention and applause. I thought it was a perfect arrangement.

Within three weeks, Nadine was gone. "I don't want that old lady hanging around!" Tony told me. "Oh, no, not her again!" he said when she appeared at the door. He began telling her, "Leave me alone! Don't come back here!" I called the agency and said she wasn't working out. I was once again on my own, but I had started the process, with Marianne now, of looking for some kind of assistance.

She and I visited small group residences in private homes, places that took in five to eight Alzheimer's patients and cared for them in a home-like setting, usually with one aide and a cook for five or six people, with a skilled caretaker stopping in for an hour once a day. This was fine for patients who were compliant and nonviolent, but Tony would surely disrupt the household and be dismissed.

"I suggest you see John, a social worker who can evaluate Tony and your situation, and offer ideas for placement," Christine said at the last support group. "He may be able to suggest a change in medication that you can ask your doctor about." I grasped at another straw, and within the week, we were in John's office.

Tony started talking as soon as John entered the room, not conversation, just talk. "When I was working I went to China have you ever been to China all that traveling my three children I tell you I am not anymore can you believe the people all around and the blue eyes let me see your eyes oh yes you have blue eyes same as me and Lizzie let me see your eyes this is my wife yes I have always I have six children you know and the planes you won't believe the planes so many...."

"Tony, Tony," repeated John, "stop. Stop just a minute. Take a breath"

Tony did not stop. He talked in a rush, without ceasing until he was close to hyperventilating. I could see his heart racing and his anxiety rising, perspiration on his forehead, as he couldn't stop himself. John held his hand up. "Stop, Tony. Excuse me. Stop!" He did.

John was able to ask me a few questions about his behavior and in a few minutes pronounced that Tony probably did not have Alzheimer's disease but fronto-temporal dementia, a rarer form of brain illness that affects the area of the brain that controls speech and behavior.

Well, what now? I thought.

John called our doctor, with whom he worked, and recommended a higher dose of Depakote, a medication to ease the anxiety. I took Tony home and immediately looked up fronto-temporal dementia on the Internet, and found that it is the most difficult type of dementia because it causes uninhibited social behavior. What I read described Tony exactly: language difficulty, either not talking at all or not being able to stop, and aphasia, the inability to articulate ideas or comprehend language, and talking to strangers, especially children.

Damage in the frontal lobe affected problem-solving, attention, behavior, and speech formation. Yes, it fit. The temporal lobe was where memory and learning took place, also gone for Tony. The back of the brain controlled the area of balance and coordination, vision, and voluntary movement. No wonder Tony still played the piano so well, and stood so straight and enjoyed our walks in the mountains. With fronto-temporal dementia a huge personality change was to be expected. Yes, undoubtedly this was a better diagnosis. But so what? Would it make a difference to the way we lived? Would this change in medication give us both the peace we sought?

Of course, the answer was "no," but I started going to another support group for caregivers of people with fronto-temporal dementia. That led to seeing specialists doing research at the University of Colorado Hospital, which led to a new MRI that showed deterioration in *all* areas of the brain, consistent with true Alzheimer's. The next time we saw the social worker, he came to the conclusion that Tony did not have frontal-temporal dementia but probably had unrecognized, undiagnosed bi-polar disorder!

The truth now, as I saw it, was that Tony's mind was *severely* impaired, so far deteriorated that a distinction between diagnoses was no longer possible, nor was it relevant. The only conclusive diagnosis could be made with autopsy.

By June first, I had hired another caregiver, Elaine, to stay with Tony several afternoons a week. She was thirty-eight, lively, and very attractive. Tony didn't understand when I said, "Elaine is coming," but he greeted her with a smile and hug when he saw her. Just right, I thought, remembering "any woman would do."

I was so happy to have a few hours of personal time that I became complacent and let my guard down. The evening after Elaine's first visit, Tony and I were getting into bed, and he began to adjust the blinds. "Tony, don't do it like that," I said. "You have to turn the blinds down towards the floor so the street lights don't shine up and in. Don't lower them all the way down. Not like that! When the window is open the breeze blows in and rattles the blinds, so please, you have to raise the blinds above the open part of the window so they are out of the wind. I'm the one who gets up and fixes them in the middle of the night when the rattling wakes us up and…"

"Don't tell me what to do!" he exploded. "I've been doing this for years! Long before you were even born! Just shut up! I'll tear the whole thing out!" he thrust his fist toward me and had I not been standing on the other side of the bed, his punch would have smashed my face. "I'm going to set this whole place on fire! I'm going to kill you! We'll both die! I hate you!" He rushed to the closet and began yanking at clothes. "I'm leaving! I can't stay here with you! I'm getting out of here!" He let out an anguished cry, turned, and crumpled onto the bed, sobbing. "I don't know where to go. I don't know what to take. I don't know.…"

I stood next to the bed, safely away from him, my body shaking with shock and fear and compassion. Then as he wept, I went to him, held him, weeping now myself, and got him safely into bed, thinking, *How long can I do this? What if I had been close enough so that his fist had hit me? This is not anger or frustration*, I thought. *He no longer has the reasoning for that. It is basic instinct, fight or flight. I threw too much information at him, gibberish, confusing nonsense that terrified him and triggered this outburst. It wasn't his fault.* I calmed him and vowed not to overload him with confusing words, and even believed it would not happen again. I took the blame for his behavior, thinking I had some control over this horrible disease. I, of course, did not.

My daughter Caroline said, when I told her of the incident, "Mom, don't wait until you have to call 911. No one would criticize you for placing Dad in a home now. You have to be careful."

But was I ready to give up being a wife? In effect ending our marriage? Wasn't it over already?

Peace followed that episode and I was euphoric with Elaine coming and giving me several hours to myself every week. I enrolled in drawing classes at the Denver Art Students League, taking a precious hour to get there and another to get back. I got my hair done. I hiked. I signed up for a writing class at the Arapahoe Community College. I went out for lunch with new friends.

Elaine came for more and more hours every week. Tony's seventy-third birthday came and went in October. We had a pleasant Thanksgiving with Marianne and her family. On Christmas Day, I got out my good dishes and served a holiday dinner around the dining room table. My sister and her husband had come from California and I invited another couple to join us. It was a party I thought I'd never have.

But I was tired. I was tired of listening and tired of eccentric things happening around the house. I was tired of looking the other way at his foolishness when we were out, and tired of hearing "Lizzie, Lizzie, Lizzie" when we were in. I was tired of being interrupted from what I was doing, whether it was cooking or taking a shower. I was tired of *explaining* what I was doing, only to have him criticize and question me, and tired of his resistance to everything I suggested. I was worn out worrying and wondering what the right decisions were, inconsequential decisions as well as the big, long-term decision that I thought about all the time, and tired of white lies and sneakiness. Tired.

And yet one night at dinner shortly after Christmas, Tony was trying to figure out where we were and who we were. Denver? Akron? Zaandam? Mother, Father? Marianne who? Which Marianne? There are so many Mariannes.

"What do they call you," he said turning to me as we sat on the couch.

"I'm Lizzie, your wife," I answered.

"Lizzie? Lizzie? You're Lizzie? Really? So, you're Lizzie! Well! Ha! Ha! You're Lizzie." He was bewildered, desperately trying to put it all together. I stared at the perplexed, vacant look, the eyebrows and his features contorted to confusion then despair when he realized he wasn't getting it. I began to cry, "Yes, I'm Lizzie! I have to be here to help you lose your mind! Who else will comfort you?" He put his arm around me while I cried and cried. "I am so sad, Tony. So sad. You have Alzheimer's and you don't know who I am. You don't know me! You don't know *you!* I have lost you. We are finished! We are done." His arm was warm around me but his face was blank, nothing.

The next day he wiped the kitchen counters for thirty minutes, and folded the towels over and over again, corner to corner, then turned the inside corners down so they wouldn't show, then the towel into thirds, then thirds again, then pounded them flat. Finally satisfied, he went upstairs to shower. I went with him to hand him his shaving cream so he wouldn't stick up his face with Fixodent, and to show him which denture went up and which down, and point him toward the shower and hand him the towel. Physically, he was fit and strong and steady on his feet. He stood before the mirror making faces and laughing at whoever was looking back at him. I felt safe with him as he hadn't had an outburst for at least two months. He still spent time playing the piano and I could still fool myself that he was my 'old' Tony.

In February my sister called from California, wanting me to come to San Francisco for a reunion luncheon she was having the end of March for the women in our family. I wanted to go. The notes of "The Third Man Theme" drifted through the house as Tony sat at the piano. And as I heard the music, the movie of the same name came to mind and I saw the giant Ferris wheel in Vienna turning and stopping. Was I in the swinging cage stuck at the top? I wanted to be at the bottom stepping out on to solid ground. Surely I could find a way to organize Tony so I could get away for a few days, maybe even a week.

CHAPTER 23

Cypress Court and the Psych Ward

Denver and Aurora, Colorado, March 2005

"WHAT DO YOU MEAN, nobody will have him? What are these places for?" I sobbed.

"Liz, we have had him here this morning just to try, to see if we could handle him. We cannot. He is too disruptive for the other residents and demands far too much attention. We cannot have him here, and if we can't have him, nobody will have him. He needs a med change, and if that doesn't work, he needs to go to a nursing home."

I sat across the desk from Christine, the administrator of Alterra, where we had first tried daycare. Had I thought Tony would be *improved* a year later?

"But he doesn't need nursing care! Look at him. He's up and around, active, talks to people, is cheerful. He doesn't belong with old people in wheelchairs!"

"Liz, a nursing home just for Alzheimer's patients is different. That's where he belongs."

Tears streaming down my cheeks, I left the building. There must be a place, a nice assisted-living place. He had stayed for a few days at the Cypress Court assisted-living place in September. They liked him there. I would call Cypress Court.

Shanda, the marketing director for Cypress Court, came to

the house and interviewed Tony. Oh, he was good! He laughed and chatted and went through his blue-eyes routine. What a delightful person he was, pleasant and cooperative, of course they would take him. We set a date to move in, Monday, April fourth.

It was too late by then for me to go to California, but the invitation had pushed me to think seriously about placing Tony somewhere where he would get good care and be as happy as possible. I understood that I would enjoy his companionship more during visits with him than I would enduring the strain of being with him constantly. I could be his wife, not his nurse.

Coinciding with this decision, his disease had advanced to the point where Tony himself began to give up. He was no longer interested in getting the mail out of the box. He wouldn't get out of the car to go for a walk on the ridge. He just sat there. He put on one shirt over another and couldn't figure out where his socks should go. The clincher, to make me know it was the right time, was a call from Elaine on Friday afternoon while I was on a long walk in Waterton Canyon.

"Liz! Come home right away! I have locked myself in the bathroom. Tony is threatening me and I am afraid! He is raising his fist and insisting that I drive him home. Hurry!" When I got home the danger had been diffused, but I knew that soon I would lose Elaine, and that it was finally time to place him.

I bought an extra-long single bed for him, and a table from Target with a drawer that I equipped with pencils, Scotch tape, paper, and paper clips, so he could play office. I found a table-top refrigerator so he could keep his bananas and pastries. I packed up some family pictures and a stuffed Panda he had gotten from the World Wildlife Fund, and I labeled his clothes. All set. Summer camp. I constantly reminded myself that it was the disease putting him there, not me.

On April fourth Shanda distracted Tony so I could leave him there without incident.

Three weeks later, April twenty-seventh, he was in the Psych Ward at the Aurora Medical Center. Out. Blotto.

There had been trouble. "Liz, we are surprised Tony is so severely demented. We didn't realize. How did you live with this so long? Last night he threatened to hit the aide when she wouldn't give him the key to go out the gate. He bopped another aide on the head. And yesterday he pushed a lady in a wheelchair all around the place, dangerously. We had a hard time getting him to stop. One helper came to me with three bruises on her arm." I was embarrassed about what Tony had done, but felt vindicated that someone else could see what I had been dealing with. I had no experience to compare Tony's behavior with others or with what he might become. The people at the facility knew.

I had been at Cypress Court with Tony on the twentieth and twenty-first, from four to eight P.M., because he was out of control during the dinner hour and sundowning time. His eyes were round, glazed over, wild with fear. I walked outside in the courtyard with him to soothe him. The aides tried to distract him so I could leave, but he stood right on my feet, grabbed at the neckline of my shirt, then picked up the yellow "wet floor" sign and held it menacingly over my head. I was finally able to leave, but came home so filled with anxiety that I ran into the house and threw up.

Cypress Court was supposed to be a happy solution, but there was no solution, just brief breaks between crises; certainly there was no "happy" in this disease. A sense of humor helps, but there is no "happy."

Shanda called me early the next day. "Liz, Tony needs a three-day med check to get his behavior under control. We can't have him here like this. We'll arrange for an ambulance to take him to the psych ward for three days, have his medications adjusted, and bring him back." I shouldn't have been surprised, but I felt like I was being swept away, everything out of control, but again, I grasped at what *could* be a new solution. "You know you can't take him home again, Liz." Shanda said. I looked up at her, startled. I hadn't thought of that. But of course, his care was beyond me. This was it.

We had opted not to use an ambulance, so he and I sat comfortably holding hands in the back seat of the car, and Marianne drove us to the Medical Center early on the twenty-seventh. It was a pleasant day, considering our mission. The admittance procedure took from eight in the morning until three in the afternoon. Every test was done to make sure Tony didn't have another disease besides the dementia. Tony loved the attention, sitting on the table, swinging his legs, laughing with the nurses, chatting cheerful nonsense with Marianne and me, through the X-rays, the blood and urine tests, EKG, CAT scan, and of course, the waiting. At three o'clock, he happily climbed into an ambulance to take him across the street to the psych ward. I sat next to him and held his hand. Marianne followed in the car.

That was the last of my cheerful husband.

In the psych ward, he was shown into his room by several enthusiastic aides. One chirpy blond woman, cracking gum, clipboard in hand, hammered a thousand questions at him. "How many pairs of socks did you bring? Let me take your blood pressure. We have to count your underwear. I have to prick your finger. Sit over here. I have to ask you a few questions. Give me your wallet. I must take your watch, and no shoelaces. Take the shoelaces out of your shoes."

It was that ominous time, four o'clock in the afternoon. He stamped his feet and stood up, stiffening his arms by his sides and clenching his fists. "Get the hell out of here! You're all bastards, sons of bitches! Just get out! You, too, Lizzie!" He lunged at me and socked me in the shoulder. I shattered into tears.

Someone shouted, "Security!"

Seeing the horror on my face, an aide turned to me. "The nurses have to protect themselves, you know." Two hefty, uniformed guards were there in a shot holding his arms.

I was terrified. "Go away! He's okay. Don't touch him!" They listened to me and left. I put my arm around him and led him to the bed. I climbed up and lay by his side until he calmed down. When it was time to leave, we walked to the foyer and I asked the nurse to distract him with cookies or something, as I had done in Cyprus Court, but she didn't understand. Tony grabbed my wrist. "Don't go! I am afraid! I can't do this!"

The head nurse called out, "Get the syringe!" The guards

were right there, pulling me away, pushing me toward the locked door and out. "Lizzie! Lizzie! Lizzie!" rang in my ears and tore my heart.

I threw myself sobbing onto the bench in the hall, where Marianne waited for me. The locked door opened and Miss Enthusiastic waved a belt at me. "Here's his belt, Honey. You can't have a belt in a psych ward. Not allowed."

The next two and a half weeks were a blur of disappointment and horror. I was asked not to visit the first day, to give him a day to adjust. My heart was racing when I walked in for that first visit, not knowing what to expect. I was buzzed in through the locked door and barely recognized him slumped over in a wheelchair, unable to hold his head up, unresponsive to my touch. This was normal, I was told. It would take time to find the right medication.

Marianne and I called or stopped in every day, seeing only deterioration. It seemed that they couldn't regulate his meds because every time he "acted out," they shot him up with emergency meds, which knocked him out, and put him in the "quiet room," where the monitor showed him hallucinating, picking things out of the air. His face was bruised black and his eye closed from a fall. "Trust us," I heard from the psychiatrist and the head nurse. "It takes time." When one of the aides had to ask me if Tony had Alzheimer's, I was livid. Didn't they know? They were treating him as strictly a psychotic case, and Alzheimer's is vastly different. Seventeen days had gone by. I wanted him out of there. Now. My trust had been misplaced.

May thirteenth, Tony was tied to a stretcher, put in an ambulance, and taken across the street to Garden Terrace, a nursing facility for the memory impaired that Marianne and I fortunately had visited a few months previously. Tears spilled down my cheeks as I stood waiting just inside the home. The stretcher pushed through the doors and rolled gently in, carrying my husband into this new place, his face black and blue, one eye swollen shut, no teeth, his hair unkempt.

CHAPTER 24

The Place

Aurora, Colorado, May 13 to June 24, 2005

THE OUTSIDE WAS NEAT, clean, and, though not inviting, presentable, with shrubbery softening the brick façade. Automatic doors opened inward to a weather foyer, and then a second set of doors slid apart slowly, automatically, to reveal a welcoming living room. In front of me were three sofas and an easy chair surrounding a table holding magazines and a plate of cookies covered with plastic wrap. I had often had Tony's favorite almond spice cookies freshly baked for him when he came home from his trips. The soft green and coral colors of the upholstery and carpet were surprisingly soothing. I had entered my husband's new home. He would never see this entry room of course, but I would, every day for what I assumed would be a long, long time.

This was a nursing home for people suffering from Alzheimer's disease. Exclusively. In the past, the word "exclusive" evoked something for the elite, like a country club. Now it meant specialized care, leaving out all others. The nurses and aides there handled the behavior and medical needs of demented people, exclusively. To the Alzheimer's patient, the fact that he was there meant he had reached the point in his disease where the people he has loved were excluded from his life, and not by choice. It meant that before long his own person would be excluded from himself. He would lose his sense of being a person.

The woman behind the curve of the reception desk recognized me and smiled. "Good morning."

"Yes," I said, avoiding her eyes. "Good morning."

At the end of the hall, past the empty ice cream parlor on the left and the lonely chapel on the right, were double doors made of steel. On the doors, gingham curtains concealed small windows embedded with security wire. I stretched to reach up and push the code buttons, 1–3–9–0. A hard, noisy shove against the metal bar on the door opened it. Sudden brightness from florescent lights glared off polished linoleum. A turn to the right, down another hall, again the coded buttons, 1–3–9–0, and a push on the metal bar to open this second set of steel doors onto the discordant activity of "West."

Max, with a fixed grin on his grizzled face, zipped up and down the hall in his geri-chair made from white PCP pipes. It formed a square around him like a playpen without a floor. The four legs were on wheels, and I watched as Max slung the canvas seat behind him so he could stand up and walk holding on to the railing around him, or sit down and shuffle, or just sit.

"Hep me! Hep me!" a woman in a geri-chair called out, blocking my way. Her wrinkled face turned up to search my eyes, her arm raised as though she were calling a taxi. "Hep me! Hep me! Oh, lady, hep me!" I patted her shoulder but avoided locking eyes. Tight, gray cornrows and pigtails on her head defied the confusion in her mind.

A repetitive clangity-clang jarred the air. Henry was at the double doors, stooped, white hair falling over his forehead, pushing an unceasing rhythm on the metal bar with the earnestness of a factory worker on the assembly line.

I turned the corner to see redheaded Martha softly swishing toward me in her housecoat and slippers. She shuffled blankly along the corridor, clinging to the handrail, crying, "Nurse! Nurse! Nurse! I'm hungry, Nurse! I'm hungry!" I turned as she passed me, noticing that her fuzzy orange hair was matted at the back of her head.

A sharp buzzer sounded an alarm on Gertrude's wheelchair.

She had tipped herself too far forward, was about to fall out, and had set off the warning. An aide was instantly there, setting her right.

Beneath the jumble of noises, the soft *ping, ping, ping* of the call button at the nurses' station gave an assurance of supervision. Two women on duty were laughing and sharing cake, the laughter a relief from the disquieting effect of the chaos.

This West wing was where newcomers were brought to evaluate their level of functioning. Tony was in bad shape when he arrived at Garden Terrace. He had not responded well to the treatment he had received at the geri-psych unit at the hospital where he had been sent for a "med check" and so was released to this Alzheimer's nursing home to ease off the high doses of medications and return to his maximum level of functioning. After two weeks, he was walking, talking, joking, feeding himself, and moving chairs around. The facility was designed for him and others like him so they could wander and feel free and accepted. This was not "assisted living," but total care to the degree it was necessary. Most residents were mobile, either on their own legs or in geri-chairs. Tony was at last in a safe place and had once again thrust me into a new world. How many "new worlds" had Tony introduced me to? Though often our interests had taken us in different directions, we always had each other to come home to for love and support. This time we were separate, each one alone. Our connection had stretched to the limit, and was about to snap.

All the rooms were the same, with the same soothing colors that I saw in the entrance room. The only distinguishing features were the window boxes containing a few identifying memorabilia of the two residents in each room. Some residents could find their own rooms. Tony could not, so I peeked in other rooms as I went down the hall, just in case he had wandered in and was napping on somebody else's bed.

Tony was not in his room, but some commotion, a scraping and bumping, drew me to the activity center. There I found him, my husband, Tony, standing tall and straight, earnestly shoving chairs around this way and that, bumping them into tables and into each other. He looked up when I called his name, smiled proudly, and went on with his work. When I touched his arm, he saw me, and in what I wanted to believe was recognition, returned the hug I gave him. He let me lead him to a bench in the bustling hallway, where we held hands and for a few minutes watched the activity. No, he did not recognize me. The concept of wife, friend, or even person was gone. But I believe there was a knowing, a kind of knowing without an idea behind it, as an infant knows his mother without knowing what a mother is. I contented myself with this belief and the hope that, though unacknowledged, he also felt a kind of comfort, with the warmth of his body touching me, his big hand gently squeezing mine.

After a few minutes, he became restless so I took his hand and led him back to the activity room and put his hands on the back of a chair and said, "Go to it, Honey. You're doing fine." I turned and walked past the Hep-me, Hep-me woman, hearing, not seeing her, sneaked around Henry at the door, and left.

"Why do you go see him when he doesn't even know you're there?" I had asked at that first support meeting in Iowa. Now I knew. I went there for me, for the warmth I felt touching him and my hope that he knew momentary peace from my nearness.

The ringing of the phone woke me at home at five-thirty one morning when Tony had been in Garden Terrace for two weeks.

"I'm sorry to call you so early," the nurse said, "but I wanted to let you know before I go off duty at six. We are moving Tony to North."

"Yes?" I said, suddenly alert, knowing "North" was the behavioral unit, the unit for those residents who have difficult behaviors and are a danger to others. "Okay. What does that mean? When will he move? What's the problem?" I knew as I spoke that Tony's life and care were completely out of my control now. Had I ever been in control? I couldn't handle him at home and they were having difficulty in the nursing home. I had to let go, more, and again.

"We are in the process of moving him now," she said. "The

North unit is half the size of this one, a maximum of only fifteen people. It is calmer, not as much noise or resident turnover. Some people have been there for several years. Tony will be happy there."

Several years… I thought. "Why now?" I asked.

"Tony is up most of the night. He goes in other folks' rooms and folds up their blankets. He unplugs their oxygen. He held the bathroom door closed in one lady's room and wouldn't let her in. He has hit the aides who try to dress or feed him. Yesterday he locked himself in the laundry room and wouldn't let anyone in. He went through the dirty clothes and threw them all over the place! Your husband's a very big and very strong man, Liz."

"Yes," I said. "I know. I see."

I got up, dressed, and went early to visit Tony in North. Now I went through *three* sets of double doors, code buttons on each. As I walked down the gleaming halls, I thought that at least we would be away from the guilt-inducing "Hep me! Hep me!"; but as I pushed open the last door, I heard, "Hep me! Hep me!" and knew she had moved, too. I would not soon be free from the guilt I felt and the despair that helplessness brings.

Tony's new room was just like the old one, his new roommate much like his old one and not a part of Tony's consciousness. Barbara, the nurse at the station, welcomed me, and I was instantly part of a new family. I quickly was united in friendship with families of the residents, bound by our common concern for the well-being of our loved ones and for each other. How quickly people thrown together by circumstances can bond. I thought of the teachers in Iran, and the Americans in Casablanca. By opening that door, I was in the midst of wandering, mostly cheerful, brainless souls.

I met Annie. Annie was one of those residents who had been there for many years, and she spent her days in a geri-chair, sometimes dressed, often half-naked, shuffling up and down the halls, gleefully shouting, "Get out of my way, you stupid bastard! Get out of here! Get the hell outta here!" Annie grabbed my hand and tugged at my simple, gold wedding band. "Gimmie that!" she cried. "That's mine! You stole it! You gimmie my ring!" I gasped, pulled my hand away, and walked quickly past her.

Often a man they called Father, with wispy white hair floating vaguely over his forehead and trousers gathered tightly at the waist of his bony frame, padded quietly beside me with his thumb and knuckles pinched fiercely onto my sleeve. He had been a priest, silent and walking. Fred, a larger, stooped man, paced the hall in slow motion, looking down at the floor, his face in a perpetual grin, his former aggression tamed for the moment.

Richard sat in his geri-chair, blocking the center of the hall, not going anywhere but reaching out to me with a friendly smile. I went up to him to shake his hand. "Watch out!" Joyce, the aide, called. "Don't get too close or he'll bop you one!" I took a quick step back as he swung at me.

This was my new community, and I got to know them all. Tony was one of them, too, but it was not a community for him. He had no awareness of the others. The residents I saw there every day had lived their lives and were gone, leaving their bodies to carry on without a brain to direct them. They knew pain and joy in the moment only or maybe in the instant only or maybe not at all. They did not come to this place to die. They came here to live. With luck, their bodies would give out as their brains had, and they would be released.

New shorts, smaller size. A piece of cake. A drawing from one of the grandchildren and sweat pants without zippers or buttons. These items became reasons for me to visit Tony every day and to feel useful, though I knew by then that he didn't need me anymore.

"He's ours now, Liz," the nurses told me. "We'll take good care of him. You go rest. Do something for yourself." A physical therapist began to work with him. An occupational therapist and a speech therapist gave him lots of the one-on-one attention he craved. These services were beyond the normal care because he had been in the hospital, and Medicare allowed up to one hundred days of rehabilitation in a nursing home after a hospital stay. I was chagrined that I had resisted a nursing home because of a preconceived idea of what it was, and because I had an unrealistically optimistic assessment of Tony's abilities. I knew I would learn eventually to let go, but he had been my total focus for so long. It was hard.

The longer, blue-sky days of June made it easier. One evening after leaving Tony, I walked in the sunshine from my car toward the mall entrance and glanced at my watch. Five o'clock. I didn't have to go home. I didn't have to be anywhere. I was free to wander in the glorious spring evening as long as I felt like it. I shook my hair as though tossing off all my cares, shaking off a role I had played the last ten years.

At home alone the next few nights, I had time to think about my life. Though the move to Denver had located me centrally among my three daughters, one in Nebraska, one in Arizona and one in Denver, I had left behind in Iowa all I had known for nearly thirty years. Essentially I was on my own—no old friends, no clubs, no job, alone. People I had met here had no expectations about who I was or what I should be or how I should dress. I was anonymous.

I had once been a foreigner in Iran, adopting the role of young wife of an international businessman. In Casablanca, I had become a socialite in a French-American community. In South Africa, I had turned silent and stoic while appearing light-hearted and cheerful, all the while enjoying my true role, mother to our three girls.

Iowa had brought a semblance of authenticity to my life, but again, living on the farm for three years had been temporary; I hadn't really been a farmer's wife. I was play acting. And now?

The roles I believed were me had been stripped away during the ten years that I was Tony's caregiver. How could I "keep up appearances" with my life in chaos? I couldn't hide. I couldn't hide Tony, and I couldn't hide myself. External conventions became completely unimportant and irrelevant. My Mary Kay business, which had given me many exuberant and dramatic years of personal development, slipped away. I felt like an imposter in my Mary Kay Director suit as I became more and more focused on coping with Tony and the chaos that Alzheimer's disease had brought to us.

During Tony's worst moments with Alzheimer's, I despaired that I was also fading away. And I believe now that is exactly what happened. Layers of me dropped away, and underneath appeared a more authentic person. By the first part of June, having been in North for nearly four weeks, Tony was walking, but unsteady on his feet. He fell frequently. When I saw him wandering the halls wearing a football helmet for protection, I cringed at this new indignity. By then he had no sense of self, slept in anyone's bed, ate with his fingers off anyone's plate with no awareness. One day I found him lying on a bed, anybody's bed, naked under the sheet, asleep, and I lay beside him. He put his arm around me, unknowing but contented. "Sweetiepie," he said. My heart leapt. What kind of awareness was still there?

Hope. It just wouldn't leave me. Hope that he would be alert when I visited. Hope that he wouldn't hurt. Now my unspoken hope was that he would fall without the helmet, that something would happen to hasten his death rather than deepen the dementia. Those last horrible stages. A backwards hope. Tony had never allowed me to abandon hope. "What if you don't find a job?" I had asked so many years ago. "Don't ever say that! It's not a possibility!" had been his response. And now I wouldn't give up on wanting peace for his troubled soul.

CHAPTER 25

Friday to Tuesday

Aurora, Colorado, June 24 to June 28, 2005

ON FRIDAY, JUNE twenty-fourth, when Tony had been in Garden Terrace for a total of six weeks, as I was leaving, I spoke to a man in the parking lot that I thought was a doctor, but who turned out to be Jim, the hospice nurse. We visited a few minutes, and as he turned to go into the building I said, "I'm sure we will be calling you sometime, but not for a long time."

"Oh, I know who Tony is. I'll have a look at him while I am in there."

The upshot of that chance meeting was that Tony was put on the hospice list the next day, Saturday, because of his extreme weight loss and because of the mottling on his skin indicating, even as Jim observed him in the dining room scooting chairs around, that he was already in the dying process.

I have learned that I can't push or shove my way through life. Life unfolds the way it's going to. Why did I meet Jim in the parking lot? How was it that he knew who Tony was? My plea for peace was being answered. The hospice team visited him on Sunday.

Monday, when I walked into the ward, the nurse called to me before I could get to Tony's room. "Liz, your husband has a swelling on the side of his neck. I don't know what it is. We have called the doctor."

I found Tony lying on his own bed, which was only a few inches off the floor so if he fell out of it he wouldn't hurt himself. He was not alert and did not respond when I entered his room and called his name and touched his cheek. The doctor told me the swelling was a painful infection, possibly due to his forgetting how to swallow, and that the infection would spread with great pain and kill him if not treated. Jim was there. Jim assured me hospice could keep Tony pain-free.

Years before, on that night long, long ago, when Tony slammed out of the kitchen door, he had shown me he wanted to leave, to walk out of his life, to get away from what was happening to him. He had said for years, "Get me out of here! I'm leaving! I have to go!" I knew he wanted to get away, to be free of the disease, so the choice to treat or not treat the infection was not a difficult one for me. I allowed hospice to assist him to leave at last his disease and the world, to leave not in anger or frustration, but in peace and relative comfort.

Ultimately, of course, his life or death was neither in my control nor his. Alzheimer's had taken over long ago. My only choice was to provide love, respect, understanding and, lacking a map, to seek the best road, to soften the sharp curves, and to walk beside him as far as I could go.

Our daughters, Caroline, Linda, and Marianne, arrived quickly and we waited together. That Tuesday evening in June, his body gently let go of what was left of his essence, until just the skin and bones were there, not much flesh. It felt warm for a few minutes, but without life. His once hefty body was sunken and his full face hollowed, so the bones jutted out under his eyes. His soft, white hair moved slightly in the breeze from the window, alive it seemed. But my husband wasn't his hair. He wasn't his body. My husband had gone, left his body and left me, behind.

I know I didn't become a widow that evening and Tony didn't die then either. Our living and dying had been all mixed up for so long that I wasn't sure which one of us was me. I know now that the border between the helper and the one who is hurting is always blurry.

Widowhood creeps insidiously over the wife of a person with Alzheimer's. She may not notice its proximity. One day he forgets that he has *just* eaten and asks, "What's for dinner?" The next week, he forgets the way home from the grocery store. Then he forgets the way *out* of the grocery store. One day he can't think of his daughter's name. Then he forgets he has a daughter, or a wife. Then he doesn't know what a wife is. Before you know it, he forgets who he is, followed by forgetting that he is someone. Then he isn't someone. He is gone but still breathing. Then, even the breath is gone.

So when did I become a widow? When did the balance of our marriage slip so heavily to one side that there was just one of us remaining, alone? I can't name the day he left me. I have been alone for a very long time.

A Stranger No More

IN AUGUST 2006, a little over a year after Tony died, I flew to Amsterdam for a family wedding and stayed on alone after the event to wander for several days in the city Tony had loved and shared with me. I was in effect saying a last goodbye to the man I had known before Alzheimer's overtook him. In that place, I wanted to recall the Tony that was healthy, the "us" that I knew then. I remembered my achy feet in four-inch heels when he had taken me by the hand and propelled me toward the *Concertgebouw*, where he had gone to rehearsals as a school boy. Pride had shone in his blue eyes as we strolled beside the canal to the spot where his school had been. Now, again, I heard his hearty laugh when powdered sugar from the *poffetjes* dusted the front of my coat. I felt his presence nearby but at the same time, I discovered I could find the way by myself.

From Amsterdam, I traveled to San Francisco, the place where I had started my life's journey. Margy, my friend for fifty-five years, my companion years ago at *Kismet*, met me for lunch in the City, not at the Plaza Hotel this time. It was gone, replaced by Levi Strauss. The City of Paris was also gone, now a Neiman Marcus. I walked with measured, adult steps down Stockton Street and saw Margy standing at the entrance to Macy's, the former I. Magnin building, her smile of greeting as warm and familiar as ever. We took the escalator up to the Cheesecake Factory on the top floor of Macy's. From our window table, we looked down on Union Square, no longer a fresh, grassy maze of hedges with noontime sprawlers, but a concrete expanse with wide steps and potted shrubs. Women in blue jeans, tank tops, and sandals jostled with women in pants suits, briefcases, and sneakers. No hats. No white gloves.

We were two old friends nearing seventy who, so quickly it seemed, had lived the lives we had once looked forward to. Fate had determined a different path for each of us, and now we giggled and wept over our stories of those fifty years.

Several hours later, we parted with hugs and promises to keep in touch, our eyes meeting with the unspoken question, "What's next?"

With furrowed brow, deep in thought, I walked up the hill to the parking garage, not humming love songs from *Kismet* this time, but hearing Tony's voice in my head. "I don't know, Lizzie. What are you going to do? You're free to do what you want. You know I'll support you whatever you decide. Go do your things, Lizzie. Go do your things."

Sunlight streamed through the sliding glass doors into my living room; there was no sound; the lid on the piano was closed; my soul was quiet. While I waited for water to boil for iced tea, I lifted the wire hook on the door of the birdcage which hung over the counter and gently put my hand inside and with my finger stroked the dust off the back of the little fabricated bird. I left the door open, promising to come back soon and wipe out the whole thing, maybe even retouch the paint. The whistle of the tea kettle startled me out of reverie. Boiling water hit the ice in the glass with a crackle. I carried the tea outside and slid onto the porch swing. My toe tapped against the stone patio and I started to sway, drifting back and forth, squeezing the small slice of lemon into my tea. *Who am I now? What happened to that young girl who had never heard of Iran, who had skipped down the street in San Francisco waiting for life to happen? Ha! 1958.*

Half a century later, lazily sipping cold tea on a sunny day, I started humming "Take my hand, I'm a stranger in paradise," and it occurred to me that with our daughters grown up and Tony gone, I had no future obligations or responsibilities. I could see nothing in the future at all. I had no expectations. Perhaps I could find that girl again. "Go do your things," he had said.

My things. As time passed, I gathered together pieces of myself. I escaped into music with season tickets to the Sunday afternoon Denver Symphony, expressed my inner self at drawing classes and writing seminars, and breathed in the holiness of nature by taking short hikes in the foothills. I wasn't lonely, but when a neighbor suggested I go to a singles dance with her, my emancipated self said, "Sure." There I rediscovered the pleasure of adult company and conversation with "well" people. Soon afterwards, in October 2006, I called Marianne on the phone. "Come over and take my picture," I said. "I'm going to go on Match.com!"

There followed several coffee and movie dates with pleasant gentlemen, but when Mark showed up at Starbucks one morning I recognized in him a spirit like my own. He and I have become partners in the truest, most inclusive sense of the word. We are sensitive to each other. He affectionately notices everything about me. He sees who I am without judgment and cradles me in warmth and richness of mind and spirit.

In July of 2008, a routine mammogram revealed breast cancer. Along with the anxiety, the premonition I had written in my journal six years before instantly flashed through my mind: some evil thing was at work in my body. Of course. No surprise. Here it was.

The day before surgery, I sauntered to the mailbox, luxuriating in the warm July sunshine. Among the circulars was an envelope addressed to "Mr. Tony Van Ingen," with a postmark and stamp from Austria. *What fun*, I thought. *Who do we know in Austria?*

I tucked my legs under me on the couch, put a cup of tea on the table next to me, picked up the letter opener, and slit the envelope. I pulled out and unfolded the letter, two pages: nicely hand-written, European style, in English.

Dear Mr. Van Ingen,

My name is Eva. I was born in Beirut in September of
1959… I wonder if you knew my mother Suzie there in
1958…. Are you are the Tony Van Ingen I heard about
growing up?… I wonder if you are my father….

Stunned! Breathless! Pictures fell out of the envelope. Eva. She
looked like Tony's sister, his mother. I read the letter again. And
again. Stared at the photos. Born September 10, 1959, eleven days
before Tony crashed my father's party welcoming me to Tehran.
What was he thinking when he put his business card in my shoe?
He was the father of a two-week-old baby! Did he know? He
couldn't have known. How could he *not* have known?

My insides shook with disbelief and shock. My hands were
sweaty. Feelings roiled inside making me gasp for breath. Poor
Eva! Tony! Didn't you trust me? Keeping a secret from me for
forty-five years. A life-long secret. Perhaps hindering the close-
ness between us I had always yearned for. The more I thought
about it the more devastated I was. He was a stranger all over
again. I couldn't tell the girls, not yet.

I called Mark.

My emotions were all mixed up, my insides quivering as I
read the letter to him over the phone. "Oh, my God," he said, but
told me to focus on the surgery and get well.

The operation, a double mastectomy with reconstruction,
had no complications. I was not afraid, only grateful that this disease had a protocol, instead of the vague suggestions for handling
Alzheimer's.

Weeks later, still disturbed about Eva's letter, I brought a
cardboard box in from the garage and sleuthed through Tony's
papers and diaries. The Tony I knew kept meticulous records.
Maybe I could find some evidence that he knew Eva's mother,
Suzie. I singled out an appointment book from 1958. Nothing. No
Suzie. Then I discovered a three-by-four-inch red pocket diary,
with a worn gold "1959" imprinted on the front, saved all these
years. Nothing in January, or in the first six months of the year.

She would have been pregnant by then, but no Suzie. I was looking very carefully now. On September 21st was "Amer. Club," and then, scrawled a few pages later, "Liz." My heart thumped as I turned the small tissue paper pages. September, October. I was nervous. November. Lebanon. There! *"Suzie,"* and again, *"Suzie,"* two weeks later. He was in Beirut and had seen Suzie, two months *after* Eva was born! He must have seen the baby. He knew.

I slid his photo off the top of my bureau and shoved it in a drawer, upside-down.

What would I tell our daughters? They idolized their father. I agonized over how to tell them without destroying their image of their dad. And of our marriage. Did they *need* to know? Could *I* keep a secret? They had a half-sister in Austria. Was that important? There was time, no hurry. I sent a brief acknowledgement to Eva, and when she asked for more information, I forwarded a biography of Tony I had written for our grandson's tenth birthday, called "When I was Ten." It included the tales of Tony's boyhood during the war in Holland, tales that he had told me repeatedly when he was in the beginning stages of Alzheimer's so he wouldn't forget.

Over the next year I began to consider our forty-five years together through a different lens. All that time he had kept a secret from me. I was left out of a part of his life. I remembered seeing him cry real tears only once, when our friend died at the age of forty-five from breast cancer. Her name was Suzie. As Tony sat on the piano bench weeping, was he remembering the Suzie he knew in Beirut and his own first daughter? How excruciating to suffer alone, and not be able to come to me for comfort.

Was our money crisis caused in part by his sending support to Suzie—and to his child? When we married, he was a twenty-eight-year-old bachelor, who had worked at a good job for many years. I assumed he would have had money saved up. I never asked him. Had he given a sum to Suzie? Had he made payments for the baby over the years? I'd never know. I like to think it was his nature to do so, and it did answer a lingering mystery about our finances still in my mind.

Did his heavy drinking start because the thought of leaving his baby was unbearable? Would it have been different if he had been able to share with me?

Had he met with Suzie in Beirut after the baby's birth to propose marriage and she said "No"?

Had Tony ever truly loved me, or was he just creating an appropriate family, according to his plan? Or did he love me and was afraid of losing me if I knew? Or had he been able to *just forget?*

I was bewildered and felt sorry for myself. I wanted to talk to someone who had known us, but part of living in so many different places meant that no one really did. Just Hannie, his sister. She knew Tony well and had known us as a couple since the beginning.

Mark encouraged me to fly to Milwaukee to see her. Once there, I poured out the story of Eva, and how betrayed I felt. "It's okay, Liz," she assured me. "Of course Tony loved you, a great deal. He was a private person. Remember, he left our family when he was thirteen to live with our grandparents in Amsterdam during the war. He has always had to take care of himself. Yes, it looks to us like his decisions were only in his self-interest. But we don't know all the circumstances. He handled the situation the best he knew how. We both know he loved his family. Consider all the things he has done for you and the girls. He met you and gave you all the love he had. He didn't let a mistake ruin his life, and it needn't ruin yours." She helped me put the facts into perspective and told me what I really wanted to hear.

Tony had loved me. Of course he had; I knew that.

But the resentment I had held in check for years now came boiling to the surface: resentment at his being gone so much, resentment that his drinking killed real companionship, and finally resentment that he disappeared into Alzheimer's before we had a chance to open up to each other.

Back in my home in Denver I saw what my sister, Katie, had seen. "Your house is a reflection of both of you," she had said. "Neither one dominates." Standing in front of the map, I stared at the black pins outlining his seventy-three years of life, much of it with me, but much of it without me, too. It was *his* map, his story.

I brought a plastic tub of photo albums in from the garage and laid them out on the couch. I flipped through age-edged pages of forty-year-old pictures and remembered, but didn't reminisce. The snapshots were just that, static clicks of the moment. I couldn't seem to get my memory beyond the literalness of the picture to the warm emotions I knew I had felt. The albums went back in the box.

Upstairs, in the top drawer of my bureau, behind the scarves and watches, lay a small, red brocade zipper bag holding my charm bracelet, not worn for many years. I found it and stretched out on the bed. Leaning on one elbow, I slithered the bracelet into my hand and dangled the charms from my fingers. *This* was where I found my story.

The Windmill. The Dutch family that loved me, a tulip parade on a misty gray day in May, the Ryksmuseum, walking through Kalverstraat, meeting Tony's school friends and staying out all night. One windmill sail is missing from the charm. When did that happen?

The Eiffel Tower. Leaving our tiny room on the Left Bank and walking hand in hand for hours, a full moon over Nôtre Dame, communicating in the accented French we had learned in Morocco.

A delicate cross and the miniature Koran, which Tony had chosen for the original bracelet, and the jade Buddha, all symbols of the wide world, differences brought together on my bracelet.

A Canadian Northwest Mounted Policeman. Niagara Falls, our little girls in the new winter parkas they would wear for two weeks before we left for South Africa, the charm and the coats purchased in spite of the financial crisis Tony alone knew was looming.

Thirty-one charms, "starters" for thinking of the fullness of our life, our affection and family, the good times, the difficult ones.

When I held that bracelet, a tenderness grew in me and I

longed to convey to Tony a fresh appreciation for the life he had provided for me and the children, not a fairy tale, a real life.

By the time a year had gone by, the shock of learning that Tony had kept a secret from me for forty-five years had mellowed. Eva had entered my consciousness and my angry disillusionment had dissipated. Now the question was not *if* to tell the girls they had a half-sister, but *when*. No ideal time, but the anniversary of the day I received the letter seemed appropriate. I felt whole again, as I shared with my family and allowed each her own individual response. I could smile now at the fairy tale I had persisted in, and could accept the fact that there were trolls under the bridge, details and secrets I would never know.

Eva and I e-mail on birthdays and Christmas and share family photos. Someday I would like to meet her to see how much like Tony she is. She is now part of our story.

Like any interpretation of history, the story shifts like sand on a beach when a wave hits it, but the music, the color, and the romance remain. *Kismet* became a symbol to me of that romance. The sense of make-believe found its way through much of my life, even to playing out the 1950s script for a husband and wife. We were a family, and though I had hoped when Tony retired we would finally drop the role-playing and be honest with each other, it didn't happen.

Together, we struggled with Alzheimer's disease; all of our family was involved, assisting, encouraging, loving. During that time I gradually *gained* in self-knowledge while Tony gradually *lost* the sense of who he was. Both of us were living moment to moment, without thought of appearances or consequences.

The facts of my story didn't change after I read Eva's letter. The light shifted, that's all, like a barely noticed layer of tarnish that darkens and dulls a neglected, once-brilliant copper tray-table. That's it. A thin film of tarnish. The luster, the color, the music, even the valiant struggles are still there beneath the surface, but now I see it all through a haze. When I walked to the mailbox that day and picked up the letter, this memoir was all but finished. *Kismet*. How prophetic is that? Fate. Our wedding photograph is still in its place on the wall in the study of my house. I look at it today again and again trying to match it up with what I know now.

Would I rewrite my story? No. As a photograph is only a snapshot of one second in a person's life, this memoir is only a record of my life as I see it now. I believe that while we live and experience new things, we can always revise our interpretation of the past. It is *Kismet*.